1968

book

A

# PHILOSOPHY OF MIND

I

# SOURCES IN CONTEMPORARY PHILOSOPHY

FRANK A. TILLMAN, CONSULTING EDITOR

HARPER & ROW, PUBLISHERS   NEW YORK AND LONDON

# PHILOSOPHY
# OF
# MIND

Edited by
STUART HAMPSHIRE
*Department of Philosophy*
*Princeton University*

*The editor is grateful to Mr. Rouald de Sousa Pernes for his assistance in the preparation of this volume.*

LIBRARY OF CONGRESS CATALOG CARD NUMBER: 66-11413

# CONTENTS

# EDITOR'S INTRODUCTION

No volume by a single scholar can recreate the incessant dialectic of contemporary philosophic inquiry; hence we are offering a series that is a collaboration of many hands. The present series is intended to provide students, teachers, and interested nonprofessionals with collections of essays in every major problem area of contemporary philosophy. Each volume is devoted to a single set of interconnected issues; each issue is currently the subject of intense philosophic discussion. The editors have been uncompromising in their attempt to bring together essays of great clarity and high technical excellence. Most of the essays were written during the last ten years, some newly written for this series; a number have already become contemporary classics. Each collection is large enough to display a cumulative diversity of viewpoint and detail.

In making relatively inaccessable essays available, this series will enable teachers of philosophy to find strategic or supplementary materials for a wide range of courses. To the student it offers the luxury of possessing essays formerly buried in bound journals or closeted in library reserves. To readers other than teachers and students, the series offers an opportunity to explore contemporary philosophy at first hand. To all readers, it offers original formulations of new ideas and fresh insight into topics of ancient ancestry.

FRANK A. TILLMAN
Vassar College

# PHILOSOPHY OF MIND

# INTRODUCTION

These articles, from journals, are intended to be representative of the wide range of contemporary inquiries in the philosophy of mind. These inquiries have been disparate both in method and in aim. Some philosophers have been concerned in recent years with bringing to light the connections between the concepts that we employ in discussions of personality, outside any scientific context. Others have been more concerned with the possibilities of fully scientific explanations of mental processes and with the concepts that might be needed in this setting. Yet a third group have in their writings exhibited both concerns. The area of possible inquiry is vast and there is obviously room for many different philosophical approaches. There is probably no field of philosophical inquiry which has attracted more attention in the last twenty years.

The vitality of the philosophy of mind at the present time probably owes something to a revised interest in ethics, and to the realisation that normative ethics is bleak and largely uninformative unless it rests on some clear and comprehensive analysis of mental concepts; it owes something to further developments in programs for scientific study of behavior; and it certainly owes something to the accidents of individual genius. Wittgenstein's polemic in the *Philosophical Investigations* against the theory of meaning, and the theory of knowledge, which had been accepted among empiricists, following Russell, has been a powerful stimulus; for this empiricist theory of meaning, and the theory of knowledge attached to it, seemed to entail a false description of the actual conditions of use of mental concepts. Wittgenstein turned attention toward an un-

1

prejudiced description of the commonplace idioms that we employ in speaking of mental processes and achievements. If one turns back to Russell's *Analysis of Mind* (1921, London: Allen) one finds that his analysis of such concepts as belief and desire rested upon a theory of meaning which has been devastatingly criticised. His analyses will no longer seem acceptable to those philosophers who have been persuaded that a careful description of our actual employment of words is at least a necessary preliminary to a clarification of concepts.

Among the specific issues within ethics and the theory of knowledge which have demanded more exact analysis of mental concepts have been the ascription of responsibility for actions; the problem of intersubjective comparisons between feelings and mental states; the limits within which a man is immune to error in describing his own sensations; the nature of sincerity in the expression and description of feeling; the notion of character and of character traits, and of human dispositions generally, and their difference from the causal properties of physical things; and the relation of pleasure to the activities enjoyed. All these issues have a traditional place in philosophy, and some of them have a long history. For example, the nature of pleasure is discussed by contemporary philosophers for very much the same reasons as it was discussed by Plato in the *Philebus* and Aristotle in *Nicomachean Ethics*. The terms in which the issue is discussed, and the theories of meaning and of knowledge presupposed, may be largely different. Many of the same distinctions, indispensable to any adequate ethics, have to be reexamined in the light of revised theories of knowledge, and therefore of self-knowledge.

No discipline other than philosophy is in a position to undertake precisely these inquiries listed above; and they are inquiries that cannot be dismissed, either as unimportant or as not admitting of definite progress. They are not unimportant, if only because some tentative, and perhaps uncritical, answers to them are assumed in most political and moral argument, or in jurisprudence, or in economics, or in psychology, or in the theory of education; they are not unimportant also for the more fundamental reason that our day-to-day thinking about ourselves and about our friends is impregnated by unexamined assumptions about the possibility of ascribing moral responsibility to criminals of different types; of comparing the states of mind of very different people; of determining a man's character, and of explaining his behavior by his character; and so on. The doubts that one may have about claims to certainty on any of these topics are not confined to philosophers influenced by a general theory of knowledge; they are also first-order doubts that arise in any responsible and reflective use of mental concepts. The philosophical doubts, suggested by theories of knowledge, are continuous with more familiar uncertainties that we have in distinguishing, for instance, the different emotions, the operations of the will, or the connections between thought and desire, or the nature of belief and of imagination. A doubt about the possibility of claiming knowledge of the external world of physical objects, through sight and touch is a *purely* philosophical doubt, in the sense that it has little hold on us when we acquire, and exchange, information in the ordinary course of affairs, or during scientific inquiry. One needs already to be puzzled by the notions of knowledge and of certainty before the full force of scepticism about the external world is understood. But the nature of the human mind, and of its relation to the body and to the whole natural order of physical things, is independently a source of puzzlement, and always stands in need of explanation.

There is a further reason why mental concepts, and the conditions of their application, always provoke philosophical doubts, and a demand for some clarification, more particularly so in our time. There is less constancy, between languages and at different periods in history, in the employment of mental concepts than in the employment of physical concepts. The prevailing conception of the human mind, or soul, has greatly changed within historical memory. Even when one reads Hume, or any eighteenth-century discussion of the passions and sentiments, one is aware that the vocabulary of personal gossip and of introspection, and therefore the vocabulary of moral appraisal, does not altogether coincide with our own. Anyone who reflects, and who learns more than one language, and who knows the literature of more than one culture and one period, knows that he has some choice within the vocabulary that he may use in thinking about his own mental states and those of others. The distinctions that he chooses to stress will be in part a matter of his own interests, and he is not constrained to make in his own thought all and only those discriminations which are familiar in the conversation and writing of his contemporaries. He may well conclude, after the kind of reflection that leads directly into philosophical argument, that some of the customary distinctions are insubstantial and illusory, survivals of beliefs about the soul that cannot be sustained; and he may have grounds for drawing distinctions that are no longer commonly recognized, or are recognized only in some other language, distinctions to which he attaches value in thinking about his own experience.

There are two distinct differences to be noticed here between knowledge of the external world and the knowledge that a man may have of his own mental states, dispositions, and processes. First, normative questions enter more directly into the choice of a vocabulary for thinking and speaking about one's own thoughts and feelings, and the thoughts and feelings of others; the questions that one will choose to ask, and the precise terms in which they are asked, will be to a greater degree determined by the opinions that one holds about that which is valuable in human experience. For example, the concepts of will, of motive, and of imagination have been differently circumscribed, and differently stressed, or even omitted altogether, in accordance with changing values. Secondly, there exists a wide range of states of mind, and processes of mind, which can only be attributed to persons who have the appropriate kind of self-knowledge or self-awareness. Only persons who draw certain distinctions and employ certain sophisticated concepts, and draw the appropriate distinctions, can experience those emotions and sentiments which are discriminated from each other by the thoughts that accompany them in the subject's mind. The emotions and sentiments that I may experience are, at least to some degree, circumscribed by the vocabulary and forms of language that I have learned in communication with others, and that I must still use in reflecting on my own inner experiences. The world of discriminable objects of reference among my inner experience is not independent of my linguistic resources and powers of discrimination, to the degree to which the world of external objects of reference is independent of my linguistic resources and powers of discrimination. In the external world the objects are there, as potential objects of reference, whether or not I have the linguistic resources, and the knowledge, to specify their differences and to be aware of them as distinguishable from each other; the knowledge that I may have about their nature does not in any way constitute, or change, their nature. But my knowledge that my sentiment can be classified in a certain way, and that it has a certain origin or source, may transform the sentiment itself, which is not, in relation to the knower, an independent object. The power and the habit of making distinctions in language is for these, here too summarily stated, reasons, not without influence on the nature and quality of a person's experience.

Within the empiricist tradition, prolonged by Russell, it was not to be doubted that a man has genuine knowledge of his own sentiments, passions, and feelings, which were conceived as kinds of transparent objects that we encounter in our experience. Such a knowledge of the so-called data of consciousness, or of experience, was taken to be the model of unquestionable knowledge of matters of fact. This kind of empirical knowledge was supposed to be unproblematical, while our claims to knowledge of the external world of physical objects was taken to be comparatively questionable and problematical. The assumption was that our feelings differ from external objects in that their surface and their substance are the same; we do not need to investigate them from different points of view in order to know definitely what they are. They are presented to us all at once, and in their entirety; there is no deceiving distance between the observer and the object, and no possibility of a distorting medium, or of a distorting angle of vision. It seemed that for these reasons we could not help knowing what our feelings are, if once the question is raised, because they must be what they seem.

But philosophers have in recent years admitted that the more complex sentiments, passions, and emotions do need to be investigated by the subject, and their elements surveyed as a pattern, before he can be sure what they are, even though they are his own. One step further beyond this recognition, one may be led to admit that the subject's awareness of a state of mind as satisfying a certain description may be a necessary condition of that description being truly applied to him. Along this path one is led into an analysis of intentional states, and of the relation between a passion, or sentiment, and its object, identified as the object by the subject. Everyone knows, pre-analytically, that there is a difference between, first, feeling uneasy and uncomfortable in circumstances when it is also true that the cause of the mental discomfort is to be found in a remark just made, and, second, being embarrassed by a remark just made. This difference between a causal relation and an intentional relation has not been found easy to analyze; yet the analysis of it must be one of the first requirements of the philosophy of mind. And this will require a more careful delineation of the different types of knowledge that a man may claim to have of his own states of mind and his own beliefs, purposes, and actions: and perhaps even a less confined conception of knowledge itself.

Lastly, there exists a new, or largely new, means of testing the adequacy of our conceptions of human freedom. The physical presence of increasingly powerful computing machines, and the accompanying theories of their potential capacities, together make the old hypothesis of *L'Homme Machine* less vague and tenuous and more tractable; relevant distinctions may suggest themselves, which could not easily or reliably have been imagined in advance of the facts. Some aspects of the multiple problems of determinism and materialism can be focussed, and made sharper and more definite. There is a small selection from the growing literature on this topic in this volume.

In any approximately complete consideration of the continuing problem of defining human freedom, in relation to present knowledge, mention would have to be made of the hypothesis of the unconscious mind, and of the claims of psychoanalytical theory to the status of a partially confirmed, or at least confirmable, scientific theory. This selection illustrates only a few of the many lines of inquiry that are now open in the philosophy of mind, in the continuing and necessary attempt to define that which is peculiar to persons.

## THE IDENTITY APPROACH TO THE MIND-BODY PROBLEM [1]

### WILFRID SELLARS

1. My primary aim in this paper is to set the stage for a discussion of some of the central themes in the so-called "identity approach" to the mind-body problem. I have particularly in mind Herbert Feigl's elaborate statement and defence of this approach in Volume II of the *Minnesota Studies*.[2] A secondary, but more constructive, purpose is to bring out some of the reasons which incline me to think that the theory is either very exciting but false, or true but relatively uninteresting.

2. I shall begin with a preliminary formulation of the identity theory which will highlight the topics I propose to discuss. Roughly put, the theory claims that what it calls "raw feels"—a technical expression which is intended to cover impressions and images pertaining to the external senses, as well as

Reprinted from *The Review of Metaphysics* (Vol. XVIII, No. 3, March 1965) by permission of the editor and Wilfrid Sellars.

[1] This paper was prepared for and presented at the Boston Colloquium for the Philosophy of Science, April 10, 1963. I am also grateful to my colleagues at the University of Pittsburgh who forced me to clarify key passages in the argument.

[2] Herbert Feigl, "The 'Mental' and the 'Physical,'" *Minnesota Studies in the Philosophy of Science*, II, 1957, pp. 370–498.

bodily sensations and feelings in a more usual sense—are identical with "brain states." It hastens to add that in speaking of "raw feels" as identical with "brain states" it does not simply mean that the very same logical subjects which have "raw feel" characteristics also have "brain state" characteristics, or that "raw feel" characteristics do not occur apart from "brain state" characteristics, but rather that the very characteristics themselves are identical. As Feigl puts it, "raw feel" universals are identical with certain "brain state" universals.

3. This rough and ready formulation of what is actually a highly sophisticated philosophical thesis blocks out three topics with which any attempt to assess the identity theory must come to grips. Each of these topics turns out on the most cursory inspection to involve highly controversial issues which are at the very center of the philosophical stage. I shall not attempt to resolve all or, indeed, any of these issues. My aim will rather be to thread my way through them in such a way as to bring out the common ground I share with the identity theory and thus make possible a meaningful joining of issues.

4. It will not have passed unnoticed in this particular climate of opinion that the identity theory as formulated above is committed to the idea that it makes sense to speak of the identity of attributes or universals. This is the first of the thorny topics on which *something* must be said. This may be the place, but it is not the time to develop a theory of abstract entities.[3] I shall simply mobilize some of the pre-analytic strands which any theory must take into account, and develop them in a way which gives the claim that "raw feel" universals are identical with certain "brain state" universals at least the appearance of being in keeping with the spirit of a scientifically oriented philosophy.

5. Universals, then, are a subset of abstract entities. Their distinctive feature is that they are expressed in language by predicates (e.g. 'red') or by predicative expressions (e.g. '3

---

[3] For the main outlines of the view I would defend, see "Abstract Entities," *Review of Metaphysics*, 17, 1963.

feet long', 'between red and yellow in color'). I shall say that predicates (under which term I shall usually include predicative expressions) 'stand for' or 'express' universals. Universals may be referred to as well as stood for or expressed. But predicates do not *refer to* universals; indeed, they are not referring expressions at all. Among the expressions which refer to universals, a particularly important role is played by those which are formed from predicates or predicative expressions which stand for or express the universals to which reference is made; thus

> Triangularity
> Being three feet long
> Being between red and yellow in color

6. Universals are public objects. They are identities not only with respect to their many instances, but also with respect to the many minds which think in terms of them, and the many languages which give expression to them. This inter-subjective and inter-linguistic character must be accounted for by any adequate theory of abstract entities. Equally important, and even more "platonistic" in tone is the distinction which must be drawn between those universals which have been "discovered" or come to be "known" and those which have not, and, within the sphere of the former, between those which are effectively taken account of by our language, and those which are not. To unpack this a bit, I shall assume that a universal is "discovered" or comes to be "known" in the course of coming to know what *use* a predicate would have to have in order to stand for or express it. The universal is *effectively taken account of* by our language if our language contains a predicative expression which actually has this use.[4]

7. Notice, therefore, that while we can refer to unknown or undiscovered universals (I drop the quotation marks from

---

[4] For the difference between these two stages compare a newly minted theory which is still but a candidate for espousal, with an accepted theory which is in day-to-day use.

these metaphorically used terms) and to universals which are not effectively taken account of by our language, only universals which are effectively taken account of by our language can be referred to by referring expressions formed from predicates which stand for or express them. Thus, although we can *refer to* the as yet unknown property of persons which would explain their telekinetic powers (supposing them to have such), our language contains no predicate which stands for or expresses this property.

8. Against this background, the following criterion for the identity of two universals can be formulated:

> Two universals are identical if, were a language to contain predicative expressions which stand for or express them, these predicative expressions would either independently have the same use, or one would be a definitional abbreviation of the other.

9. Clearly, much of the burden of the above distinctions is borne by the word "use" and the phrase "the same use." My general strategy is clear. It is to connect "realistic" talk about universals with "nominalistic" talk about linguistic expressions. My further strategy would be to connect talk about the use of expressions with talk about uniformities in the occurrence of linguistic inscriptions, and, therefore, to build a bridge to "behavioral criteria of synonymy." But that is strategy for a war and not a battle. Here I shall limit myself to pointing out that the patterns of use I have primarily in mind are (1) the reporting or observation pattern; (2) the consequence pattern. The latter is, roughly, the pattern which would find its explicit formulation in what Carnap calls 'transformation rules', L-transformation rules, P-transformation rules and others. I add "and others" to Carnap's list because it is not clear that it is an exhaustive classification. Other possible candidates are "bridge laws" and "correspondance rules."

10. I pointed out above that we can refer to universals for which we have no corresponding predicates. There are two

types of case, one of which is, for our purposes uninteresting. Thus there is a sense in which it can be said that there are color universals for which we have no predicates. We can imagine that we had no predicate for the color between red and yellow. It should be noticed, however, that while we might not have had the predicate "orange" we might well have had the predicate expression "between red and yellow in color." And, indeed, for a person to be in the logical space of color is for him to know how to use predicate expressions adequate to the job of *introducing* predicates in the narrower sense, such as "orange."

11. The interpretation of statements asserting the identity of universals where the logical space of the universals is in this sense familiar is relatively straightforward. Consider, for example the schema:

The universal which. . . . = the universal which. . . .

We can distinguish two forms the descriptions might take: (a) Each locates a universal with respect to a point outside the logical space of the universal located. Thus,

The color of Plato's beard = the color of your father's moustache.

Here, if we have the relevant information we can go from one of the descriptions either directly to an illustrating name of the universal, i.e. a name formed appropriately from the predicative expression which stands for it, thus

The color of Plato beard = orange (i.e. being orange)

or to a description which locates the universal with respect to the logical space to which it belongs, thus

The color of Plato's beard = the color between red and yellow

(b) This last identity statement gives us an example of the second form the descriptions might take. In it at least one of them locates a universal in a manner internal to the logical space to which it belongs. From an identity statement of this form, for example the above, we can move, given that we have a predicate—say, 'orange'—which expresses the universal located as between red and yellow, to an identity statement

  The color of Plato's beard = orange

in which a *description* is identified with a *nominatum* as in the paradigm of identification:

  The author of Waverly = Scott.

If we do not have such a predicate, we at least have the predicate expression 'between red and yellow in color,' and could *introduce* a predicate having the use of 'orange'—which does not mean that the latter would be "short for" 'between red and yellow in color' any more than proper names are "short for" their criteria.

12. But the important case of referring to universals for which we have no corresponding predicates is that in which we refer to what I have called unknown or undiscovered universals. Consider, thus,

  A. The property which an adequate theory of telekinesis—
     if we but had it—would ascribe to persons having this
     power.

Contrast this with

  B. The property which the theory (current) of chemical
     interactions assigns to catalysts.

In B it is implied that we have a predicate in our language which stands for or expresses the property in question. Not so in case A. There the property in question is referred to by relating it to the properties expressed by the predicates of the science of telekinesis at its operational and instantially inductive level. The logical space of these empirical constructs is not that of the properties to which access would be gained by constructing a sound theory of telekinetic phenomena.

13. In general, then, the universals which it is the task of theoretical science to "discover" are referred to *via* a reference to the unborn or undeveloped theory, the predicates of which would stand for or express them, and, therefore, *via* a reference to the logical space of the empirical properties of the phenomena to be explained by the theory.

14. Yet the predicates of even sketchily developed theories express or stand for universals. Here it is essential to note that as a theory develops, its predicates cannot, in general, be said to continue to stand for or express the same universals. This brings me to a fundamental point which adds an element of symmetry to our previous classification of universals. To the classification (which highlights the temporal dimension);

    1. Not yet discovered.
    2. Discovered or known:
        a Not yet effectively taken account of by our language
        b Effectively taken account of by our language

we must now add a third heading under 2

        c No longer effectively taken account of by our language

and a new major category:

    3. Lost, or, so to speak, undiscovered universals

15. These considerations strongly suggest that the objective or "platonistic" status I am ascribing to universals might be construed in a Peircean way as relative to the continuing scientific community. Thus, if on hearing the above proliferation of universals, one is tempted to expostulate, 'which of these universals really exist!' I would reply by calling Peirce's characterization of a true proposition as one that the continuing scientific community would ultimately accept—and then changing the subject.

## II

16. Now if the claims of the identity theory are placed in the framework of the above distinctions, it is clear that the theory can scarcely intend to assert the identity of "raw feel" universals with certain "brain state" universals which are effectively taken account of by existing language. For on the above analysis, this would involve that some "brain state" predicates currently have the same use as "raw feel" predicates. And this is obviously not the case. The claim must, surely, rather be that among the universals which would find expression in the predicates of a to be developed "brain state" theory, some are identical with "raw feel" universals.

17. At first sight, this is hardly much better. For, it might be urged, how could any predicates in a "brain state" theory have the same use as "raw feel" predicates? After all, the latter doesn't even presuppose the knowledge that there are such things as brains! But before we take up this and other objections, we must explore the notion of a "raw feel" universal.

## III

18. The "rawness" of "raw feels" is their non-conceptual character. The sense in which "raw feels" (e.g. a feeling of warmth) are "of something" is not to be assimilated to the intentionality of thoughts. To say that they are non-conceptual is, of course, not to deny that they can be referred to and characterized by the use of concepts, or even, directly responded to by concepts in direct self-knowledge. 'Non-conceptual' does not mean non-conceptualized.

19. The word "feel" in the expression "raw feel" is an extension to all sense modalities of a use of the word "feel" which has its ultimate source in such contexts as

1. He felt the hair on the back of his neck bristle.

In this primary context, 'to feel' is clearly a cousin of 'to see,' and feeling in this sense can properly be classified as a mode of perception. Notice that feeling in this sense is conceptual; a propositional attitude. One would, perhaps, be more comfortable about this remark if the example had been,

> 2. He felt that the hair on the back of his neck was bristling.

The relation between 1 and 2 is an interesting and important topic in the philosophy of perception. I shall simply assume on the present occasion that 1 is a stronger form of 2 which emphasizes the non-inferential character of the experience.

20. Notice that to ascribe a perceptual propositional attitude to a person in the form,

> 3. He perceived that-p

is to endorse the proposition involved in the attitude. We can, however, ascribe the same propositional attitude in a non-endorsing way by using such locutions as

> 4. He thought he perceived that-p
> 5. It seemed to him that he perceived that-p
> 6. It appeared to him that-p
> 7. He was under the (perceptual) impression that-p

None of these is *completely* neutral with respect to endorsement. They all tend to imply the falsity of the proposition involved in the attitude, and have other overtones which are irrelevant to my purpose. I shall make a technical use of 7 in which it will imply neither the truth nor the falsity of the proposition involved in the perceptual propositional attitude. In this usage the statements,

> 8. He was under the tactual impression that the hair at the back of his neck was bristling
> 9. He was under the visual impression that there was a red and triangular physical object in front of him

ascribe perceptual propositional attitudes while making no commitment concerning the truth or falsity of the proposition involved in the attitude.

21. Now a classical theme in the philosophy of perception is that the truth of statements such as 9 imply the occurrence of something which is variously called a '(visual) sensation' (a sensation of a red triangle) or a '(visual) impression' (an impression of a red triangle), where this occurrence is understood to be a non-conceptual episode which *somehow* has the perceptible qualities which the corresponding conceptual episode, i.e. the propositional attitude takes to be exemplified in the world of perceptible things. Thus, the fact that a person is under the visual impression that a certain stick in water is bent is taken to imply that he is having a visual impression of a bent object. I shall assume that this is true. This does not mean that I accept the "sense datum inference," for it should not be assumed that to have a visual impression is to sense a sense datum as these terms are used in classical sense-datum theories.

22. Notice that visual impressions are classified by the use of the word "of" followed by the phrase which would appear in the statement of the propositional attitudes which imply their occurrence, thus

> Impression of a red and triangular object

corresponds to

> Impression that there is a red and triangular object in front of one.

The idea that there are such non-conceptual episodes was put to use in explaining, for example, how a straight stick (in water) can look bent, and a red object (in green light) look black. It was postulated that the propositional attitude expressed by

> He is under the visual impression that there is a black object in a certain place

involves, among other things, (a) the occurrence of an impression of a black object, (b) the occurrence of the thought that there is a black object in a certain place, and thought (or perceptual judgment, as it was called) being evoked by the impression. Roughly speaking, *impressions that* were construed as conceptual responses to *impressions of*. To this was added the idea that while in standard conditions viewing red objects results in an impression of a red object, and viewing bent objects results in an impression of a bent object, in non-standard conditions (e.g. viewing a straight stick in water) the viewing of an object that is not bent may result in an impression of a bent object, and the viewing of an object that is not red may result in an impression of a red object.

23. Although the examples I have been using come from vision, exactly the same distinctions were in the case of feeling. Here 'feelings of . . .' are the counterparts of 'visual impressions of . . .' We can therefore understand the philosophical use of the expression "raw feel" as an extension to all modes of perception of an expression which stands for the non-conceptual kind of episode which explains why a person can be under the impression that he is being pricked by something sharp when in fact this is not the case.

24. I pointed out in 22 that sense impressions or raw feels are classified according to the perceptible qualities which are ascribed to some part of the world by the perceptual propositional attitudes which they evoke, and which characterize their standard causes. As I see it, the "of" phrases in

Sense impression of a red triangle
Raw feel of being pricked by a sharp object

are adjectives which, in addition to classifying raw feels *extrinsically* by their causes and effects, also classify them with reference to their intrinsic character.

25. How are we to understand the intrinsic character of raw feels? Obviously the sense impression of red triangle is not, in the literal sense, either red or triangular; nor is the raw feel of being pricked by a sharp object a being pricked by a sharp object. The most that can be said is that the families

of qualities and relations which intrinsically characterize raw
feels or sense impressions correspond in a certain way the
families of qualities and relations which characterize perceptible
objects and processes.[5] I shall return to this point later. For
the moment I shall simply say that the logical space of the
qualities and relations which characterize raw feels is, in certain
respects, isomorphic with the logical space of the perceptible
qualities and relations of physical objects and processes. It
would be useful, therefore, to introduce predicates for raw
feels which are formed from predicates which stand for perceptible qualities and relations by adding the subscript 's'.
Thus a triangular $_s$ impression or raw feel would be one which
in standard conditions is brought about by viewing a triangular
object and which, *ceteris paribus*, results in being under the
impression that a triangular object is before one.[6]

26. It will have been noticed that even my characterization
of the intrinsic properties of raw feels has been, so to speak,
extrinsic. For I characterized them in terms of their corre-
spondence with the perceptible qualities and relations of physical objects and processes. It might be inferred from this that
I think of our access to the logical space of impressions as
indirect, as based upon a prior access to the logical space of
perceptible qualities and relations. I shall postpone taking a
stand of my own on this matter, and limit myself for the
moment to pointing out that the type of identity theory I am
examining rejects this suggestion and insists that our access
to the logical space of sense impressions or raw feels is direct

---

[5] The scholastics took the different, and ultimately unsatisfactory
tack of holding that the characteristics are the same, but that the mode
of exemplification is different. For an analysis of the Thomist-Aristotelian
approach to this question see my "Being and Being Known," *Proceedings
of the American Catholic Philosophical Association*, 1960, reprinted as
Chapter II of *Science, Perception and Reality*, Routledge and Kegan
Paul, 1963.

[6] For an elaboration and defense of these distinctions, see Chapter
II, sections 22 ff., and Chapter III, section VI of *Science, Perception and
Reality*; also "Reply to Aune" in a forthcoming volume of essays edited
by Hector Castañeda to be published by the Wayne State University Press.

and, indeed, is the presupposition of our access to the logical space of physical objects and processes. It insists, indeed, that the qualities and relations of "raw feels" are "directly given" and that physical objects and their properties are "existential hypotheses" whose reality is guaranteed by the fine job they do of saving the appearances.

27. Finally a categorical point about raw feels which is implicit in the preceding remarks. They are construed as "pure episodes" and are contrasted with dispositions and mongrel categorical-hypothetical states. It should be noticed that the fact that one has in some sense "privileged access" to a state of oneself doesn't by itself imply that this state is a pure episode. Children can be trained to respond linguistically to short-term dispositional states of their organism, e.g. anger. Nor, as this point in turn suggests, need "privileged access" be construed in terms of classical theories of the given. The identity theory we are examining, however, is committed to the idea that raw feels are pure episodes and that raw-feel facts are "given" in something like the classical sense.

## IV

28. Before taking the bull by the horns, a word or two about the other terms of the identities envisaged by the identity theory. It will be remembered that according to the theory, raw feel universals are identical with certain brain state universals. Which brain state universals? Indeed, which brains?

29. For there is, in the first place, the brain as an empirical object to which empirical properties definable in observation terms can be ascribed. Can raw feel universals be identical with universals which characterize the empirical brain? They cannot, of course, be identical with any universals expressed by empirical predicates defined in terms of the publicly observable features of the brain, for raw feels are pure episodes which are public only in the sense that others can infer that which is given to oneself. (What authorizes the inference is, of course, a classic question.) Nevertheless it is important to see that

there is a sense in which it is perfectly legitimate to suppose that raw feels *are identical with* certain states of the empirical brain. This, for the simple reason that it makes sense to suppose that they *are* states of the empirical brain. Imagine a person who has been defleshed and deboned, but whose nervous system is alive, intact and in functioning order. Imagine its sensory nerves hooked up with input devices and its motor nerves hooked up with an electronic system which enables it to communicate. Without expanding on this familiar science fiction, let me simply suggest that we think of what we ordinarily call a person as a nervous system clothed in flesh and bones. In view of what we know, it makes perfectly good sense to introduce the term "core person" for the empirical nervous system, and to introduce a way of talking according to which raw feels and, for that matter, thoughts are in the first instance states of "core persons" and only derivatively of the clothed person.

30. I submit that in this sense most scientifically oriented philosophers think of raw feels and thoughts as brain states. But while the thesis that raw feel universals *are*, in this sense, brain states and therefore trivially[7] identical with certain brain state universals is almost undoubtedly *true*, it is relatively non-controversial and unexciting. If the issue is put in these large scale terms, only those who demand really distinct logical subjects for the sense-impressions and the material states of persons —thus Cartesian dualists—would demur. Aristotelians and Strawsonians could take it in their stride.

31. For the claim that raw feels (or even thoughts) are in this sense identical with brain states simply transfers the episodes and dispositions initially attributed to persons to the central nervous system, now conceived of as a core person. All of the important philosophical problems pertaining to the relation of mental states to physical states remain.

32. These considerations give proper perspective to the fact that according to the identity theory in the more challeng-

---

[7] Compare the trivial move from 'shapes are properties of physical objects' to 'shapes are identical with certain properties of physical objects.'

ing form in which it is currently defended, the brain state universals which are identical with raw feel universals, are universals which would be expressed by certain predicates of an as yet to be elaborated *theory* of brain activity. Thus, instead of making the relatively unexciting claim that raw feel universals are identical with certain brain state universals, where this reduces to the claim that raw feel universals *are* brain state universals (i.e., ascribable to brains as core persons) the identity theory in question claims that raw feel universals are not only brain state universals in this unexciting sense, but are identical with certain complex micro-physical universals to be 'discovered' in the course of developing a scientific theory of brains.

33. Thus the question arises, "Is it reasonable to suppose that the scientific study of brains will lead to the discovery of brain state universals which are identical with raw feel universals?" And to this question we are strongly tempted to answer 'no!' For interpreted along the lines sketched at the beginning of this paper it becomes, "Would an adequate theory of brains contain predicates which had the same use as raw feel predicates?" And the idea that this might be so has a most implausible ring. It will be useful to formulate some of the objections which this idea tends to arouse.

34. The first is that since predicates which would stand for the relevant brain state universals are *ex hypothesi* theoretical predicates, they would not have the avowal or reporting use which is characteristic of some, if not all, raw feel predicates. To this objection the identity theorist replies that once the theory was developed, people could be trained to respond to the brain states in question with the predicates of the theory—which would thus gain an avowal use.

35. The second objection is that raw-feel predicates do not have a theoretical use, or, to put it in the material mode, raw feels are not theoretical entities. Here the identity theorist might reply that the *other*-ascriptive use of raw-feel predicates is, in effect, a theoretical use. The force of this reply will be explored subsequently.

36. The third objection is the challenge "How can a predicate (e.g. 'having an impression of a red and triangular surface') which applies to a single logical subject (a person) have the same use as a predicate which applies to a multiplicity of scientific objects (micro-physical entities)?" The effect of this challenge is to make the point that the identity theory involves not only the identity of raw feel universals with certain brain state universals, but of persons with systems of scientific objects. The identity theorist can be expected to reply that it is enough for his purposes if raw feel universals which differ only in this categorical respect from the raw feel universals expressed by predicates which apply to persons as single logical subjects are identical with certain brain state universals. We shall leave this reply untouched, although we shall return to something like it at the end of our argument.

37. The fourth objection, however, is the most familiar and goes to the heart of the matter. "How," it asks, "can a property which is in the logical space of neurophysiological states be identical with a property which is not?" Otherwise put, "How could a predicate defined in terms of neurophysiological primitives have the same use as (be synonymous with) a predicate which is not?" To *this* question the inevitable answer is "It could not."

## V

38. It might seem, as it has to many, that this is the end of the matter. The identity theory is absurd, and that is all there is to it. And, indeed, the identity theory as we have so far described it has no obvious defense against this standard objection. Yet it is not difficult to discern the fundamental strategy of the identity theorist in the fact of this objection. It consists in an appeal to a supposed analogy between the speculatively entertained identity of raw feel universals with brain state universals, and the once speculative but now established identity of chemical universals with certain micro-physical universals. The story is a familiar one, and I shall not bore

you with the details.[8] The relevant points are quickly made. Suppose $U_c$ is a certain universal which the predicate '$P_c$' in the chemical theory current at time T stands for. And suppose that this chemical theory has a degree of sophistication essentially that of chemical theory today, but that micro-physics current at T is rudimentary. An 'identity theorist' puts forward at T the thesis that chemical universals will turn out to be identical with certain to-be-discovered micro-physical universals, i.e. universals which would be expressed by the predicates of a more sophisticated micro-physics. An opponent raises the following objections:

1. How can micro-physical predicates which are not tied to Chem Lab observables have the same use as chemical predicates which are?

The 'identity theorist' replies that once the theory is developed, these defined micro-physical predicates are given this new use, and therefore acquire a chemical-theoretical role.

2. How can the predicates of current chemical theory, which have no definitional tie to micro-physical primitives have the same use as any predicates of future micro-physical theory which will have such a tie?

This objection corresponds to the fourth and most telling objection to the mind-body identity theorist. And once again the objection is, in a certain sense, decisive. But here the 'identity theorist' has available to him a move which is, at first sight, not available in the raw feel, brain state case. He can argue that *both* of the universals involved in the identification are *to be discovered* universals, the chemical ones as well as the micro-physical ones. Roughly, the identity claim takes the form,

The universals which will be expressed at T by the predicates of a more adequate theory of chemical processes are identical

[8] See my paper on "Theoretical Explanation" in B. Baumrin (ed.) *Philosophy of Science*, New York, 1963.

with the universals which would be expressed at T by the
predicates of a more adequate micro-physical theory.

and while the universals which the predicates of chemical
theory current at T express would not be identical with micro-
physical universals, the universals which would be expressed
by its more powerful successor might be.

39. For just as universals can be "discovered" and "given
effective expression in our language" by our coming to use
predicates in various ways, so universals can be "abandoned"
by no longer finding expression in our language, and even
lost. A chemical predicate which at T did not stand for a micro-
physical universal may come to do so at T. And the chemical
universal for which it stood at T may be left in the lurch for
a more sophisticated face.

40. The situation can be represented as one in which
chemical theoretic predicates cease to stand for universals
which are merely constantly co-exemplified with micro-physical
universals ("bridge laws") and come to stand for micro-physical universals. The identification is *made* rather than *discovered*
—though the possibility of identification is discovered.

# VI

41. Is anything like this move possible in the raw feel,
brain state case? Can the identity of raw feel universals with
brain state universals be assimilated to the identity of chemical
and micro-physical universals? Can raw feel predicates and
brain state predicates be regarded as on the move towards a
possible synonymity as was correctly predicted for the predicates of chemical and micro-physical theory? Summarily put,
can raw feels be *reduced* to neurophysiological states?

42. This suggestion runs up against the obvious objection
that according to typical identity theories, raw feel predicates,
at least in their first person use, are as *untheoretical* as predicates can be. Unlike the predicates of chemical theory, they are
not on the move towards a more adequate logical space which

they might come to express. Like the Bostonian, they are *there*. This is often put by saying that they "label" directly given qualities and relations.

43. And even if the identity theorist were to hold that the *other*-ascriptive use of raw feel predicates is to be reconstructed as involving something like a common sense theory which postulates them as inner episodes to account for the perceptual behavior (including verbal behavior) of *others*, so that the identification of the raw feels of *others* with neurophysiological states would be immune to this objection, the latter would still apply to any attempt to identify the theoretical 'raw feels' of others with the (supposedly) radically *non-theoretical* raw feels of first person discourse. But no identity theorist worth his salt would restrict his thesis to the raw feels of others.

44. Suppose that at this point the identity theorist switches his tactics to conform to his reductionist strategy and abandons the thesis of givenness. In other words, he now argues that instead of the use of raw-feel predicates being a confluence of two autonomous uses, a *self*-ascriptive use in which they "label given universals" and an *other*-ascriptive use in which they can be compared to theoretical predicates, there is one basic use in which they can be compared to predicates in a common sense theory of perceptual behavior; that is *anybody*-ascriptive use, and that such avowal or reporting use as raw feel predicates have is a dimension of use which is built on and presupposes this anybody-ascriptive common sense theoretical use. Would not this complete the parallel with the chemistry-physics model? For if both raw feel and brain state predicates are in a suitably broad sense *theoretical* predicates, can we not conceive of a reduction of raw feel theory to brain state theory?

45. If the concept of reduction is construed on the model of the physics-chemistry case, then, as I see it, the answer is "No." For reduction in this sense is a *special case* of the identification of universals located with respect to two theoretical structures which are expected to merge. A second alternative must be taken into account. Roughly, instead of the primitive

predicates of the reduced theory ending up as *defined* predicates in the unified theory—which is the chemistry-physics case
—these primitive predicates could perfectly well end up as
*primitive* predicates once more in the unified theory. On this
alternative, the *to-be-discovered* sense impression universals
would be no more complex than the sense impression universals
expressed by current sense impression predicates; they would
have a different categorical framework, and be nomologically
related to (but *not* analysable into) universals expressed by
other primitive predicates in the to-be-achieved unified sense
impression, brain state theory. While all these predicates—including sense impression predicates—would be physicalistic in
a broad sense (physical$_1$) as belonging to a spatio-temporal–
nomological framework of scientific explanation, they would
not be physicalistic in that narrower sense (physical$_2$) in which
to be physicalistic is to belong to a set of predicates adequate
to the theoretical description of non-living matter.[9] As I see it,
then in the never-never land of ideal brain state theory the
logical space of sense-impressions would, so to speak, be transposed into a new key and located in a new context. It would
not, however, have become internally more complex in the
way in which the logical space of chemical properties becomes
internally more complex by virtue of their identification with
micro-physical properties. That is to say, there would be no
increase in complexity with respect to what might be called
the factual content of sense impression universals: such in-
creased complexity as occurred would be of a logical character. Roughly, the new sense impression universals would be
exemplified not by single logical subjects (persons) but rather
by manifold of logical subjects which might be called—bor-

---

[9] For the distinction here drawn between 'physical$_1$' and 'physical$_2$'
see "The Concept of Emergence" by Paul E. Meehl and Wilfrid Sellars
in Vol. I of *Minnesota Studies in the Philosophy of Science.* According to
the view I would defend, the to-be-discovered raw-feel universals are
physical$_1$ but not physical$_2$. Feigl, on the other hand, is strongly inclined
to argue that they are physical$_2$ and to make this claim essential to any
identity theory worth the name.

rowing a term without its philosophical commitments—sensa.[10]

46. But if sense-impression or raw-feel theory is to merge with brain-state theory, the latter phrase must be used in its proper sense of "theory adequate to explain the properties of empirical brains as 'core persons'" and freed from any commitment to the idea that neurophysiological theory is of necessity a theory the scientific objects of which are nerves which are reducible, along with their properties, to systems of micro-*physical* entities in a sense which implies that all the predicates of an ideal neurophysiology would be definable in terms of micro-physical primitives none of which apply *exclusively* to micro-physical systems which are the theoretical counterparts of brains.[11]

47. Thus, if the objects of brain state theory are conceived to be reducible to micro-physical objects (however un-thingish) by an adequate micro-physical theory, the latter phrase must connote *not* 'micro-theory adequate to the explanation of *inanimate* physical objects' (as if often tends to do), but rather 'micro-theory adequate to the explanation of any physical object, animate or inanimate.'

48. It is my conviction that a theory which is to explain the properties of core persons will involve a family of families of predicates which would be a categorial transformation, but not substantive reduction, of raw feel predicates, and which would apply only to systems of scientific objects which are the theoretical counterparts at the most fundamental level of empirical brains. In other words I accept the identity theory only in its *weak* form according to which raw feels or sense impressions are states of core persons, for as I see it, the logical space of raw feels will reappear transposed *but unreduced* in a theoretical framework adequate to the job of explaining what core persons can do. In my opinion such a theory is not yet even on the horizon.

[10] For a development of this point see *Science, Perception and Reality*, pp. 100–105; 190–196.

[11] Compare the distinction drawn above (45) between physical$_1$ and physical$_2$ primitives.

49. The plausibility of the more radical interpretation of the reducibility of neurophysiology to micro-physics rests on the fact that if one thinks of 'sense impressions' or 'raw feels' as theoretical constructs introduced for the purpose of explaining simple 'discriminative behavior' such as is found in white rats, then one would indeed find no reason to suppose that the postulated states might not be conceived of as reducible along the lines described in 46. After all, we can conceive of—and even construct—machines which can perform these discrimina⁊ tions. It is therefore crucial to my thesis to emphasize that sense impressions or raw feels are common sense theoretical constructs introduced to explain the occurrence *not* of white rat type discriminative behavior, *but rather of perceptual propositional attitudes,* and are therefore bound up with the explanation of why human language contains families of predicates having the logical properties of words for perceptible qualities and relations. In this radically transformed sense, then, I would defend the thesis of concept empiricism according to which the content and structure of our *concepts* of the perceptible qualities of things is derived from the presence of this content and structure in the world—though I would reject the idea that the derivation involves an 'act of abstraction.'[12]

50. I shall conclude with a brief mention of other facets of the problem. Perhaps the most important of these is the fact that the logical space of the perceptible qualities and relations of physical things and processes on which that of the attributes and relations of raw feels is modeled, is, in an important sense, *closed.* Perceptible qualities and relations are, as the identity theory indirectly acknowledges, pure occurrent qualities and relations. They are neither dispositional nor mongrel states. To say of a physical object that it is red and triangular is not to ascribe a power or disposition to it, though it is, in a very strong sense, to imply that it has certain powers and disposi-

[12] For an elaboration of this point see section III of "Philosophy and the Scientific Image of Man" in Robert Colodny (ed.) *Frontiers of Science and Philosophy,* Pittsburgh, 1962, reprinted as Chapter I in *Science, Perception and Reality.*

tions. Now it is not the "internal structure" of the families of occurrent perceptible qualities and relations which generate the demand for theoretical explanation, but rather the nomological structure of the changes and interactions of the physical things and processes to which these qualities and relations belong. Roughly, it is not such facts, expounded in a 'phenomenology' of sensible qualities and relations, as that to be orange is to be between red and yellow in color which demand scientific explanation, but rather such nomological facts as that black objects sink further into snow than white objects when the sun is shining.[13] And when physical theory explains the powers and dispositions of perceptible things and processes by "identifying" perceptible things and processes with systems of micro-physical objects, the "identification" is not to be construed as involving a *reduction* of perceptible qualities and relations to the qualities and relations of scientific objects, but rather as a *correlation* of these two sets of qualities and relations by means of "bridge laws." On the other hand, a realistic interpretation of theoretical entities—such as has been presupposed throughout the argument of this paper—requires that physical objects and processes be reducible to, i.e. *identifiable with* (rather than merely correlated with) systems of scientific objects.

51. But how can it be maintained that perceptible things *but not the perceptible qualities and relations in terms of which all their empirical properties are defined* are, in the strict sense reducible? The answer, surely, must be that once again the chemistry-physics paradigm is inadequate.

52. Scientific Realism maintains the *in principle* replaceability of the framework of perceptible things by a framework of scientific objects which contains highly derived counterparts of the inductively established *causal properties* of the former. But while Scientific Realism grants that the framework of scientific objects also contains highly derived counterparts of the *occurrent perceptible qualities* of perceptible things, it need

---

[13] Cf. William Kneale, *Probability and Induction*, Oxford, 1949, pp. 78 ff.

not and, if my argument is correct, must not hold that these qualities are reducible to, i.e. replaceable by, their counterparts in micro-physical theory—as in the chemistry-physics case. The intrinsic structure of their 'closed' logical space (50) requires rather that they be *relocated*. This relocation involves a simultaneous move on the sense-impression front. For the qualities and relations which are irreducible to their counterparts in the micro-physics of the objects of perception, *are* reducible, i.e. identifiable with, the qualities and relations which, I have contended (45–48), must be postulated in an adequate theoretical explanation of the nature and function of sense impressions or 'raw feels.'[14]

# MIND-BODY IDENTITY, PRIVACY, AND CATEGORIES

### RICHARD RORTY

## 1. Introductory

Current controversies about the Mind-Body Identity Theory form a case-study for the investigation of the methods practised by linguistic philosophers. Recent criticisms of these methods question that philosophers can discern lines of demarcation between "categories" of entities, and thereby diagnose "conceptual confusions" in "reductionist" philosophical theories. Such doubts arise once we see that it is very difficult, and perhaps impossible, to draw a firm line between the "conceptual" and the "empirical," and thus to differentiate between a statement embodying a conceptual confusion and one that expresses a surprising empirical result. The proponent of the Identity

[14] I have explored the conceptual problems involved in this "relocation" of the perceptible qualities of common sense things in a number of places, most recently in the essay referred to in footnote 12. See also the concluding sections of Chapter III ("Phenomenalism") in *Science, Perception and Reality*.

Reprinted from *The Review of Metaphysics* (Vol. XIX, No. 1, September 1965) by permission of the editor and Richard Rorty.

Theory (by which I mean one who thinks it sensible to assert that empirical inquiry will discover that *sensations* (not thoughts) are identical with certain brain-processes[1]) holds that his opponents' arguments to the effect that empirical inquiry *could* not identify brain-processes and sensations are admirable illustrations of this difficulty. For, he argues, the classifications of linguistic expressions that are the ground of his opponents' criticism are classifications of a language which is as it is because it is the language spoken at a given stage of empirical inquiry. But the sort of empirical results that would show brain processes and sensations to be identical would also bring about changes in our ways of speaking. These changes would make these classifications out of date. To argue against the Identity Theory on the basis of the way we talk now is like arguing against an assertion that supernatural phenomena are identical with certain natural phenomena on the basis of the way in which superstitious people talk. There is simply no such thing as a method of classifying linguistic expressions that has results guaranteed to remain intact despite the results of future empirical inquiry. Thus in this area (and perhaps in all areas) there is no method which will have the sort of magisterial neutrality of which linguistic philosophers fondly dream.

In this paper I wish to support this general line of argument. I shall begin by pressing the claims of the analogy between mental events and supernatural events. Then I shall try to rebut the objection which seems generally regarded as

---

[1] A proponent of the Identity Theory is usually thought of as one who predicts that empirical inquiry *will* reach this result—but few philosophers in fact stick their necks out in this way. The issue is not the truth of the prediction, but whether such a prediction makes sense. Consequently, by "Identity Theory" I shall mean the assertion that it does make sense.

I include only sensations within the scope of the theory because the inclusion of thoughts would raise a host of separate problems (about the reducibility of intentional and semantic discourse to statements about linguistic behavior), and because the form of the Identity Theory which has been most discussed in the recent literature restricts itself to a consideration of sensations.

fatal to the claims of the Identity Theory—the objection that "privacy" is of the essence of mental events, and thus that a theory which holds that mental events might *not* be "private" is *ipso facto* confused. I shall conclude with some brief remarks on the implications of my arguments for the more general metaphilosophical issues at stake.

## 2. The Two Forms of the Identity Theory

The obvious objection to the identity theory is that "identical" either means a relation such that

$$(x) \quad (y) \quad [(x = y) \supset \quad (F) \quad (Fx \equiv Fy)]$$

(the relation of "strict identity") or it does not. If it does, then we find ourselves forced into

> saying truthfully that physical processes such as brain processes are dim or fading or nagging or false, and that mental phenomena such as after-images are publicly observable or physical or spatially located or swift.[2]

and thus into using meaningless expressions, for

> we may say that the above expressions are meaningless in the sense that they commit a category mistake; i.e., in forming these expressions we have predicated predicates, appropriate to one logical category, of expressions that belong to a different logical category. This is surely a conceptual mistake.[3]

But if by "identical" the Identity Theory does *not* mean a relation of strict identity, then what relation *is* intended? How does it differ from the mere relation of "correlation" which, it is admitted on all sides, might without confusion be said to hold between sensations and brain processes?

Given this dilemma, two forms of the identity theory may

---

[2] James Cornman, "The Identity of Mind and Body," *Journal of Philosophy*, 59 (1962), p. 490.
[3] Cornman, p. 491.

be distinguished. The first, which I shall call the *translation* form, grasps the first horn, and attempts to show that the odd-sounding expressions mentioned above do not involve category mistakes, and that this can be shown by suitable translations into "topic-neutral" language of the sentences in which these terms are originally used.[4] The second, which I shall call the *disappearance* form, grasps the second horn, and holds that the relation in question is not strict identity, but rather the sort of relation which obtains between, to put it crudely, existent entities and non-existent entities when reference to the latter once served (some of) the purposes presently served by reference to the former—the sort of relation that holds, e.g., between "quantity of caloric fluid" and "mean kinetic energy of molecules." There is an obvious sense of "same" in which what used to be called "a quantity of caloric fluid" is *the same thing* as what is now called a certain mean kinetic energy of molecules, but there is no reason to think that all features truly predicated of the one may be sensibly predicated of the other.[5] The translation form of the theory holds that if we really understood what we were saying when we said things like "I am hav-

[4] Cf. J. J. C. Smart, "Sensations and Brain Processes," reprinted in *The Philosophy of Mind*, ed. Chappell (Prentice-Hall, Englewood Cliffs, 1962), pp. 160–172, esp. pp. 166–68, and especially the claim that "When a person says 'I see a yellowish-orange after-image' he is saying something like this: 'There is something going on which is like what is going on when I have my eyes open, am awake, and there is an orange illuminated in good light in front of me, that is, when I really see an orange,'" (p. 167). For criticisms of Smart's program of translation, see Cornman, *op. cit.*; Jerome Shaffer, "Could Mental States Be Brain Processes?," *Journal of Philosophy* 58 (1961), pp. 812–822; Shaffer, "Mental Events and the Brain," *Journal of Philosophy* 60 (1963), pp. 160–166. See also the articles cited in the first footnote to Smart's own article.

[5] No statement of the disappearance form of the theory with which I am acquainted is as clear and explicit as Smart's statement of the translation form. See, however, Feyerabend, "Mental Events and the Brain," *Journal of Philosophy* 60 (1963), pp. 295–296, and "Materialism and the Mind-Body Problem," *The Review of Metaphysics* 17 (1963), pp. 49–67. See also Wilfrid Sellars, "The Identity Approach to the Mind-Body Problem," included in this volume. My indebtedness to this and other writings of Sellars will be obvious in what follows.

ing a stabbing pain" we should see that since we are talking
about "topic-neutral" matters, we might, for all we know, be
talking about brain-processes. The disappearance form holds
that it is unnecessary to show that suitable translations (into
"topic-neutral" language) of our talk about sensations can be
given—as unnecessary as to show that statements about quan-
tities of caloric fluid, when properly understood, may be seen
to be topic-neutral statements.[6]

From the point of view of this second form of the theory,
it is a mistake to assume that "X's are nothing but Y's" entails
"All attributes meaningfully predicable of X's are meaningfully
predicated of Y's," for this assumption would forbid us ever to
express the results of scientific inquiry in terms of (in Cornman's useful phrase) "cross-category identity."[7] It would seem
that the verb in such statements as "Zeus's thunderbolts are dis-
charges of static electricity" and "Demoniacal possession is a
form of hallucinatory psychosis" is the "is" of identity, yet
it can hardly express *strict* identity. The disappearance form
of the Identity Theory suggests that we view such statements as
elliptical for e.g., "What people used to call 'demoniacal possession' is a form of hallucinatory psychosis," where the relation
in question *is* strict identity. Since there is no reason why
"what people call 'X'" should be in the same "category" (in
the Rylean sense) as "X," there is no need to claim, as the
translation form of the theory must, that topic-neutral translations of statements using "X" are possible.

In what follows, I shall confine myself to a discussion and
defense of the disappearance form of the theory. My first reason
for this is that I believe that the analysis of "Sensations are
identical with certain brain-processes" proposed by the disap-

[6] Both forms agree, however, on the requirements which would have
to be satisfied if we are to claim that the empirical discovery in question
has been made. Roughly, they are (1) that one-one or one-many correlations could be established between every type of sensation and some
clearly demarcated kind(s) of brain-processes; (2) that every known
law which refers to sensations would be subsumed under laws about
brain-processes; (3) that new laws about sensations be discovered by
deduction from laws about brain-processes.

[7] Cornman, p. 492.

pearance form (*viz.*, "What people now call 'sensations' are identical with certain brain-processes") accomplishes the same end as the translation form's program of topic-neutral translation—namely, avoiding the charge of "category-mistake!" while preserving the full force of the traditional materialist position. My second reason is that I believe that an attempt to defend the translation form will inevitably get bogged down in controversy about the adequacy of proposed topic-neutral translations of statements about sensations. There is obviously a sense of "adequate translation" in which the topic-neutrality of the purported translations *ipso facto* makes them inadequate. So the proponent of the translation form of the theory will have to fall back on a weaker sense of "adequate translation." But the weaker this sense becomes, the less impressive is the claim being made, and the less difference between the Identity Theory and the non-controversial thesis that certain brain-processes may be constantly correlated with certain sensations.

### 3. The Analogy between Demons and Sensations

At first glance, there seems to be a fatal weakness in the disappearance form of the Identity Theory. For normally when we say "What people call 'X's' are nothing but Y's" we are prepared to add that "There are no X's." Thus when, e.g., we say that "What people call 'caloric fluid' is nothing but the motion of molecules" or "What people call 'witches' are nothing but psychotic women" we are prepared to say that there are no witches, and no such thing as caloric fluid. But it seems absurd to say that there might turn out to be no such things as sensations.

To see that this disanalogy is not fatal to the Identity Theory, let us consider the following situation. A certain primitive tribe holds the view that illnesses are caused by demons— a different demon for each sort of illness. When asked what more is known about these demons than that they cause illness, they reply that certain members of the tribe—the witch-doctors —can see, after a meal of sacred mushrooms, various (intangible) humanoid forms on or near the bodies of patients. The witch-doctors have noted, for example, that a blue demon with a long nose accompanies epileptics, a fat red one accompanies sufferers from pneumonia, etc. They know such further facts as that the fat red demon dislikes a certain sort of mold which the witch-doctors give people who have pneumonia. (There are various competing theories about what demons do when not causing diseases, but serious witch-doctors regard such speculations as unverifiable and profitless.)

If we encountered such a tribe, we would be inclined to tell them that there are no demons. We would tell them that diseases were caused by germs, viruses, and the like. We would add that the witch-doctors were not seeing demons, but merely having hallucinations. We would be quite right, but would we be right on *empirical* grounds? What empirical criteria, built into the demon-talk of the tribe, go unsatisfied? What predictions which the tribesmen make fail to come true? If there are none, a sophisticated witch-doctor may reply that all modern science can do is to show (1) that the presence of demons is constantly correlated with that of germs, viruses, and the like, and (2) that eating certain mushrooms sometimes makes people think they see things that aren't really there. This is hardly sufficient to show that there are no demons. At best, it shows that if we forget about demons, then (a) a simpler account of the cause and cure of disease and (b) a simpler account of why people make the perceptual reports they do, may be given.

What do we reply to such a sophisticated witch-doctor? I think that all that we would have left to say is that the simplicity of the accounts which can be offered if we forget about demons *is* an excellent reason for saying that there are no demons. Demon-discourse is one way of describing and predicting phenomena, but there are better ways. We *could* (as the witch-doctor urges) tack demon-discourse on to modern science by saying, first, that diseases are caused by the compresence of demons and germs (each being a necessary, but neither a sufficient, condition) and, second, that the witch-doctors (unlike drunkards and psychotics) really do see intangible beings (about whom, alas, nothing is known save their visual appearances). If we did so, we would retain all the predictive and explanatory advantages of modern science. We would know as much about the cause and cure of disease, and about hallucinations, as we did before. We would, however, be burdened with problems which we did not have before: the problem of why demons are visible only to witch-doctors, and the problem of why germs cannot cause diseases all by themselves. We avoid both problems by saying that demons do not exist. The witch-doctor may remark that this use of Occam's Razor has the same advantage as that of theft over honest toil. To such a remark, the only reply could be an account of the practical advantages gained by the use of the Razor in the past.

Now the Identity Theorist's claim is that sensations may be to the future progress of psycho-physiology as demons are to modern science. Just as we now want to deny that there are demons, future science may want to deny that there are sensations. The only obstacle to replacing sensations discourse with brain-discourse seems to be that sensation-statements have a reporting as well as an explanatory function. But the demon case makes clear that the discovery of a new way of explaining the phenomena previously explained by reference to a certain sort of entity, *combined with a new account of what is being reported by observation-statements about that sort of entity*, may give good reason for saying that there are no entities of that sort. The absurdity of saying "Nobody has ever felt a pain" is no greater than that of saying "Nobody has ever seen a demon," *if* we have a suitable answer to the question "What *was* I reporting when I said I felt a pain?" To this question, the science of the future may reply "You were reporting the occurrence of a certain brain-process, and it would make life simpler for us if you would, in the future, *say* 'My C-fibers are firing' instead of saying 'I'm in pain.'" In so saying, he has as good a *prima facie* case as the scientist who answers the witch-doctor's question "What *was* I reporting when I reported a demon?" by saying "You were reporting the content of your hallucination, and it would make life simpler if, in the future, you would describe your experiences in those terms."

Given this *prima facie* analogy between demons and sensations, we can now attend to some disanalogies. We may note, first, that there is no simple way of filling in the blank in "What people called 'demons' are nothing but ——————." For neither "hallucinatory contents" nor "germs" will do. The observational and the explanatory roles of "demon" must be distinguished. We need to say something like "What people who reported seeing demons were reporting was simply the content of their hallucinations," and *also* something like "What people explained by reference to demons can be explained better by reference to germs, viruses, etc." Because of the need for a relatively complex account of how we are to get along without reference to demons, we cannot *identify* "What we called 'demons'" with anything. So, instead, we simply deny their existence. In the case of sensations, however, we can give a relatively simple account of how to get along in the future. Both the explanatory *and* the reporting functions of statements about sensations can be taken over by statements about brain-processes. Therefore we are prepared to identify "What we called 'sensations'" with brain-processes, and to say "What we called 'sensations' turn out to be nothing but brain-processes."

Thus this disanalogy does not have the importance which it appears to have at first. In both the demon case and the sensation case, the proposed reduction has the same pragmatic consequences: namely, that we should stop asking questions about the causal and/or spatio-temporal relationships holding between the "reduced" entities (demons, sensations) and the rest of the universe, and replace these with questions about the relationships holding between certain other entities (germs, hallucinatory experiences, brain-processes) and the rest of the universe. It happens, for the reasons just sketched, that the proposed reduction is put in the form of a denial of existence in one case, and of an identification in another case. But "There are no demons" and "What people call 'sensations' are nothing but brain processes" can both equally well be paraphrased as "Elimination of the referring use of the expression in question ('demon,' 'sensation') from our language would leave our ability to describe and predict undiminished."

Nevertheless, the claim that there might turn out to be no such thing as a "sensation" seems scandalous. The fact that a witch-doctor might be scandalized by a similar claim about demons does not, in itself, do much to diminish our sense of shock. In what follows, I wish to account for this intuitive implausibility. I shall argue that it rests *solely* upon the fact that elimination of the referring use of "sensation" from our language would be in the highest degree *impractical*. If this can be shown, then I think that the Identity Theorist will be cleared of the charge of "conceptual confusion" usually leveled against him. Rather than proceeding directly to this argument, however, I shall first consider a line of argument which has often been used to show that he *is* guilty of this charge. Examining this line of argument will permit me to sketch in greater detail what the Identity Theorist is and is not saying.

## 4. The Eliminability of Observation Terms

The usual move made by the opponents of the Identity Theory is to compare suggested reduction of sensations to brain-processes to certain other cases in which we say that "X's turn out to be nothing but Y's." There are two significantly different classes of cases and it might seem that the Identity Theorist confuses them. First, there is the sort of case in which both "X" and "Y" are used to refer to observable entities, and the claim that "What people called 'X's' are nothing but Y's" is backed up by pointing out that the statement "This is an X" commits one to an empirically false proposition. For example, we say that "What people called 'unicorn horns' are nothing but narwhal horns," and urge that we cease to respond to a perceptual situation with "This is a unicorn horn." We do this because "This is a unicorn horn" commits one to the existence of unicorns, and there are, it turns out, no unicorns. Let us call this sort of case *identification of observables with other observables.* Second, there is the sort of case in which "X" is used to refer to an observable entity and "Y" is used to refer to an unobservable entity. Here we do not (typically) back up the claim that "What people called 'X's' are nothing but Y's" by citing an empirically false proposition presupposed by "This is an X." For example, the statement that "What people call 'tables' are nothing but clouds of molecules" does not suggest, or require as a ground, that people who say "This is a table" hold false beliefs. Rather, we are suggesting that something *more* has been found out about the sort of situation reported by "This is a table." Let us call this second sort of case *identification of observables with theoretical entities.*

It seems that we cannot assimilate the identification of sensations with brain-processes to either of these cases. For, unlike the typical case of identification of observables with other observables, we do not wish to say that people who have reported sensations in the past have (necessarily) any empirically disconfirmed beliefs. People are not wrong about sensations in the way in which they were wrong about "unicorn horns." Again, unlike the typical case of the identification of observables with theoretical entities, we do not want to say that brain-processes are "theoretical" or unobservable. Furthermore, in cases in which we identify an observable *X* with an unobservable *Y*, we are usually willing to accept the remark that "That does not show that there are no X's." The existence of tables is not (it would seem) impugned by their identification with clouds of electrons, as the existence of unicorn horns is impugned by their identification with narwhal horns. But a defender of the Disappearance Form of the Identity Theory *does* want to impugn the existence of sensations.

Because the claim that "What people call 'sensations' may turn out to be nothing but brain-processes" cannot be assimilated to either of these cases, it has been attacked as trivial or incoherent. The following dilemma is posed by those who attack it: either the Identity Theorist claims that talk about sensations presupposes some empirically disconfirmed belief (and what could it be?) or the "identity" which he has in mind is the uninteresting sort of identity which holds between tables and clouds of molecules (mere "theoretical replaceability").

The point at which the Identity Theorist should attack this dilemma is the premise invoked in stating the second horn —the premise that the identification of tables with clouds of molecules does not permit us to infer to the non-existence of tables. This premise is true, but *why* is it true? That there is room for reflection here is apparent when we place the case of tables side-by-side with the case of demons. If there is any point to saying that tables are nothing but clouds of molecules it is presumably to say that, in principle, we could stop making a referring use of "table," and of any extensionally equivalent term, and still leave our ability to describe and predict undiminished. But this would seem just the point of (and the justification for) saying that there are no demons. Why does the realization that nothing would be lost by the dropping of "table" from our vocabulary still leave us with the conviction that there are tables, whereas the same realization about demons leaves us with the conviction that there are no demons? I suggest that the only answer to this question which will stand examination is that although we could *in principle* drop "table," it would be monstrously inconvenient to do so, whereas it is both possible in principle and convenient in practice to drop "demon." The reason "But there still are tables" sounds so plausible is that nobody would dream of suggesting that we stop reporting our experiences in table-talk and start reporting them in molecule-talk. The reason "There are no demons" sounds so plausible is that we are quite willing to suggest that the witch-doctors stop reporting their experiences in demon-talk and start reporting them in hallucination-talk.

A conclusive argument that this practical difference is the *only* relevant difference would, obviously, canvass all the other differences which might be noted. I shall not attempt this. Instead, I shall try to make my claim plausible by sketching a general theory of the conditions under which a term may cease to have a referring use without those who made such a use being convicted of having held false beliefs.

Given the same sorts of correlations between X's and Y's, we are more likely to say "X's are nothing but Y's" when reference to X's is habitually made in non-inferential reports, and more likely to say "There are no 'X's' when such reference is never or rarely made. (By "non-inferential report" I mean a statement in response to which questions like "How did you know?" "On what evidence do you say . . . ?" and "What leads you to think . . . ?" are normally considered misplaced and unanswerable, but which is nonetheless capable of empirical confirmation.) Thus we do not say that the identification of temperature with the kinetic energy of molecules shows that there is no such thing as temperature, since "temperature" originally (i.e., before the invention of thermometers) stood for something which was always reported non-inferentially, and still is frequently so reported. Similarly for all identifications of familiar macro-objects with unfamiliar micro-objects. But since in our culture-circle we do not *habitually* report non-inferentially the presence of caloric fluid, demons, etc., we do not feel unhappy at the bald suggestion that there are no such things.

Roughly speaking, then, the more accustomed we are to "X" serving as an observation-term (by which I mean a term habitually used in non-inferential reports) the more we prefer, when enquiry shows the possibility of accounting for the phenomena explained by reference to X's without such reference, to "identify" X's with some sort of Y's, rather than to deny existence to X's *tout court*. *But the more grounds we have for such identification, the more chance there is that we shall stop using "X" in non-inferential reports,* and thus the greater chance of our eventually coming to accept the claim that "there are no X's" with equanimity. This is why we find borderline cases, and gradual shifts from assimilations of X's to Y's to an assertion that X's do not exist. For example, most people do not report the presence of pink rats non-inferentially (nor inferentially, for that matter), but some do. The recognition that they are in the minority helps those who do so to admit that there are no pink rats. But suppose that the vast majority of us had always seen (intangible and uncatchable) pink rats;

would it not then be likely that we should resist the bald assertion that there are no pink rats and insist on something of the form "pink rats are nothing but . . ." ? It might be a very long time before we came to drop the habit of reporting pink rats and begin reporting hallucinations instead.

The typical case-history of an observation-term ceasing to have a referring use runs the following course: (1) X's are the subjects of both inferential and non-inferential reports;[8] (2) empirical discoveries are made which enable us to subsume X-laws under Y-laws and to produce new X-laws by studying Y's; (3) inferential reports of X's cease to be made; (4) non-inferential reports of X's are reinterpreted either (4a) as reports of Y's, *or* (4b) as reports of mental entities (thoughts that one is seeing an X, hallucinatory images, etc.); (5) non-inferential reports of X's cease to be made (because their place is taken by non-inferential reports either of Y's or of thoughts, hallucinatory images, etc.); (6) we conclude that there simply are no such things as X's.

This breakdown of stages lets us pick out two crucial conditions that must be satisfied if we are to move from "X's are nothing but Y's" (stage 2) to "there are no X's" (stage 6). These conditions are;

A. The Y-laws must be *better* at explaining the kinds of phenomena explained by the X-laws (not just equally good). Indeed, they must be sufficiently better so that *the inconvenience of changing one's linguistic habits by ceasing to make inferential reports about X's is less than the inconvenience of going through the routine of translating one's X-reports into Y-reports in order to get satisfactory explanations of the phenomena in question.* If this condition is not satisfied, the move from stage (2) to stage (3) will not be made, and thus no later move will be made.

---

[8] Note that if X's are *only* referred to in inferential reports—as in the case of "neutrons" and "epicycles," no philosophically interesting reduction takes place. For in such cases there is no hope of getting rid of an explanandum; all we get rid of is a putative explanation.

B. Either Y-reports may themselves be made non-inferentially, or X-reports may be treated as reports of mental entities. For we must be able to have some answer to the question "What *am* I reporting when I non-inferentially report about an X?," and the only answers available are "you're reporting on a Y" or "you're reporting on some merely mental entity." If neither answer is available, we can move neither to (4a) nor to (4b), nor, therefore, on to (5) and (6).

Now the reason we move from stage (2) to stage (3) in the case of demons is that A is obviously satisfied. The phenomena which we explained by reference to the activity of demons are so much better explained in other ways that it is simpler to stop inferring to the existence of demons altogether than to continue making such inferences, and then turning to laws about germs and the like for an explanation of the behavior of the demons. The reason why we do *not* move from (2) to (3) (much less to (6)) in the case of temperature or tables is that explanations formulated in terms of temperatures are so good, on the ground which they were originally intended to cover, that we feel no temptation to stop talking about temperatures and tables merely because we can, in some cases, get more precise predictions by going up a level to laws about molecules. The reason why we move on from (3) to (4) in the case of demons is that the alternative labeled (4b) is readily available —we can easily consign experiences of demons to that great dumping-ground of out-dated entities, the Mind. There were no experiences of demons, we say, but only experiences of mental images.

Now it seems obvious that, in the case of sensations, A will not be satisfied. The inconvenience of ceasing to talk about sensations would be so great that only a fanatical materialist would think it worth the trouble to cease referring to sensations. If the Identity Theorist is taken to be predicting that some day "sensation," "pain," "mental image," and the like will drop out of our vocabulary, he is almost certainly wrong. But if he is saying simply that, at no greater cost than an inconvenient linguistic reform, we *could* drop such terms, he is entirely justified. And I take this latter claim to be all that traditional materialism has ever desired.

Before leaving the analogy between demons and sensations, I wish to note one further disanalogy which an opponent of the Identity Theory might pounce upon. Even if we set aside the fact that A would not be satisfied in the case of sensations, such an opponent might say, we should note the difficulty in satisfying B. It would seem that there is no satisfactory answer to the question "What *was* I non-inferentially reporting when I reported on my sensations?" For neither (4a) nor (4b) seems an available option. The first does not seem to be available because it is counter-intuitive to think of, e.g., "I am having my C-fibers stimulated," as capable of being used to make a non-inferential report. The second alternative is simply silly —there is no point in saying that when we report a sensation we are reporting some "merely mental" event. For sensations are *already* mental events. The last point is important for an understanding of the *prima facie* absurdity of the disappearance form of the Identity Theory. The reason why most statements of the form "there might turn out to be no X's at all" can be accepted with more or less equanimity in the context of forecasts of scientific results is that we are confident we shall always be able to "save the phenomena" by answering the question "But what about all those X's we've been accustomed to observe?" with some reference to thoughts-of-X's, images-of-X's, and the like. Reference to mental entities provides non-inferential reports of X's with something to have been about. But when we want to say "There might turn out to be no mental entities at all," we cannot use this device. This result makes clear that if the analogy between the past disappearance of supernatural beings and the possible future disappearance of sensations is to be pressed, we must claim that alternative (4a) is, appearances to the contrary, still open. That is, we must hold that the question "What *was* I non-inferentially reporting when I non-inferentially reported a stabbing pain?" can be sensibly answered "You were reporting a stimulation of your C-fibers."

Now why should this *not* be a sensible answer? Let us begin by getting a bad objection to it out of the way. One can imagine someone arguing that this answer can only be given if a stimulation of C-fibers is strictly identical with a stabbing pain, and that such strict identification involves category-mistakes. But this objection presupposes that "A report of an X is a report of a Y" entails that "X's are Y's." If we grant this presupposition we shall not be able to say that the question "What was I reporting when I reported a demon?" is properly answered by "You were reporting the content of an hallucination which you were having." However, if we ask why this objection is plausible, we can see the grain of truth which it embodies and conceals. We are usually unwilling to accept "You were reporting a Y" as an answer to the question "What *was* I non-inferentially reporting when I non-inferentially reported an X?" unless (a) Y's are themselves the kind of thing we habitually report on non-inferentially, and (b) there does not exist already an habitual practice of reporting Y's non-inferentially. Thus we accept "the content of an hallucination" as a sensible answer because we know that such contents, being "mental images," are just the sort of thing which does get non-inferentially reported (once it is recognized for what it is) and because we are not accustomed to making non-inferential reports in the form "I am having an hallucinatory image of . . ."[9] To take an example of answers to this sort of question that are *not* sensible, we reject the claim that when we report on a table we are reporting on a mass of whirling particles, for either we think we know under what circumstances we should make such a report, and know that these circumstances do not obtain, or we believe that the presence of such particles can only be inferred and never observed.

[9] Note that people who *become* accustomed to making the latter sort of reports may no longer accept explanations of their erroneous non-inferential reports by reference to hallucinations. For they know what mental images are like, and they know that *this* pink rat was not an hallucinatory content. The more frequent case, fortunately, is that they just cease to report pink rats and begin reporting hallucinations, for their hallucinations no longer deceive them.

The oddity of saying that when I think I am reporting on a stabbing pain I am actually reporting on a stimulation of my C-fibers is similar to these last two cases. We either imagine a situation in which we can envisage ourselves non-inferentially reporting such stimulation (periscope hitched up to a microscope so as to give us a view of our trepanned skull, overlying fibers folded out of the way, stimulation evident by change in color, etc.), or else we regard "stimulation of C-fibers" as not the sort of thing which *could* be the subject of a non-inferential report (but inherently a "theoretical" state of affairs whose existence can only be inferred, and not observed). In either case, the assertion that we have been non-inferentially reporting on a brain-process all our lives seems absurd. So the proponent of the disappearance form of the Identity Theory must show that reports of brain-processes are neither incapable of being non-inferential nor, if non-inferential, necessarily made in the way just imagined (with the periscope-microscope gadget) or in some other peculiar way. But now we must ask who bears the burden of proof. Why, after all, should we think that brain-processes are *not* a fit subject-matter for non-inferential reports? And why should it not be the case that the circumstances in which we make non-inferential reports about brain-processes are just those circumstances in which we make non-inferential reports about sensations? For this will in fact be the case if, when we were trained to say, e.g., "I'm in pain" we were in fact being trained to respond to the occurrence within ourselves of a stimulation of C-fibers. If this is the case, the situation will be perfectly parallel to the case of demons and hallucinations. We *will*, indeed, have been making non-inferential reports about brain-processes all our lives *sans le savoir*.

This latter suggestion can hardly be rejected *a priori*, unless we hold that we can only be taught to respond to the occurrence of A's with the utterance "A!" if we were able, prior to this teaching, to be aware, when an A was present, that it was present. But this latter claim is plausible only if we assume that there is an activity which can reasonably be called "awareness" prior to the learning of language. I do not wish to fight once again the battle which has been fought by Wittgenstein and many of his followers against such a notion of awareness. I wish rather to take it as having been won, and to take for granted that there is no *a priori* reason why a brain-process is inherently unsuited to be the subject of a non-inferential report. The distinction between observation-terms and non-observation-terms is relative to linguistic practices (practices which may change as inquiry progresses), rather than capable of being marked out once and for all by distinguishing between the "found" and the "made" elements in our experience. I think that the recognition of this relativity is the first of the steps necessary for a proper appreciation of the claims of the Identity Theory. In what follows, I want to show that this first step leads naturally to a second: the recognition that the distinction between *private* and *public* subject-matters is as relative as that between items signified by observation-terms and items not so signified.

The importance of this second step is clear. For even if we grant that reports of brain-processes may be non-inferential, we still need to get around the facts that reports of sensations have an epistemological peculiarity that leads us to call them reports of *private* entities, and that brain-processes are intrinsically *public* entities. Unless we can overcome our intuitive conviction that a report of a private matter (with its attendant infallibility) cannot be identified with a report of a public matter (with its attendant fallibility), we shall not be able to take seriously the claim of the proponents of the disappearance form of the Identity Theory that alternative (4a) is open, and hence that nothing prevents sensations from disappearing from discourse in the same manner, and for the same reasons, as supernatural beings have disappeared from discourse. So far in this paper I have deliberately avoided the problem of the "privacy" of sensations, because I wished to show that if this problem *can* be surmounted, the Identity Theorist may fairly throw the burden of proof onto his opponent by asking whether a criterion can be produced which would show that the identification of sensations and brain-processes involves a conceptual confusion, while absolving the claim that demons do not exist of such a confusion. Since I doubt that such a criterion *can* be produced, I am inclined to say that if the problem about "privacy" is overcome, then the Identity Theorist has made out his case.

## 5. The "Privacy" Objection

The problem that the privacy of first-person sensation reports presents for the Identity Theory has recently been formulated in considerable detail by Baier.[10] In this section, I shall confine myself to a discussion of his criticism of Smart's initial reply to this argument. Smart holds that the fact that "the language of introspective reports has a different logic from the logic of material processes" is no objection to the Identity Theory, since we may expect that empirical inquiry can and will change this logic:

> It is obvious that until the brain-process theory is much improved and widely accepted there will be no *criteria* for saying "Smith has an experience of such-and-such a sort" except Smith's introspective reports. So we have adopted a rule of language that (normally) what Smith says goes.[11]

Baier thinks that this reply "is simply a confusion of the privacy of the subject-matter and the availability of external evidence."[12] Baier's intuition is that the difference between a language-stratum in which the fact that a report is sincerely made is sufficient warrant for its truth, and one in which this situation does not obtain, seems so great as to call for an explanation —and that the only explanation is that the two strata concern different subject-matters. Indeed Baier is content to let the mental-physical distinction stand or fall with the distinction

---

[10] Kurt Baier, "Smart on Sensations," *Australasian Journal of Philosophy*, 40 (1962), pp. 57–68.

[11] Smart, "Sensations and Brain Processes," p. 169.

[12] Baier, p. 63.

between "private" subject-matters and "public" subject-matters, and he therefore assumes that to show that "introspective reports are necessarily about something private, and that being about something private is *incompatible with being* about something public"[13] is to show, once and for all, that the Identity Theory involves a conceptual confusion. Baier, in short, is undertaking to show that "once private, always private."

He argues for his view as follows:

> To say that one day our physiological knowledge will increase to such an extent that we shall be able to make absolutely reliable encephalograph-based claims about people's experiences, is only to say that, if carefully checked, our encephalograph-based claims about 'experiences' will always be *correct,* i.e. will make the *same claims* as a *truthful* introspective report. If correct encephalograph-based claims about Smith's experiences contradict Smith's introspective reports, we shall be entitled to infer that he is *lying.* In that sense, what Smith says will no longer go. But we cannot of course infer that he is making a mistake, for that is nonsense . . . *However good the evidence may be, such a physiological theory can never be used to show to the sufferer that he was mistaken in thinking that he had a pain, for such a mistake is inconceivable.* The sufferer's epistemological authority must therefore be better than the best physiological theory can ever be. Physiology can therefore never provide a person with more than *evidence* that someone else is having an experience of one sort or another. It can never lay down *criteria* for saying that someone is having an experience of a certain sort. Talk about brain-processes therefore must be about something other than talk about experiences. Hence, introspective reports and brain-process talk cannot be merely different ways of talking about the same thing.[14]

Smart's own reply to this line of argument is to admit that

13 Baier, p. 59.
14 Baier, pp. 64–65; italics added.

No physiological evidence, say from a gadget attached to my skull, could make me withdraw the statement that I have a pain when as a matter of fact I feel a pain. For example, the gadget might show no suitable similarities of cerebral processes on the various occasions on which I felt a pain . . . I must, I think, agree with Baier that if the sort of situation which we have just envisaged did in fact come about, then I should have to reject the brain-process thesis, and would perhaps espouse dualism.[15]

But this is not the interesting case. The interesting case is the one in which suitable similarities are in fact found to occur —the same similarities in all subjects—until one day (long after all empirical generalizations about sensations *qua* sensations have been subsumed under physiological laws, and long after direct manipulation of the brain has become the exclusive method of relieving pain) somebody (call him Jones) thinks he has no pain, but the encephalograph says that the brain-process correlated with pain did occur. (Let us imagine that Jones himself is observing the gadget, and that the problem about whether he might have made a mistake is a problem for Jones; this eliminates the possibility of lying.) Now in most cases in which one's observation throws doubt on a correlation which is so central to current scientific explanations, one tries to eliminate the possibility of observational error. But in Baier's view it would be absurd for Jones to do this, for "a mistake is inconceivable." Actually, however, it is fairly clear what Jones' first move would be—he will begin to suspect that he does not know what pain is—i.e., that he is not using the word "pain" in the way in which his fellows use it.[16]

So now Jones looks about for independent verification of the hypothesis that he does not use "I am in pain" incorrectly. But here he runs up against the familiar difficulty about the

[15] Smart, "Brain Processes and Incorrigibility—a Reply to Professor Baier," *Australasian Journal of Philosophy*, 40 (1962), p. 68.

[16] This problem will remain, of course, even if Jones merely *thinks* about whether he is in pain, but does not say anything.

vocabulary used in making introspective reports—the difficulty of distinguishing between "misuse of language" and "mistake in judgment"—between (a) recognizing the state of affairs which obtains for what it is, but describing it wrongly because the words used in the description are not the right words, and (b) being able to describe it rightly once it is recognized for what it is, but not in fact recognizing it for what it is (in the way in which one deceived by an illusion does not recognize the situation for what it is). If we do not have a way of determining which of these situations obtains, we do not have a genuine contrast between misnaming and misjudging. To see that there is no genuine contrast in this case, suppose that Jones was not burned prior to the time that he hitches on the encephalograph, but now he is. When he is, the encephalograph says that the brain-process constantly correlated with pain-reports occurs in Jones' brain. However, although he exhibits pain-behavior, Jones thinks that he does not feel pain. (But, now as in the past, he both exhibits pain-behavior and thinks that he feels pain when he is frozen, stuck, struck, racked, etc.) Now is it that he does not know that *pain* covers what you feel when you are burned as well as what you feel when you are stuck, struck, etc.? Or is it that he really does not feel pain when he is burned? Suppose we tell Jones that what he feels when he is burned is *also* called "pain." Suppose he then admits that he does feel *something*, but insists that what he feels is quite *different* from what he feels when he is stuck, struck, etc. Where does Jones go from here? Has he failed to learn the language properly, or is he correctly (indeed infallibly) reporting that he has different sensations than those normally had in the situation in question? (Compare the parallel question in the case of a man who uses "blue" in all the usual ways except that he refuses to grant that blue is a color—on the ground that it is so different from red, yellow, orange, violet, etc.)

The only device which would decide this question would be to establish a convention that anyone who sincerely denied that he felt a pain while exhibiting pain-behavior and being burned *ipso facto* did not understand how to use "pain." This denial would *prove* that he lacked such an understanding. But this would be a dangerous path to follow. For not to understand when to use the word "pain" in non-inferential reports is presumably to be unable to know which of one's sensations to call a "pain." And the denial that one felt pain in the circumstances mentioned would only prove such inability if one indeed *had* the sensation normally called a pain. So now we would have a public criterion, satisfaction of which would count as showing that the subject had such a sensation—i.e., that he felt a pain even though he did not think that he did. But if such a criterion exists, its application overrides any contradictory report that he may make—for such a report will be automatically disallowed by the fact that it constitutes a demonstration that he does not know what he is talking about. The dilemma is that either a report about one's sensations which violates a certain public criterion is a sufficient condition for saying that the reporter does not know how to use "pain" in the correct way, or there is no such criterion. If there is, the fact that one cannot be mistaken about pains does not entail that sincere reports of pain cannot be over-ridden. If there is not, then there is no way to answer the question formulated at the end of the last paragraph, and hence no way to eliminate the possibility that Jones may not know what pain is. Now since the *a priori* probability that he does not is a good deal higher than the *a priori* probability that the psycho-physiological theory of Jones' era is mistaken, this theory has little to fear from Jones. (Although it would have a great deal to fear from a sizable accumulation of cases like Jones.')

To sum up this point, we may look back at the italicized sentence in the above quotation from Baier. We now see that the claim that "such a mistake is inconceivable" is an ellipsis for the claim that a mistake, made *by one who knows what pain is*, is inconceivable, for only this expanded form will entail that when Jones and the encephalograph disagree, Jones is always right. But when formulated in this way our infallibility about our pains can be seen to be empty. Being infallible about something would be useful only if we could draw the usual distinction between misnaming and misjudging, and, having ascertained that we were not misnaming, know that we were not misjudging. But where there are no criteria for misjudging (or to put it more accurately, where in the crucial cases the criteria for misjudging turn out to be the same as the criteria for misnaming), then to say that we are infallible is to pay ourselves an empty compliment. Our neighbors will not hesitate to ride rough-shod over our reports of our sensations unless they are assured that we know our way around among them, and we cannot satisfy them on this point unless, up to a certain point, we tell the same sort of story about them as they do. The limits of permissible stories are flexible enough for us to be able to convince them occasionally that we have odd sensations, but not flexible enough for us to use these surprising sensations to break down, at one blow, well-confirmed scientific theories. As in the case of other infallible pronouncements, the price of retaining one's epistemological authority is a decent respect for the opinions of mankind.

Thus the common-sense remark that first-person reports always will be a better source of information about the occurrence of pains than any other source borrows its plausibility from the fact that we normally do not raise questions about a man's ability to use the word "pain" correctly. Once we *do* raise such questions seriously (as in the case of Jones), we realize that the question (1) "Does he know which sensations are called 'pains'?" and (2) "Is he a good judge of whether he is in pain or not?" are simply two ways of asking the same question—viz., "Can we fit his pain-reports into our scheme for explaining and predicting pains?" or, more bluntly, "Shall we disregard his pain-reports or not?" And once we see this we realize that if "always be a better source of information" means "will never be over-ridden on the sort of grounds on which presumed observational errors are over-ridden elsewhere in science," then our common-sensical remark is probably false. If "always be a better source of information" means merely "can only be over-ridden on the basis of a charge of misnaming, and never on the basis of a charge of misjudging," then our common-sensical remark turns out to depend upon a distinction that is not there.

This Wittgensteinian point that sensation-reports must conform to public criteria or else be disallowed may also be brought out in the following way. We determine whether to take a surprising first-person report of pain or its absence seriously (that is, whether to say that the sensation reported is something that science must try to explain) by seeing whether the reporter's over-all pattern of pain-reporting is, by the usual behaviorial and environmental criteria, normal. Now suppose that these public criteria (for "knowing how to use 'pain'") change as physiology and technology progress. Suppose, in particular, that we find it convenient to speed up the learning of contrastive observation predicates (such as "painful," "tickling," etc.) by supplying children with portable encephalographs-cum-teaching-machines which, whenever the appropriate brain-process occurs, murmur the appropriate term in their ears. Now "appropriate brain-process" will start out by meaning "brain-process constantly correlated with sincere utterances of 'I'm in pain' by people taught the use of 'pain' in the old rough-and-ready way." But soon it will come to mean, "the brain-process which we have always programmed the machine to respond to with a murmur of 'pain.'" (A meter is (now, but was not always) what matches the Standard Meter; intelligence is (now, but was not always) what intelligence tests test; pains will be (but are not now) what the Standard "Pain"-Training Program calls "pain.") Given this situation, it would make sense to say things like "You say you are in pain, and I'm sure you are sincere, but you can see for yourself that your brain is not in the state to which you were trained to respond to with "Pain," so apparently the training did not work, and you do not yet understand what pain is." In such a situation, our "inability to be mistaken" about our pains would remain, but our "final epistemological authority" on the subject would be gone, for there would be a standard procedure for over-riding our reports. Our inability to be mistaken is, after all, no more than our ability to have such hypothetical statements as "If you admit that I'm sincere and that I know the language, you have to accept what I say" accepted by our fellows. But this asset can only be converted into final epistemological authority if we can secure both admissions. Where a clear-cut public criterion *does* exist for "knowing the language," inability to be mistaken does not entail inability to be over-ridden.

Now Baier might say that if such criteria did exist, then we should no longer be talking about what we presently mean by "pains." I do not think that this needs to be conceded,[17] but suppose that it is. Would this mean that there was now a subject-matter which was not being discussed—viz., the private subject-matter the existence of which Baier's argument was intended to demonstrate? That we once had contact with such a subject-matter, but lost it? These rhetorical questions are meant to suggest that Baier's explanation of the final epistemological authority of first-person reports of pains by the fact that this "logic" is "a function of this type of subject-matter" rather than, as Smart thinks, a convention is an explanation of the obscure by the more obscure. More precisely, it will not be an explanation of the epistemological authority in question— but only an unenlightening redescription of it—unless Baier can give a meaning to the term "private subject-matter" other than "kind of thing which is reported in reports which cannot be over-ridden." These considerations show the need for stepping back from Baier's argument and considering the criteria which he is using to demarcate distinct subject-matters.

[17] My reasons for thinking this concession unnecessary are the same as those presented in some recent articles by Hilary Putnam: cf. "Minds and Machines," *Dimensions of Mind*, ed. Hook (Collier Books, New York, 1961), pp. 138–161, esp. pp. 153–160; "The Analytic and the Synthetic," *Minnesota Studies in the Philosophy of Science*, III, pp. 358–397; "Brains and Behavior," in *Analytic Philosophy*, II, ed. R. J. Butler (Blackell's, Oxford, 1965).

## 6. "Privacy" as a Criterion of Categorial Demarcation

The closest Baier comes to giving a definition of "private subject-matter" is to say that

> We must say that "I have a pain" is about "something private," because in making this remark we report something which is (1) *necessarily owned* . . . is (2) *necessarily exclusive and unsharable* . . . (3) *necessarily imperceptible by the senses* . . . (4) *necessarily asymmetrical*, for whereas it makes no sense to say "I could see (or hear) that I had a pain," it makes quite good sense to say "I could see (or hear) that *he* had a pain"; (5) something about the possession of which the person who claims to possess it could not possibly examine, consider, or weigh any evidence, although other people could . . . and lastly (6) it is something about which the person whose private state it is has final epistemological authority, for it does not make sense to say "I have a pain unless I am mistaken."[18]

Now this definition of "something private" entails that nothing could be private except a state of a person, and is constructed to delimit all and only those states of a person which we call his "mental" states. To say that mental states are private is to say simply that mental states are described in the way in which mental states are described. But it is not hard to take *any* Rylean category of terms (call it *C*), list all the types of sentence-frames which do and do not make sense when their gaps are filled with terms belonging to this category, and say that "something C" is distinguished by the fact that it is "necessarily X," "necessarily Y," etc., where "X" and "Y" labels for the fact that certain sentence-frames will or will not receive these terms as gap-fillers. For example, consider the thesis that:

> We must say that 'The devil is in that corner' is about 'something supernatural' because in making this report we report

[18] Baier, "Smart on Sensations," p. 60; The numbers in parentheses have been added.

something which is *necessarily intangible,* since it makes no
sense to ask about the texture of his skin, not *necessarily simply located,* since it does not follow from the fact that a supernatural being is in the corner that the same supernatural being
is not simultaneously at the other side of the globe, *necessarily
immortal,* since it does not make sense to say that a supernatural being has died, *necessarily perceptible to exorcists,*
since it would not make sense to say that a man was an
exorcist and did not perceive the devil when he was present ...

Are devils hallucinations? No, because when one reports an
hallucination one reports something which, though intangible,
is simply-located, is neither mortal nor immortal, and is not
always perceptible to exorcists. Are reports of devils reports of
hallucinations? No, because reports of devils are reports of
something supernatural, and reports of hallucinations are reports
of something private. Is it simply because we lack further
information about devils that we take exorcists' sincere reports
as the best possible source for information about them? No,
for this suggestion confuses the supernatural character of the
subject-matter with the availability of external evidence. Those
without the supernatural powers with which the exorcist is
gifted may find ways of gathering *evidence* for the presence
of supernatural beings, but they can never formulate an over-
riding and independent *criterion* for saying that such a being
is present. Their theories might become so good that we might
sometimes say that a given exorcist was *lying,* but we could
never say that he was *mistaken.*

If this pastiche of Baier's argument seems beside the point,
it is presumably either (1) because the language-game I have
described is not in fact played, or else (2) because "necessarily intangible, not necessarily simply-located, necessarily
immortal, and necessarily perceptible to exorcists" does not
delimit a subject-matter in the way in which "necessarily owned,
exclusive, imperceptible by the senses, asymmetrical, etc., etc.,"
does. In (1) one has to ask "what if it *had* been played?"
After all, if the technique of detecting distinct subject-matters
which Baier uses is a generally applicable technique, and not

just constructed *ad hoc* to suit our Cartesian intuitions, then it ought to work on imaginary as well as real language games. But if it is, we ought to be able to formulate rules for applying it which would tell us *why* (2) is the case. For if we cannot, and if the language-game described once was played, then Baier's objection to the Identity Theory is an objection to the theory that reports of visible supernatural beings are reports of hallucinations. Baier gives no more help in seeing what these rules would be. But I think that the root of Baier's conviction that "something private" is a suitable candidate for being a "distinct subject-matter" is the thesis that certain terms are *intrinsically* observation predicates, and signify, so to speak, "natural explananda." When in quest of such predicates we look to the "foundations" of empirical knowledge, we tend to rapidly identify "observation predicate" with "predicate occurring in report having final epistemological authority" with "predicate occurring in report about something private." This chain of identifications leaves us with the suspicion that if there were no longer a private subject-matter to be infallible about, the whole fabric of empirical inquiry about public matters would be left up in the air, unsupported by any absolute epistemological authority. The suggestion that the distinction between items reportable in infallible reports and items not so reportable is "ultimate," or "irreducible," or "categorical," owes its intuitive force to the difficulty of imagining a stage in the progress of inquiry in which there was not *some* situation in which absolute epistemological authority about *something* would be granted to *somebody*.

There probably, indeed, could *not* be such a stage, for inquiry cannot proceed if everything is to be doubted at once, and if inquiry is even to get off the ground we need to get straight about what is to be questioned and what not. These practical dictates show the kernel of truth in the notion that inquiry cannot proceed without a foundation. Where we slide from truth into error is in assuming that certain items are *naturally* reportable in infallible reports, and thus assume that the items presently so reportable always were and always will be reportable (and conversely for items not presently so reportable). A pain looks like the paradigm of such an item, with the situation described by "seems to me as if I were seeing something red" almost as well-qualified. But in both cases, we can imagine situations in which we should feel justified in over-riding sincere reports using these predicates. More important, we see that the device which we should use to justify ourselves in such situations—viz., "The reporter may not know how to use the word . . ."—is one which can apply in *all* proposed cases. Because this escape-hatch is always available, and because the question of whether the reporter does know how to use the word or does not is probably not itself a question which could ever be settled by recourse to any absolute epistemological authority, the situation envisaged by Baier—namely, the body of current scientific theory foundering upon the rock of a single over-riding report—can probably never arise. Baier sees a difference in kind between the weight of *evidence* produced by such a theory and the single, authoritative, *criterion* provided by such a report. But since there can be no over-riding report until the ability of the speaker to use the words used in the report is established, and since this is to be established only by the weight of the evidence and not by recourse to any single criterion, this difference in kind (even though it may indeed be "firmly embedded in the way we talk" for millennia) is always capable of being softened into a difference of degree by further empirical inquiry.

## 7. Reductionist Philosophical Theories and Categorial Distinctions

In the preceding sections of this paper I have constantly invoked the fact that language changes as empirical discoveries are made, in order to argue that the thesis that "what people now call 'sensations' might be discovered to be brain-processes" is sensible and unconfused. The "deviance" of a statement of this thesis should not, I have been urging, blind us to the facts that (a) entities referred to by expressions in one Rylean category may also be referred to by expressions in another, (b) expressions in the first category may drop out of the language once this identity of reference is realized, and (c) the thesis in question is a natural way of expressing the result of this realization in the case of "sensation" and "brain-process." Now a critic might object that this strategy is subject to a *reductio ad absurdum.* For the same fact about linguistic change would seem to justify the claim that *any* statement of the form (S) "What people call 'X's' may be discovered to be Y's" is *always* sensible and unconfused. Yet this seems paradoxical, for consider the result of substituting, say "neutrino" for "X" and "mushroom" for "Y." If the resulting statement is not conceptually confused, what statement is?

In answer to this objection, I should argue that it is a mistake to attribute "conceptual confusions" to *statements.* No statement can be known to express a conceptual confusion simply by virtue of an acquaintance with the meanings of its component terms. Confusion is a property of people. Deviance is a property of utterances. Deviant utterances made by using sentences of the form (S) *may* be token confusion on the part of the speaker about the meanings of words, but it may simply indicate a vivid (but unconfused) imagination, or perhaps (as in the neutrino-mushroom case) merely idle fancy. Although the making of such statements may be *prima facie* evidence of conceptual confusion—i.e., of the fact that the speaker is insufficiently familiar with the language to find a non-deviant way of making his point—this evidence is only *prima facie*, and questioning may bring out evidence pointing the other way. Such questioning may show that the speaker actually has some detailed suggestions about possible empirical results which would point to the discovery in question, or that he has no such suggestions, but is nevertheless not inclined to use the relevant words in any *other* deviant utterances, and to cheerfully admit the deviance of his original utterance. The possibility of such evidence, pointing to imagination or to fancy rather than to confusion, shows that from the fact that certain questions are typically asked, and certain statements typically made,

by victims of conceptual confusion, it does not follow that all
those who use the sentences used to ask these questions or to
make these statements are thus victimized.

This confusion about confusion is due to the fact that
philosophers who propound "reductionist" theories (such as
"There is no insensate matter," "There are no minds," "There
are no physical objects," etc.) ) often *have* been conceptually
confused. Such theories are often advocated as solutions to
pseudo-problems whose very formulation involves deviant uses
of words—uses which in fact result from a confusion between
the uses of two or more senses of the same term, or between
two or more related terms (e.g., "name" and "word") or
between the kind of questions appropriately asked of entities
referred to by one set of terms and the kind appropriately asked
of entities referred to by another. (That these deviant uses *are*
the result of such confusion, it should be noticed, is only capable of being determined by questioning of those who use them—
and we only feel *completely* safe in making this diagnosis when
the original user has, in the light of the linguistic facts drawn
to his attention, admitted that his putative "problem" has been
dissolved.) Because reductionist theories may often be choked
off at the source by an examination of uses of language, anti-
reductionist philosophers have lately become prone to use "conceptual confusion" or "category mistake" as an all-purpose
diagnosis for any deviant utterance in the mouth of a philosopher. But this is a mistake. Predictions of the sort illustrated
by (S) may be turned to confused purposes, and they may
be made by confused people. But we could only infer with certainty from the deviance of the utterance of a sentence of the
form (S) to the conceptual confusion of the speaker if we had
a map of the categories which are exhibited in all possible
languages, and were thus in a position to say that the cross-
category identification envisaged by the statement was eternally
impossible. In other words, we should only be in a position
to make this inference with certainty if we knew that empirical
inquiry could *never* bring about the sort of linguistic change
which permits the non-deviant use of "There are no X's" in the

case of the "X's" to which the statement in question refers. But philosophers are in no position to say that such change is impossible. The hunt for categorial confusions at the source of reductionist philosophical theories is an extremely valuable enterprise. But their successes in this enterprise should not lead linguistic philosophers to think that they can do better what metaphysicians did badly—namely, prove the irreducibility of entities. Traditional materialism embodied many confusions, but at its heart was the unconfused prediction about future empirical inquiry which is the Identity Theory. The confusions may be eradicated without affecting the plausibility or interest of the prediction.[19]

# ROBOTS: MACHINES OR ARTIFICIALLY CREATED LIFE? [1]

HILARY PUTNAM

Those of us who passed many (well- or ill-spent?) childhood hours reading tales of rockets and robots, androids and telepaths, galactic civilizations and time machines, know all too well that robots—hypothetical machines that simulate human behavior, often with an at least roughly human appearance—can be friendly or fearsome, man's best friend or worst enemy. When friendly, robots can be inspiring or pathetic—they can overawe us with their superhuman powers (and with their greater than human virtue as well, at least in the writings of some authors), or they can amuse us with their stupidities and naivete. Robots have been "known" to fall in love, go mad (power- or other-

[19] I have been greatly helped in preparing this paper by the comments of Richard Bernstein, Keith Gunderson, Amélie Rorty, and Richard Schmitt.

Reprinted from *The Journal of Philosophy* (Vol. LXI, No. 21, November 12, 1964), by permission of the editor and Hilary Putnam.
[1] This paper was presented in a symposium on "Minds and Machines" at the sixty-first annual meeting of the American Philosophical Association, Eastern Division, December 28, 1964.

wise), annoy with oversolicitousness. At least in the literature
of science fiction, then, it is possible for a robot to be "conscious"; that means (since 'consciousness,' like 'material object'
and 'universal,' is a philosopher's stand-in for more substantial
words) to have feelings, thoughts, attitudes, and character traits.
But is it really possible? If it is possible, what are the necessary
and sufficient conditions? And why should we philosophers
worry about this anyway? Aren't the mind-body problem, the
problem of other minds, the problem of logical behaviorism,
the problem: What did Wittgenstein really mean in the private-
language argument? (and why should one care?), more than
enough to keep the most industrious philosopher of mind busy
without dragging in or inventing the Problem of the Minds of
Machines?—These are my concerns in this paper.

The mind-body problem has been much discussed in the
past thirty-odd years, but the discussion seems to me to have
been fruitless. No one has really been persuaded by *The Concept
of Mind* that the relation of university to buildings, professors,
and students is a helpful model for the relation of mind to body,
or even for the relation of, say, *being intelligent* to individual
speech-acts. And Herbert Feigl informs me that he has now
himself abandoned his well-known "identity theory" of the
mind-body relation. The problem of other minds has been
much more fruitful—the well-known and extremely important
paper by Austin is ample testimony to that—but even that
problem has begun to seem somewhat stale of late. What I
hope to persuade you is that the problem of the Minds of
Machines will prove, at least for a while, to afford an exciting
new way to approach quite traditional issues in the philosophy
of mind. Whether, and under what conditions, a robot could
be conscious is a question that cannot be discussed without at
once impinging on the topics that have been treated under the
headings Mind-Body Problem and Problem of Other Minds.
For my own part, I believe that certain crucial issues come to
the fore almost of their own accord in this connection—issues
which *should* have discussed by writers who have dealt
with the two headings just mentioned, but which have not

been—and, therefore, that the problem of the robot becomes almost obligatory for a philosopher of mind to discuss.

Before starting I wish to emphasize, lest any should mis-understand, that my concern is with how we should speak about humans and not with how we should speak about machines. My interest in the latter question derives from my just-mentioned conviction: that clarity with respect to the "borderline-case" of robots, if it can only be achieved, will carry with it clarity with respect to the "central area" of talk about feelings, thoughts, consciousness, life, etc.

## Minds and Machines

In an earlier paper,[2] I attempted to show that a problem *very* analogous to the mind-body problem would automatically arise for robots. The same point could easily have been made in connection with the problem of other minds. To briefly review the argument: conceive of a community of robots. Let these robots "know" nothing concerning their own physical make-up or how they came into existence (perhaps they would arrive at a robot Creation Story and a polytheistic religion, with robot gods on a robot Olympus). Let them "speak" a language (say, English), in conformity with the grammatical rules and the publicly observable semantic and discourse-analytical regularities of that language. What might the role of psychological predicates be in such a community?

In the paper referred to, I employed a simple "evincing" model for such predicates. Since this model is obviously *over*-simple, let us tell a more complicated story. When a robot sees something red (something that evokes the appropriate internal state in the robot) he calls it "red." Our robots are supposed to be capable of inductive reasoning and theory construction. So a robot may discover that something he called red was not really red. Then he will say "well, it looked red." Or, if he is in the appropriate internal state for red, but knows on the

[2] "Minds and Machines," in Sidney Hook, ed., *Dimensions of Mind* (New York: NYU Press, 1960), pp. 148–179.

basis of cross-inductions from certain other cases that what he "sees" is not really red, he will say "it *looks* red, but it isn't really red." Thus he will have a distinction between the physical reality and the visual appearance, just as we do. But the robot will never say "that looks as if it looked red, but it doesn't really look red." That is, there is no notion in the robot-English of an *appearance of an appearance of red*, any more than there is in English. Moreover, the reason is the same: that any state which cannot be discriminated from "looks-red" *counts* as "looks-red" (under normal conditions of linguistic proficiency, absence of confusion, etc). What this illustrates, of course, is that the "incorrigibility" of statements of the form "that looks red" is to be explained by an elucidation of the logical features of such discourse, and not by the metaphor of "direct" access.

If we assume that these robots are unsophisticated scientifically, there is no reason for them to know more of their own internal constitution than an ancient Greek knew about the functioning of the central nervous system. We may imagine them developing a sophisticated science in the course of centuries, and thus eventually arriving at tentative identifications of the form: "when a thing 'looks red' to one of us, it means he is in internal state 'flip-flop 72 is on'." If these robots also publish papers on philosophy (and why should a robot not be able to do considerably better than many of our students?), a lively discussion may ensue concerning the philosophical implications of such discoveries. Some robots may argue, "*obviously,* what we have discovered is that 'seeing red' *is* being in internal state 'flip-flop 72 on'"; others may argue, "*obviously,* what you made was an *empirical* discovery; the *meaning* of 'it looks red' isn't the same as the *meaning* of 'flip-flop 72 is on'; hence the *attributes* (or states, or conditions, or properties) 'being in the state of seeming to see something red' and 'having flip-flop 72 on' are *two* attributes (or states, or conditions, or properties) and not *one*"; others may argue "when I have the illusion that something red is present, nothing red is physically there. Yet, in a sense, I *see* something red. What I see, I *call* a sense datum. The sense datum is red. The flip-flop isn't red. So, *obviously,* the

sense datum can't be identical with the flip-flop, on or off."
And so on. In short, robots can be just as bad at philosophy
as people. Or (more politely), the *logical* aspects of the Mind-
Body Problem are aspects of a problem that *must* arise for any
computing system satisfying the conditions that (1) it uses
language and constructs theories; (2) it does not initially
"know" its own physical make-up, except superficially; (3) it
is equipped with sense organs, and able to perform experiments; (4) it comes to know its own make-up through empirical
investigation and theory construction.

## Some Objections Considered

The argument just reviewed seems extremely simple. Yet
some astonishing misunderstandings have arisen. The one that
most surprised me was expressed thus: "As far as I can see, all
you show is that a robot could simulate human *behavior*." This
objection, needless (hopefully)-to-say, misses the point of the
foregoing *completely*. The point is this: that a robot or a computing machine can, *in a sense*, follow rules (Whether it is the
same sense as the sense in which a man follows rules, or only
analogous, depends on whether the particular robot can be
said to be "conscious," etc., and thus on the central question of
this paper.); that the meaning of an utterance is a function of
the rules that govern its construction and use; that the rules
governing the *robot* utterances 'I see something that looks red'
and 'flip-flop 72 is on' are quite different. The former utterance
may be correctly uttered by any robot which has "learned" to
discriminate red things from non-red things correctly, judged
by the consensus of the other robots, and which finds itself in
the state that signals the presence of a red object. Thus, in the
case of a normally constructed robot, 'I see something that
looks red' may be uttered whenever flip-flop 72 is on, *whether
the robot "knows" that flip-flop 72 is on or not*. 'Flip-flop 72 is
on' may be correctly (reasonably) uttered only when the robot
"knows" that flip-flop 72 is on—i.e., only when it can *conclude*
that flip-flop 72 is on from empirically established theory together with such observation statements as its conditioning may

prompt it to utter, or as it may hear other robots utter. 'It looks red' is an utterance for which it does not and cannot give reasons. 'Flip-flop 72 is on' is an utterance for which it can give reasons. And so on. Since these semantic differences are the same for the robot as for a human, any argument from the semantic nonequivalence of internal (physical)-state statements and "looks" statements to the character of mind or consciousness must be valid for the robot if it is valid for a human. (Likewise the argument from the alleged fact that there is "a sense of *see*" in which one can correctly say "I see something red" in certain cases in which nothing red is physically present.)

Besides the misunderstandings and nonunderstandings just alluded to, some interesting objections have been advanced. These objections attempt to break the logical analogy just drawn by me. I shall here briefly discuss two such objections, advanced by Prof. Kurt Baier.

Baier's first argument[3] runs as follows: The connection between my visual sensation of red and my utterance 'it looks as if there is something red in front of me' (or whatever) is *not* merely a causal one. The sensation does not *merely* evoke the utterance; I utter the utterance because I *know* that I am having the sensation. But the robot utters the utterance because he is *caused* to utter it by his internal state (flip-flop 72 being on). Thus there is a fundamental disanalogy between the two cases.

Baier's second argument is as follows: Certain *qualia* are *intrinsically* painful and others are *intrinsically* pleasurable. I cannot conceive of an intrinsically unpleasant quale *Q* being exactly the same for someone else "only he finds it pleasurable." However, if a robot is programmed so that it *acts as if* it were having a pleasant experience when, say, a certain part of its anatomy jangles, it could easily be reprogrammed so that it would act as if it were having a painful, and not a pleasant,

[3] These arguments come from an unpublished paper by Baier, which was read at a colloquium at the Albert Einstein College of Medicine in 1962.

experience upon those occasions. Thus the counterparts of "qualia" in the robot case—certain physical states—lack an essential property of qualia: they cannot be *intrinsically* pleasurable or painful.

Can a robot have a sensation? Well, it can have a "sensation." That is, it can be a "model" for any psychological theory that is true of human beings. If it is a "model" for such a theory, then when it is in the internal state that corresponds to or "realizes" the psychological predicate "has the visual sensation of red," it will act as a human would act (depending also on what other "psychological" predicates apply). That is, "flip-flop 72 being on" does not have to *directly* (uncontrollably) "evoke" the utterance 'It looks as if there is something red in front of me.' I agree with Baier that so simple an "evincing" model will certainly not do justice to the character of such reports—but not in the case of robots either!

What is it for a person to "know" that he has a sensation? Since only philosophers talk in this way, no uniform answer is to be expected. Some philosophers identify having a sensation and knowing that one has it. Then "I know I have the visual sensation of red" just means "I have the visual sensation of red," and the question "Can the robot *know* that he has the 'sensation' of red?" means "Can the robot have the 'sensation' of red?"—a question which we have answered in the affirmative. (I have not argued that "sensations" are *sensations*, but only that a thorough-going logical analogy holds between sensation-talk in the case of humans and "sensation"-talk in the case of robots.) Other philosophers (most recently Ayer, in *The Concept of a Person*) have argued that to *know* one has a sensation one must be able to describe it. But in this sense, too, a robot can know that he has a "sensation." If knowing that *p* is having a "multi-tracked disposition" to appropriate sayings and question-answerings and behavings, as urged by Ryle in *The Concept of Mind*, then a robot can know anything a person can. A robot, just as well as a human, could participate in the following dialogue:

A. Describe the visual sensation you just mentioned.
B. It is the sensation of a large red expanse.
A. Is the red uniform—the same shade all over?
B. I think so.
A. Attend carefully!
B. I am!

Unfortunately for this last argument, Ryle's account of knowing is incorrect; no specifiable disposition to sayings and behavings, "multi-tracked" or otherwise, can *constitute* a knowing-that in the way in which certain specifiable arrangements and interrelationships of buildings, administrators, professors, and students will constitute a university. "Knowing that," like being in pain and like preferring, is only mediately related to behavior: knowing that *p* involves being disposed to answer certain questions correctly *if I want to, if I am not confused,* etc. And wanting to answer a question correctly is being disposed to answer it correctly *if I know the answer, if there is nothing I want more,* etc.—Psychological states are characterizable only in terms of their relations to each other (as well as to behavior, etc.), and not as dispositions which can be "unpacked" without coming back to the very psychological predicates that are in question. But this is not fatal to our case. A robot, too, can have internal states that are related to each other (and only indirectly to behavior and sensory stimulation) as required by a psychological theory. Then, when the robot is in the internal state that realizes the predicate "knows that *p*" we may say that the robot "knows" that *p*. Its "knowing" may not be *knowing*—because it may not "really be conscious"—that is what we have to decide; but it will play the role in the robot's behavior that *knowing* plays in human behavior. In sum, for any sense in which a human can "know that he has a sensation" there will be a logically and semantically analogous sense in which a robot can "know" that he has a "sensation." And this is all that my argument requires.

After this digression on the logical character of "knowing," we are finally ready to deal with Baier's first argument. The argument may easily be seen to be a mere variant of the "water-on-the-brain" argument (you can have water on the brain but not water on the mind; hence the mind is not the brain). One can know that one has a sensation without knowing that one is in brain-state $S$; hence the sensation cannot be identical with brain-state $S$. This is all the argument comes to. But, since "knowing that" is an intensional context, a robot can correctly say "I don't know that flip-flop 72 is on (or even what a 'flip-flop' is, for that matter)," even in situations in which it can correctly assert, "I have the 'sensation' of red." It can even assert: "I 'know' that I have the 'sensation' of red." If it follows in the human case that the sensation of red is not identical with the brain-state $S$, then by the same argument from the same semantical premises, the robot philosopher can conclude that the "sensation" of red is not identical with "flip-flop 72 being on." The robot philosopher too can argue: "I am not merely *caused* to utter the utterance 'It looks as if there is something red in front of me' by the occurrence of the 'sensation'; part of the causation is also that I '*understand*' the words that I utter; I 'know' that I am having the 'sensation'; I 'wish' to report my 'sensation' to other robots; etc." And, indeed, I think that Baier and the robot philosopher are both right. Psychological attributes, whether in human language or in robot language, are simply *not* the same as physical attributes. To say that a robot is angry (or "angry") is a quite different predication from the predication "such and such a fluid has reached a high concentration," even if the latter predicate "physically realizes" the former. Psychological theories say that an organism has certain states which are *not* specified in "physical" terms, but which are taken as primitive. Relations are specified between these states, and between the totality of the states and sensory inputs ("stimuli") and behavior ("responses"). Thus, as Jerry Fodor has remarked,[4] it is part of the "logic" of psychological theories that (physically) *different* structures may obey

[4] "Psychological Explanation," to appear in a . . . collection edited by Max Black.

(or be "models" of) the *same* psychological theory. A robot and a human being may exhibit "repression" or "inhibitory potential" in exactly the same sense. I do not contend that 'angry' is a primitive term in a psychological theory; indeed, this account, which has been taken by some as a reaction to Ryle-ism, seems to me to create puzzles where none should exist (if 'angry' is a theoretical term, then "I am angry" must be a *hypothesis!*); but I do contend that the patterns of correct usage, in the case of an ordinary-language psychological term, no more presuppose or imply that there is an *independently* specifiable state which "realizes" the predicate, or, if there is one, that it is a *physical* state in the narrow sense (definable in terms of the vocabulary of present-day physics), or, if there is one, that it is the *same* for all members of the speech community, than the postulates of a psychological theory do. Indeed, there could be a community of robots that did *not* all have the same physical constitution, but did all have the same *psychology;* and such robots could *univocally* say "I have the sensation of red," "you have the sensation of red," "he has the sensation of red," even if the three robots referred to did not "physically realize" the "sensation of red" in the same way. Thus the *attributes:* having the "sensation" of red and "flip-flop 72 being on" are simply *not* identical in the case of the robots. If Materialism is taken to be the denial of the existence of "nonphysical" attributes, then Materialism is false even for robots!

Still, Baier might reply: if I say that a robot has the "sensation" of red, I mean that he is in *some* physical state (a "visual" one) that signals to him the presence of red objects; if I say that a human has the sensation of red, I do not mean that he is necessarily in some special *physical* state. *Of course,* there is a *state* I am in when and only when I have the sensation of red—namely, the state of having a sensation of red. But this is a remark about the logic of 'state,' and says *nothing* about the meaning of 'sensation of red.'

I think that this is right. When *we* say: "that robot has the 'sensation' of red." there are (or would be) implications that are not present when we talk about each other. But that is because we think of the robots *as* robots. Let us suppose that the robots do *not* "think" of themselves as robots; according to their theory, they have (or possibly have) "souls." Then, when a robot says of another robot "he has the 'sensation' of red" (or something in more ordinary language to this effect), the implication will *not* be present that the other robot must be in any special *physical* state. Why should it not be an open possibility for the robot scientists and philosophers that they will *fail* to find "correlates" at the physical level for the various sensations they report, just as it is an open possibility for us that we will fail to find such correlates? To carry the analogy one final step further: if the robots go on to manufacture ROBOTS (i.e., robots that the robots themselves regard as *mere* robots), a robot philosopher will sooner or later argue: "when I say that a ROBOT 'thinks that something is red,' or that something 'looks red' to a ROBOT, all that I mean is that the ROBOT is in a certain kind of *physical* state (admittedly, one specified by its *psychological* significance, and not by a direct physical-chemical description). The ROBOT must be able to discriminate red from non-red things, and the state in question must figure in a certain rather-hard-to-describe way in the discrimination process. But when I say that a fellow *person* (robot) 'thinks that something is red,' etc., I do not mean that he is necessarily in any special kind of physical state. Thus, in the only philosophically interesting sense of 'sensation,' persons (robots) have 'sensations' and ROBOTS do not." I conclude that Baier's first argument does not break my analogy.

The second argument seems to me to rest on two dubious premises. Granted, if the physical correlate of a given painful quale $Q$ is something peripheral, then my brain could be "reprogrammed" so that the event would become the physical correlate of some pleasurable psychological state; if the correlate is a highly structured state of the whole brain, then such reprogramming may well be impossible. Thus the premise: Let $S$ be the state of the robot's brain that "realizes" some "pleasure quale"; then, in principle, the robot's brain could always be reprogrammed so that $S$ would "realize" a "painful quale" instead—seems to be simply false. (The other dubious premise is the existence of *intrinsically* pleasant and painful qualia. This is supposed to be introspectively evident, but I do not find it so.)

## Should Robots Have Civil Rights?

Throughout this paper I have stressed the possibility that a robot and a human may have the same "psychology"—that is, they may obey the same psychological laws. To say that two organisms (or systems) obey the same psychological laws is not at all the same thing as to say that their behavior is similar. Indeed, two people may obey the same psychological laws and exhibit *different* behavior, even given similar environments in childhood, partly because psychological laws are only statistical and partly because crucial parameters may have different values. To know the psychological laws obeyed by a species, one must know how *any* members of that species *could* behave, given the widest variation in all the parameters that are capable of variation at all. In general, such laws, like all scientific laws, will involve abstractions—terms more or less remote from direct behavioral observation. Examples of such terms have already been given: repression, inhibitory potential, preference, sensation, belief. Thus, to say that a man and a robot have the same "psychology" (are *psychologically isomorphic*, as I will also say) is to say that the behavior of the two *species* is most simply and revealingly analyzed, at the psychological level (in abstraction from the details of the internal physical structure), in terms of the *same* "psychological states" and the same hypothetical parameters. For example, if a human being is a "probabilistic automaton," then any robot with the same "machine table" will be psychologically isomorphic to a human being. If the human brain is simply a neural net with a certain program, as in the theory of Pitts and McCulloch, then a robot whose "brain" was a similar net, only constructed of flip-flops rather than of neurons, would have exactly the same psychology as a human. To avoid question-begging, I will consider psychology as a science that describes the behavior of any species of systems whose behavior is amenable to behavioral analysis, and interpretation in terms of molar behavioral "constructs" of the familiar kind (stimulus, response, drive, saturation, etc.). Thus, saying that a robot (or an octopus) has a *psychology* (obeys psychological laws) does not imply that it is necessarily conscious. For example, the mechanical "mice" constructed by Shannon have a psychology (indeed, they were constructed precisely to serve as a model for a certain psychological theory of conditioning), but no one would contend that they are alive or conscious. In the case of Turing Machines, finite automata, etc., what I here call "psychological isomorphism" is what I referred to in previous papers as "sameness of functional organization."

In the rest of this paper, I will imagine that we are confronted with a community of robots which (who?) are psychologically isomorphic to human beings in the sense just explained. I will also assume that "psychophysical parallelism" holds good for human beings and that, if an action can be explained psychologically, the corresponding "trajectory" of the living human body that executes that action can be explained (in principle) in physical-chemical terms. The possibility of constructing a robot psychologically isomorphic to a human being does not depend on this assumption; a robot could be psychologically isomorphic to a disembodied spirit or to a "ghost in a machine" just at well, if such there were; but the conceptual situation will be a little less confusing if we neglect *those* issues in the present paper.

Let Oscar be one of these robots, and let us imagine that Oscar is having the "sensation" of red. Is Oscar having the sensation of red? In more ordinary language: is Oscar *seeing* anything? Is he thinking, feeling anything? Is Oscar Alive? Is Oscar Conscious?

I have referred to this problem as the problem of the "civil rights of robots" because that is what it may become, and much faster than any of us now expect. Given the ever-accelerating rate of both technological and social change, it is entirely possible that robots will one day exist, and argue "we *are* alive; we *are* conscious!" In that event, what are today only philosophical prejudices of a traditional anthropocentric and mentalistic kind would all too likely develop into conservative political attitudes. But fortunately, we today have the advantage of being able to discuss this problem disinterestedly, and a little more chance, therefore, of arriving at the correct answer.

I think that the most interesting case is the case in which (1) "psychophysical parallelism" holds (so that it can at least be contended that *we* are just as much "physical-chemical systems" as robots are), and (2) the robots in question are psychologically isomorphic to us. This is surely the most favorable case for the philosopher who wishes to argue that robots of "a sufficient degree of complexity" would (not just *could*, but necessarily *would*) be conscious. Such a philosopher would presumably contend that Oscar had sensations, thoughts, feelings, etc., in just the sense in which we do and that the use of "raised-eyebrow" quotes throughout this paper whenever a psychological predicate was being applied to a robot was unnecessary. It is this contention that I wish to explore, not with the usual polemical desire to show either that materialism is correct and, hence (?), that such robots as Oscar would be conscious or to show that all such questions have been resolved once and for all by *Philosophical Investigations*, God but give us the eyes to see it, but rather with my own perverse interest in the logical structure of the quaint and curious bits of discourse that philosophers propound as "arguments"—and with a perhaps ultimately more serious interest in the relevant semantical aspects of our language.

### Anti-civil-libertarian Arguments

Some of the arguments designed to show that Oscar *could not* be conscious may be easily exposed as bad arguments. Thus, the *phonograph-record argument:* a robot only "plays" behavior in the sense in which a phonograph record plays music. When we laugh at the joke of a robot, we are really appreciating the wit of the human programmer, and not the wit of the robot. The *reprogramming argument:* a robot has no real character of its own. It could at any time be reprogrammed to behave in the reverse of the way it has previously behaved. But a human being who was "reprogrammed" (say, by a brain operation performed by a race with a tremendously advanced science), so as to have a new and completely predetermined set of responses, would no longer be a human being (in the full sense), but a monster. The *question-begging argument:* the so-called "psychological" states of a robot are in reality just physical states. But *our* psychological states are *not* physical states. So it could only be in the most Pickwickian of senses that a robot was "conscious."

The first argument ignores the possibility of robots that *learn.* A robot whose "brain" was merely a library of predetermined behavior routines, each imagined in full detail by the programmer, would indeed be uninteresting. But such a robot would be incapable of learning anything that the programmer did not know, and would thus fail to be psychologically isomorphic to the programmer, or to any human. On the other hand, if the programmer constructs a robot so that it will be a model of certain psychological laws, he will *not,* in general, know how it will behave in real-life situations, just as a psychologist might know all of the *laws* of human psychology, but still be no better (or little better) than anyone else at predicting how humans will behave in real-life situations. Imagine that the robot at "birth" is as helpless as a new-born babe, and that it acquires our culture by being brought up with humans. When it reaches the stage of inventing a joke, and we laugh, it is simply not true that we are "appreciating the wit of the programmer." What the programmer invented was not a joke, but a system which could one day produce new jokes. The second argument, like the first, assumes that "programmed" behavior must be wholly predictable and lack all spontaneity. If I "reprogram" a criminal (via a brain operation) to become a good citizen, but without destroying his capacity to learn, to develop, to change (perhaps even to change back into a criminal some day), then I have certainly not created a "monster." If Oscar is psychologically isomorphic to a human, then Oscar can be "reprogrammed" to the extent, and only to the extent, that a human can. The third argument assumes outright that psychological predicates never apply to Oscar and to a human in the same sense, which is just the point at issue.

All these arguments suffer from one unnoticed and absolutely crippling defect. They rely on just two facts about robots: that they are artifacts and that they are deterministic systems of a physical kind, whose behavior (including the "intelligent" aspects) has been preselected and designed by the artificer. But it is purely contingent that these two properties are *not* properties of human beings. Thus, if we should one day discover that *we* are artifacts and that our every utterance was anticipated by our superintelligent creators (with a small "c"), it would follow, if these arguments were sound, that *we* are not conscious! At the same time, as just noted, these two properties are *not* properties of *all* imaginable robots. Thus these arguments fail in two directions: they might "show" that *people* are *not* conscious—because people might be the wrong sort of robots— while simultaneously failing to show that some robots are not conscious.

## Pro-civil-libertarian Arguments

If the usual "anti-civil-libertarian" arguments (arguments against conceding that Oscar is conscious) are bad arguments, *pro*-civil-libertarian arguments seem to be just about nonexistent! Since the nineteenth century, materialists have contended that "consciousness is just a property of matter at a certain stage of organization." But as a semantic analysis this contention is hopeless (psychophysical parallelism is certainly not *analytic*), and as an identity theory it is irrelevant. Suppose that Feigl had been correct, and that sensation words *referred* to events (or "states" or "processes") definable in the language of physics. (As I remarked before, Feigl no longer holds this view.) In particular, suppose 'the sensation of red' *denotes* a brain process. (It is, of course, utterly unclear what this supposition comes to. We are taught the use of "denotes" in philosophy by being told that 'cat' denotes the class of all cats, and so on; and then some philosophers say " 'the sensation of red' denotes a class of brain processes," as if *this* were now supposed to be clear! In fact, all we have been told is that " 'the sensation of red' denotes a brain process" is true just in case " 'the sensation of red' *is* a brain process" is true. Since this latter puzzling assertion was in turn explained by the identity theorists in terms of the distinction between *denotation* and *connotation,* nothing has been explained.) Still, this does not show that Oscar is conscious. Indeed, Oscar may be psychologically isomorphic to a human without being at all similar in physical-chemical construction. So we may suppose that Oscar does not have "brain processes" at all and, hence, (on this theory) that Oscar is *not* conscious. Moreover, if the physical "correlate" of the sensation of red (in the case of a human) is $P_1$, and the physical correlate of the "sensation" of red (in the case of Oscar) is $P_2$, and if $P_1$ and $P_2$ are *different* physical states, it can nonetheless be maintained that, when Oscar and I both "see something that looks red" (or "have the sensation of red," to use the philosophical jargon that I have allowed myself in this paper), we are in the *same* physical state, namely the *disjunction* of $P_1$ and $P_2$. How do we decide whether "the sensation of red" (in the case of a human) is "identical" with $P_1$ or "identical" with $P_1 \vee P_2$? Identity theorists do not tell me anything that helps me to decide.

Another popular theory is that ordinary-language psychological terms, such as 'is angry' (and, presumably, such quasi-technical expressions as 'has the sensation of red') are *implicitly defined by a psychological theory.* On this view, it would follow from the fact that Oscar and I are "models" of the same psychological (molar behavioral) theory that psychological terms have *exactly the same sense* when applied to me and when applied to Oscar.

It may, perhaps, be granted that there is something that could be called an "implicit psychological theory" underlying the ordinary use of psychological terms. (That an angry man will behave aggressively, unless he has strong reasons to repress his anger and some skill at controlling his feelings; that insults tend to provoke anger; that most people are not very good at controlling strong feelings of anger; are examples of what might be considered "postulates" of such a theory. Although each of these "postulates" is quasi-tautological, it might be contended that the conjunction of a sufficient number of them has empirical consequences, and can be used to provide empirical explanations of observed behavior.) But the view that the whole meaning of such a term as 'anger' is fixed by its place in such a theory seems highly dubious. There is not space in the present paper to examine this view at the length that it deserves. But one or two criticisms may indicate where difficulties lie.

To assert that something contains phlogiston is (implicitly) to assert that certain laws, upon which the concept of phlogiston depends, are correct. To assert that something is electrically charged is in part to assert that the experimental laws upon which the concept of electricity is based and which electrical theory is supposed to explain, are not radically and wholly false. If the "theory" upon which the term anger "depends" really has empirical consequences, then even to say "I am angry" is in part to assert that these empirical consequences are not radically and wholly false. Thus it would not be absurd, if 'anger' really *were* a theoretical term, to say "I think that I am very angry, but I'm not sure" or "I think that I have a severe pain, but I'm not sure" or "I think that I am conscious but I'm not sure," since one might well not be sure that the experimental laws implied by the "psychological theory" implicit in ordinary language are in fact correct. It would also not be absurd to say: "perhaps there is not really any such thing as anger" or "perhaps there is not really any such thing as pain" or "perhaps there is not really any such thing as being conscious." Indeed, no matter how certain I might be that I have the sensation of red, it might be proved *by examining other people* that I did *not* have that sensation and that in fact there was no such thing as having the sensation of red. Indeed, "that *looks like* the sensation of red" would have a perfectly good use—namely, to mean that my experience is as it would be if the "psychological theory implicit in ordinary language" were true, but the theory is not in fact true. These consequences should certainly cast doubt on the idea that "psychological terms in ordinary language" really are "theoretical constructs."

It is obvious that "psychological terms in ordinary language" have a *reporting use*. In the jargon of philosophers of science, they figure in *observation statements*. "I am in pain" would be such a statement. But clearly, a term that figures in observational reports has an observational use, and that use must enter into its meaning. Its meaning cannot be fixed merely by its relation to other terms, in abstraction from the actual speech habits of speakers (including the habits upon which the reporting use depends).

The first difficulty suggests that the "psychological theory" that "implicitly defines" such words as 'anger' has in fact *no* nontautological consequences—or, at least, no empirical consequences that could not be abandoned without changing the meaning of these words. The second difficulty then further suggests that the job of fixing the meaning of these words is only partially done by the logical relationships (the "theory"), and is completed by the reporting use.

A third difficulty arises when we ask just what it is that the "psychological theory implicit in ordinary language" is supposed to be *postulating*. The usual answer is that the theory postulates the existence of certain *states* which are supposed to be related to one another and to behavior as specified in the theory. But what does 'state' mean? If 'state' is taken to mean physical state, in the narrow sense alluded to before, then psychophysical parallelism would be implied by an arbitrary "psychological" assertion, which is obviously incorrect. On the other hand, if 'state' is taken in a sufficiently wide sense so as to avoid this sort of objection, then (as Wittgenstein points out) the remark that "being angry is being in a certain psychological state" *says nothing whatsoever*.

In the case of an ordinary scientific theory (say, a physical theory), to postulate the existence of "states" $S_1, S_2, \ldots, S_n$ satisfying certain postulates is to assert that one of two things is the case: either (1) physical states (definable in terms of the existing primitives of physical theory) can be found satisfying the postulates; or (2) it is necessary to take the new predicates $S_1, \ldots, S_n$ (or predicates in terms of which they can be defined) as additional primitives in physical science, and widen our concept of "physical state" accordingly. In the same way, identity theorists have sometimes suggested that "molar psychological theory" *leaves it open* whether or not the states it postulates are physical states or not. But if physical states *can* be found satisfying the postulates, then they are the ones referred to by the postulates. 'State' is then a methodological term, so to speak, whose status is explained by a perspicuous representation of the procedures of empirical theory construction and confirmation. This solution to our third difficulty reduces to the identity theory under the supposition that psychophysical paralellism holds, and that physical states *can* be found "satisfying" the postulates of "molar behavioral psychology."

Even if this solution to the third difficulty is accepted, however, the first two difficulties remain. To be an empirically confirmable scientific theory, the "molar behavioral theory" implicit in the ordinary use of psychological terms must have testable empirical consequences. If the ordinary-language psychological terms really designate states postulated by this theory, then, if the theory is radically false, we must say there are no such "states" as being angry, being in pain, having a sensation, etc. And this must always remain a possibility (on this account), no matter what we observe, since no finite number of observations can deductively establish a scientific theory properly so-called. Also, the reporting role of "psychological" terms in ordinary language is not discussed by this account. If saying "I am in pain" is simply ascribing a *theoretical* term to myself, then this report is in part a *hypothesis,* and one which may always be false. This account—that the ordinary use of "psychological" terms presupposes an empirical theory, and one which may be radically false—has recently been urged by Paul Feyerabend. Feyerabend would accept the consequence that I have rejected as counterintuitive: that there may not really be any pains, sensations, etc., in the customary sense. But where is this empirical theory that is presupposed by the ordinary use of "psychological" terms? Can anyone state *one* behavioral law which is clearly empirical and which is presupposed by the concepts of sensation, anger, etc.? The empirical connection that exists, say, between being in pain and saying "ouch," or some such thing, has sometimes been taken (by logical behaviorists, rather than by identity theorists) to be such a law. I have tried to show elsewhere,[5] however, that no such law is really required to be true for the application of the concept of pain in its customary sense. What entitles us to say that a man is in pain in our world may not entitle one to say that he is in pain in a different world; yet the *same* concept of pain may be applicable. What I contend is that to understand any "psychological" term, one must be implicitly familiar with a network of *logical* relationships, and one must be adequately trained in the reporting use of that word. It is also necessary, I believe, that one be prepared to accept first-person statements by other members of one's linguistic community involving these predicates, at least when there is no *special* reason to distrust them; but this is a general convention associated with discourse, and not part of the meaning of any particular word, psychological or otherwise. Other general conventions associated with discourse, in my opinion, are the acceptance of not-too-bizarre rules of inductive inference and theory confirmation and of certain fundamental rules of deductive inference. But these things, again, have to do with one's discourse *as a whole* not being linguistically deviant, rather than with one's understanding any particular word. If I am not aware that someone's crying out (in a certain kind of context) is a sign that he is in pain, I can be *told*. If I refuse (without good reason), to believe what I am told, it can be pointed out to me that, when I am in that context (say, my finger is burnt), *I* feel pain, and no condition known by me to be relevant to the feeling or nonfeeling of pain is different

---

[5] In "Brains and Behavior." The character of psychological concepts is also discussed by me in "The Mental Life of Some Machines," to appear in a . . . collection edited by Hector Neri Castañeda.

in the case of the Other. If I *still* feel no inclination to ascribe pain to the Other, then my whole concept of discourse is abnormal—but it would be both a gross understatement and a misdiagnosis to say that I "don't know the meaning of 'pain.'"

I conclude that "psychological" terms in ordinary language are *not* theoretical terms. Moreover, the idea that, if psychophysical parallelism is correct, then it is analytic that pain *is* the correlated brain-state is not supported by a shred of linguistic evidence. (Yet this is a consequence of the combined "identity theory-theoretical term" account as we developed it to meet our third difficulty.) I conclude that any attempt to show that Oscar is conscious (analytically, relative to our premises) along these lines is hopeless.

## Ziff's Argument

So far all the arguments we have considered, on both sides of the question: Is Oscar conscious?, have been without merit. No sound consideration has been advanced to show that it is false, given the meaning of the words in English and the empirical facts as we are assuming them, that Oscar is conscious; but also no sound consideration has been advanced to show that it is true. If it is a violation of the rules of English to say (without "raised-eyebrow quotes") that Oscar is in pain or seeing a rose or thinking about Vienna, we have not been told *what* rules it violates; and if it is a violation of the rules of English to *deny* that Oscar is conscious, given his psychological isomorphism to a human being, we have likewise not been told what rules it violates. In this situation, it is of interest to turn to an ingenious ("anti-civil-libertarian") argument by Paul Ziff.[6]

Ziff wishes to show that it is false that Oscar is conscious. He begins with the undoubted fact that if Oscar is not alive

---

[6] I take the liberty of reporting an argument used by Ziff in a conversation. I do not wish to imply that Ziff necessarily subscribes to the argument in the form in which I report it, but I include it because of its ingenuity and interest.

he cannot be conscious. Thus, given the semantical connection between 'alive' and 'conscious' in English, it is enough to show that Oscar is not *alive*. Now, Ziff argues, when we wish to tell whether or not something is alive, we do *not* go by its *behavior*. Even if a thing looks like a flower, grows in my garden like a flower, etc., if I find upon taking it apart that it consists of gears and wheels and miniaturized furnaces and vacuum tubes and so on, I say "what a clever mechanism," not "what an unusual plant." It is *structure,* not *behavior* that determines whether or not something is alive; and it is a violation of the semantical rules of our language to say of anything that is clearly a mechanism that it is "alive."

Ziff's argument is unexpected, because of the great concentration in the debate up to now upon *behavior,* but it certainly calls attention to relevant logical and semantical relationships. Yet I cannot agree that these relationships are as clear-cut as Ziff's argument requires. Suppose that we construct a robot— or, let me rather say, an *android,* to employ a word that smacks less of mechanism—out of "soft" (protoplasm-like) stuff. Then, on Ziff's account, it may be perfectly correct, if the android is sufficiently "life-like" in structure, to say that we have "synthesized life." So, given two artifacts, both "models" of the same psychological theory, both completely deterministic physical-chemical systems, both designed to the same end and "programmed" by the designer to the same extent, it may be that we must say that one of them is a "machine" and not conscious, and the other is a "living thing," (albeit "artificially created") and conscious, simply because the one consists of "soft stuff" and the other consists of "hardware." A great many speakers of English, I am sure (and I am one of them), would find the claim that this dogmatic decision is required by the meaning of the word 'alive' quite contrary to their linguistic intuitions. I think that the difficulty is fundamentally this: a plant does not exhibit much "behavior." Thus it is natural that criteria having to do with *structure* should dominate criteria having to do with "behavior" when the question is whether or not something that looks and "behaves" like a plant is really a living

thing or not. But in the case of something that looks and behaves like an *animal* (and especially like a *human being*), it is
natural that criteria having to do with behavior—and not just
with actual behavior, but with the *organization* of behavior,
as specified by a psychological theory of the thing—should play
a much larger role in the decision. Thus it is not unnatural that
we should be prepared to argue, in the case of the "pseudo-
plant," that "it isn't a living thing because it is a mechanism,"
while some are prepared to argue, in the case of the robot, that
"it isn't a *mere* mechanism, because it is *alive*," and "it is alive,
because it is conscious," and "it is conscious because it has the
same behavioral organization as a living human being." Yet
Ziff's account may well explain why it is that many speakers are
not convinced by these latter arguments. The tension between
conflicting criteria results in the "obviousness," to some minds,
of the robot's "machine" status, and the equal "obviousness,"
to other minds, of its "artificial-life" status.

There is a sense of 'mechanism' in which it is clearly
analytic that a mechanism cannot be alive. Ziff's argument can
be reduced to the contention that, on the normal interpretation
of the terms, it is analytic in English that something whose
*parts* are all mechanisms, in this sense, likewise cannot be alive.
If this is so, then no English speaker should suppose that he
could even *imagine* a robot *thinking*, being *power-mad*, *hating
humans*, or *being in love*, any more than he should suppose that
he could imagine a married bachelor. It seems evident to me
(and indeed to most speakers) that, absurdly or not, we *can*
imagine these things. I conclude, therefore, that Ziff is wrong:
it may be *false*, but it is not a *contradiction*, to assert that Oscar
is alive.

### The "Know-Nothing" View

We have still to consider the most traditional view on our
question. According to this view, which is still quite widely held,
*it is possible that Oscar is conscious, and it is possible that he is
not conscious.* In its theological form, the argument runs as follows: I am a creature with a body and a soul. My body happens

to consist of flesh and blood, but it might just as well have been a machine, had God chosen. Each voluntary movement of my body is correlated with an activity of my soul (how and why is a "mystery"). So, it is quite possible that Oscar has a soul, and that each "voluntary" movement of his mechanical body is correlated in the same mysterious way with an activity of his soul. It is also possible—since the laws of physics suffice to explain the motions of Oscar's body, without use of the assumption that he has a soul—that Oscar is but a lifeless machine. There is absolutely no way in which we can know. This argument can also be given a nontheological (or at least apparently nontheological) form by deleting the reference to God, and putting 'mind' for 'soul' throughout. To complete the argument, it is contended that I know what it *means* to say that Oscar has a "soul" (or has a pain, or the sensation of red, etc.) *from my own case.*

One well-known difficulty with this traditional view is that it implies that it is also possible that other humans are not really conscious, even if they are physically and psychologically isomorphic to me. It is contended that I can know with *probability* that other humans are conscious by the "argument from analogy." But in the inductive sciences, an argument from analogy is generally regarded as quite weak unless the conclusion is capable of further and independent inductive verification. So it is hard to believe that our reasons for believing that other persons are conscious are very strong ones if they amount simply to an analogical argument with a conclusion that admits of *no* independent check, observational, inductive, or whatever. Most philosophers have recently found it impossible to believe *either* that our reasons for believing that other persons are conscious are that weak *or* that the possibility exists that other persons, while being admittedly physically and psychologically isomorphic (in the sense of the present paper) to myself, are not conscious. Arguments on this point may be found in the writings of all the major analytical philosophers of the present century. Unfortunately, many of these arguments depend upon quite dubious theories of meaning.

The critical claim is the claim that it follows from the fact
that I have had the sensation of red, I can imagine this sensation, "I know what it is like," that I can understand the assertion that Oscar has the sensation of red (or any other sensation
or psychological state). In a sense, this is right. I *can*, in one
sense, understand the *words*. I can parse them; I don't think
"sensation of red" means *baby carriage*, etc. More than that:
I know what I would experience if I were conscious and
psychologically as I am, but with Oscar's mechanical "body"
in place of my own. How does this come to be so? It comes
to be so, at least in part, because we have to learn from experience what our own bodies are like. If a child were brought up
in a suitable kind of armor, the child might be deceived into
thinking that it was a robot. It would be harder to fool him
into thinking that he had the internal structure of a robot,
but this too could be done (fake X-rays, etc.). And when I
"imagine myself in the shoes of a (conscious) robot," what I
do, of course, is to imagine the sensations that I might have
if I were a robot, or rather *if I were a human who mistakenly
thought that he was a robot.* (I look down at my feet and see
bright metal, etc.)

Well, let us grant that in this sense we *understand* the sentence "Oscar is having the sensation of red." It does not follow
that the sentence possesses a truth value. We understand the
sentence "the present King of France is bald," but, on its
normal interpretation in English, the sentence has no truth
value under present conditions. We can give it one by adopting
a suitable convention—for example, Russell's theory of descriptions—and more than one such suitable convention exists. The
question really at issue is *not* whether we can "understand"
the sentences "Oscar is conscious" (or "has the sensation of
red" or "is angry") and "Oscar is not conscious," in the sense
of being able to use them in such contexts as "I can perfectly
well picture to myself that Oscar is conscious," but whether
there really is an intelligible sense in which one of these sentences is true, on a normal interpretation, and the other false
(and, in that case, whether it is also true that we can't tell
which).

Let us revert, for a moment, to our earlier fantasy of ROBOTS—i.e., second-order robots, robots created by robots and regarded by robots as *mere* ROBOTS. As already remarked, a robot philosopher might very well be led to consider the question: Are ROBOTS conscious? The robot philosopher "knows," of course, just what "experiences" he would have if he were a "conscious" ROBOT (or a robot in a ROBOT suit). He can "perfectly well picture to himself that a ROBOT could have "sensation." So he may perfectly well arrive at the position that it is logically possible that ROBOTS have sensations (or, rather, "sensations") and perfectly possible that they do not, and moreover he can never know. What do we think of this conclusion?

It is clear what we should think: we should think that there is not the slightest reason to suppose (and every reason not to suppose) that there is a special property, "having the 'sensation' of red," which the ROBOT may or may not have, but which is inaccessible to the robot. The robot, knowing the physical and psychological description of the ROBOT, is in a perfectly good position to answer all questions about the ROBOT that may reasonably be asked. The idea that there is a further question (class of questions) about the ROBOT which the robot cannot answer, is suggested to the robot by the fact that these alleged "questions" are grammatically well formed, can be "understood" in the sense discussed above, and that the possible "answers" can be "imagined."

I suggest that our position with respect to robots is *exactly* that of robots with respect to ROBOTS. There is not the slightest reason for us, either, to believe that "consciousness" is a well-defined property, which each robot either *has* or *lacks*, but such that it is not possible, on the basis of the physical description of the robot, or even on the basis of the psychological description (in the sense of "psychological" explained above), to *decide* which (if any) of the robots possesses this property and which (if any) fail to possess it. The rules of "robot language" may well be such that it is perfectly possible for a robot to "conjecture" that ROBOTS have "sensations" and also perfectly possible for a robot to conjecture that ROBOTS do not have "sensations." It does not follow that the physical and psychological description of the ROBOTS is "incomplete," but only that the concept of "sensation" (in "raised-eyebrow quotes") is a well-defined concept only when applied to robots. The question raised by the robot philosopher: Are ROBOTS "conscious"? calls for a decision and not for a discovery. The decision, at bottom, is this: Do I treat ROBOTS as fellow members of my linguistic community, or as machines? If the ROBOTS are accepted as full members of the robot community, then a robot can find out whether a ROBOT is "conscious" or "unconscious," "alive" or "dead" in just the way he finds out these things about a fellow robot. If they are rejected, then nothing *counts* as a ROBOT being "conscious" or "alive." Until the decision is made, the statement that ROBOTS are "conscious" has no truth value. In the same way, I suggest, the question: Are robots conscious? calls for a decision, on our part, to treat robots as fellow members of our linguistic community, or not to so treat them. As long as we leave this decision unmade, the statement that robots (of the kind described) are conscious has no truth value.

If we reject the idea that the physical and psychological description of the robots is incomplete (because it "fails to specify whether or not they are conscious"), we are not thereby forced to hold either that "consciousness" is a "physical" attribute or that it is an attribute "implicitly defined by a psychological theory." Russell's question in the philosophy of mathematics: If the number 2 is not the set of all pairs, then what on earth is it? was a silly question. Two is simply the second number, and nothing else. Likewise, the materialist question: If the attribute of "consciousness" is not a physical attribute (or an attribute implicitly defined by a psychological theory) then what on earth is it? is a silly question. Our psychological concepts in ordinary language are as we have fashioned them. The "framework" of ordinary-language psychological predicates is what it is and not another framework. *Of course* materialism is false; but it is so *trivially* false that no materialist should be bothered!

*Conclusion*

In this paper, I have reviewed a succession of failures: failures to show that we *must* say that robots are conscious, failures to show that we *must* say they are not, failures to show that we *must* say that we can't tell. I have concluded from these failures that there is no correct answer to the question: Is Oscar conscious? Robots may indeed have (or lack) properties unknown to physics and undetectable by us; but not the slightest reason has been offered to show that they do, as the ROBOT analogy demonstrates. It is reasonable, then, to conclude that the question that titles this paper calls for a decision and not for a discovery. If we are to make a decision, it seems preferable to me to extend our concept so that robots *are* conscious—for "discrimination" based on the "softness" or "hardness" of the body parts of a synthetic "organism" seems as silly as discriminatory treatment of humans on the basis of skin color. But my purpose in this paper has not been to improve our concepts, but to find out what they are.

# BELIEF AND WILL

## H. H. PRICE

There are various familiar expressions which suggest that believing has some characteristics in common with action. This has led certain philosophers to maintain that belief is something voluntary, and they have spoken of "the will to believe." Indeed, we all agree with these philosophers up to a point. We all agree that there is such a thing as "wishful thinking"; and the sort of thinking here referred to is believing, or at any rate half-believing. Again, when we are confronted

Reprinted from *Proceedings of the Aristotelian Society, Supplementary Volume* (Vol. XXVIII, 1954) by permission of the editor and H. H. Price.

by some doubtful and complex question, one person may sum up his conclusion about it by saying "I believe that p" and another may say "I prefer to believe that q." In such a case we should all admit that a man can properly be said to choose which of several alternative answers he will believe.

Some philosophers, however, have gone farther. They have not only maintained that believing, or some believing, is voluntary. They have also maintained that belief is at least sometimes a matter of moral obligation; that there are circumstances in which a man *ought* to believe a proposition p or disbelieve a proposition q. Here they are not using the word "ought" in what might be called its intellectually-normative sense, a mild and harmless sense which would worry nobody. They do not just mean that it would be reasonable for Mr. A to believe the proposition p, given the evidence which he has. They mean that he is morally obliged to believe it, that he will be morally blameworthy if he fails to believe it, and still more so if he disbelieves it. As we shall see later, they even think that in some circumstances a man is morally obliged to believe a proposition p even though the evidence which he has may be unfavourable to it; or that he is morally obliged to go on believing it as firmly as before, even when the evidence for the proposition is weakened, or the evidence against it is strengthened, as a result of some new piece of information he has acquired. These doctrines about a duty to believe are strange and even alarming. But there are certain common ways of speaking and thinking about belief which lead very naturally in that direction. Perhaps it may be of some interest to consider them and to ask what their implications are. As I have said, they are ways of speaking and thinking which suggest that believing has something in common with action.

Let us begin with the word "cannot." As there are things we cannot do, there are also propositions which we cannot believe. "I just cannot believe that." "Nothing would induce me to believe it." Sometimes this inability is attributed to another person, not to ourselves. "The story is true, but naturally *he* cannot believe it." And sometimes we say this kind of thing without specifying any particular believer. There are propositions which no one can believe. They are just unbelievable. Thus it is just unbelievable that at 11 p.m. on January 1st the temperature on the roof of the Air Ministry in London was 85 deg. Fahrenheit.

The interesting thing about this inability or incapacity to believe is that we regard it as the upper limit of a scale of increasing difficulty in believing. It may be easy, or quite easy, to believe such and such a proposition; or it may be rather difficult to believe, or very difficult; or it may be almost impossible to believe; or finally, quite impossible. These phrases about degrees of difficulty are sometimes used quite generally, without reference to a particular believer. It is not very easy, or it is rather difficult, to believe that there are Abominable Snowmen in the Himalayas. But sometimes a man says of himself "It is difficult for *me* to believe that." And sometimes he says it of another specified person or class of persons. It is very difficult for an Englishman to believe that the Dutch contributed a good deal to the defeat of the Spanish Armada in 1588, and perhaps it is not very easy for a Dutchman to believe that the English did. It is difficult for the Senior Tutor of St. Benedict's College to believe that the college hockey team will be defeated in tomorrow's hockey match, though perhaps he can just bring himself to believe it.

We may next notice that there are several different sorts of situation in which the phrase "cannot believe" is used. When it is said that such and such a thing cannot be done or cannot happen, it is always appropriate to ask "Why?" Statements of impossibility are elliptical. When we say that something is impossible (cannot be done, cannot happen) we mean that there is something else, not at the moment specified, which prevents it or precludes it. And it is always appropriate to ask what this preventing factor is.

Now sometimes what prevents a man from believing a proposition p, what *makes* him unable to believe it, is just the fact that he is taking a reasonable attitude to this proposition. There are two ways in which this may happen, corresponding to the two criteria which we use for deciding whether a belief is reasonable, the consistency criterion on the one hand, and the evidential criterion on the other. If it is reasonable for me to believe p, then p must be consistent with all the other propositions I believe. And further, the evidence which I have must be on balance favourable to p.

Let us first consider the consistency criterion. Obviously, that fact that p is inconsistent with some other proposition q which I believe is not by itself a sufficient ground to justify me in saying "I cannot believe p." It will only justify me in saying "I cannot *both* believe p *and* believe q." It might be, then, that the reasonable course is to reject q and accept p, or again to suspend judgement about both.

But what if the proposition p is *internally* inconsistent? Surely in this case, at any rate, the consistency criterion will be enough by itself to justify me in saying "I cannot believe that?" Suppose a fisherman tells me that he caught a warm-blooded fish in the River Cherwell to-day. Surely I am justified in saying "I simply cannot believe it?"

Nevertheless, it is logically possible that the man did catch a creature which looked like a fish, lived in water, had scales and fins, and yet was warm-blooded; and that the only way he could think of for describing it was this *paradoxical*, i.e., logically-inconsistent, expression "a warm-blooded fish." He would have been wiser, perhaps to make the inconsistency perfectly plain and obvious. He should have followed the example of Professor Wisdom's man who was asked whether it was raining and replied "It is and it isn't." He should have said "What I caught was a fish and yet it was not." But then, surely, I should have been all the more justified in saying "I cannot believe it?" Well, if the inconsistency of his statement was my sole justification for saying so, my inability to believe him would no doubt have been reasonable, but it would also have been imperceptive. I should be showing an insensitiveness to the limitations and imperfections of language.

What I ought to say is "What do you mean?" or "How

do you mean?" Perhaps he will then explain that the creature had some or many of the characteristics of a fish, but was also warm-blooded. When he has given his explanation I shall still say "I cannot believe your story," and my inability to believe it will still be reasonable. But the grounds of this reasonableness are now quite different from what they were at first. There is no longer any inconsistency in his story, now that he has explained what he meant. It is logically possible that there should be a creature which is in many ways like a trout and yet is warm-blooded. If I *now* say "I cannot believe that," I say so not on logical grounds, but on evidential ones. It is now the evidential criterion of reasonableness, and not the consistency criterion, which justifies my inability to believe. It is empirically improbable, very improbable indeed, that there should be such a creature as he describes. All the knowledge I have about living creatures, and all the testimony I have been able to get from zoological experts, is evidence against the man's story.

I would suggest, then, that when the proposition we are considering is about matters of fact (i.e., is not a proposition of logic or of pure mathematics) the evidential criterion of reasonableness, and not the consistency criterion, is much the more important of the two. If we cannot believe the proposition, our inability to believe it must be justified in the end on *evidential* grounds.

Nevertheless, when reasonable people are unable to believe a proposition, because of the very strong evidence they have against it, the proposition may happen to be true all the same. Similarly when they say, and say reasonably, that they have *difficulty* in believing a proposition (because of the strong, though not overwhelmingly strong, evidence which they have against it) the proposition may happen to be true. Here I cannot forbear to mention the duck-billed platypus. A creature which lays eggs, has a ducklike beak, and fur, and four webbed feet—how *could* there be such an animal? When the creature was first reported, it was very reasonable for people to say "We just cannot believe this story." Moreover, it was especially

reasonable for experts to say it. All the then available zoological
evidence made it very improbable that such a beast should
exist. What one is reasonably incapable of believing may nevertheless be true. There is therefore a sense in which it may be
right, sometimes—reasonable or "right and proper"—to disbelieve a proposition which is in fact true; and equally, of
course, to believe a proposition which is in fact false.

There is indeed a connection between believing reasonably and believing truly. (I shall have more to say about it
later.) If there were not, there would not be much point in
being reasonable about one's beliefs or one's disbeliefs. If you
believe reasonably, your beliefs as a whole are likely, in the
long run, to be more often true than false. But obviously this
does not entail that if you believe reasonably *all* your beliefs
will be true. And similarly, if or so far as you are reasonable
in your believing, the propositions you are *unable* to believe are
likely to be on the whole and in the long run false rather than
true. But this again does not entail that *all* the propositions
which you are reasonably incapacitated from believing are false.
In one's inability to believe, as in one's believing, one may on
occasion be reasonable but mistaken. Similarly, in both cases
alike, one may be unreasonable but correct. What makes me
unable to believe a proposition p may be pure prejudice or
stupidity or sheer cussedness; but p may be false for all that.
What makes it easy for me to believe another proposition q
may be something equally unreasonable; nevertheless, q may
happen to be true.

It was worth while to explain that inability to believe
something *can* be perfectly reasonable, just because it is so
very often unreasonable or at any rate non-reasonable. When a
man says "I cannot believe p," "nothing would induce me to
believe it," what prevents him from believing it, very often, is
not that he has strong evidence against the proposition, nor yet
the fact that he has detected an internal inconsistency in it, but
just some emotion or desire which he has. He cannot believe
the proposition because he so much *wants* it to be false, or

because the situation would be so upsetting or shocking or terrifying if the proposition were true. He just cannot believe that the train will arrive late, because he will get into so much trouble if it does. Some people cannot believe that the works of John Bunyan have any merit at all, because he came from Bedford and they have such an intense dislike for that town and everything to do with it. This same dislike makes them unable, or hardly able, to believe that the road which passes through Bedford is the shortest route from Oxford to Cambridge. A more serious sort of example, which I shall discuss later, is one in which much stronger emotions are involved— stronger in the sense both of being more intense and of being more deeply rooted, as it were, in our emotional life. Newman says somewhere that a man cannot believe that his most intimate friend is false to him. Again, in time of war a fervent patriot cannot believe that his country was the aggressor, and up to the last moment he cannot believe that it is going to be defeated.

I am not sure, however, whether this "cannot" is always a pure and simple inability—i.e., whether it always means that it just is not in the person's power to believe the proposition. What makes me doubt this is the fact that in such circumstances we sometimes say not just "I cannot believe it" but "I cannot and will not believe it" ("I can't believe it, and what is more, I won't").

This conjunctive statement or conjunctive expression of attitude is rather puzzling. At first sight there even seems to be a logical inconsistency in it. Surely if it makes sense to say "I will not believe it" (i.e., "I have resolved not to") then it must be true that I *can* believe it—the very thing which the first part of my utterance denies. If I resolve not to do X, or refuse to do it, surely X must be something which I am able to do. If a man says "I won't get up" surely he is thereby admitting that he is able to get up. He has the power to get up, but he refuses to exercise it. You can only refuse to exercise a power if you do actually have it, or at least assume that you have.

But when a man says "I can't and won't believe this," perhaps "I can't" means something like "I cannot afford to," rather than "I am unable to" or "am incapable of." If one cannot afford to do something, or cannot afford to allow it to happen, it is of course in one's power to do it or to allow it to happen. And so it makes perfectly good sense to add "and what is more I *will not* do it" or "I *will not* allow it to happen."

Now "cannot" *is* sometimes an abbreviation for "cannot afford to." I cannot go out for a long walk in the country to-day. I haven't got the time, because I must finish writing a lecture. By saying "I cannot" I do not mean at all that it is not in my power to go. It certainly is. I could perfectly well get into my car the next minute and drive out to the Chiltern Hills and spend the whole day in the woods looking for woodcocks. And just because it *is* in my power to go, it would make sense to add "I will not go," i.e., "I have resolved not to."

Similarly, there are propositions which a man cannot afford to believe, and therefore will not believe. He is not likely to say himself that he cannot afford to believe a proposition p, though other people may say this in talking about him. What he says, probably, is just "I cannot believe it," which might mean, and more usually would mean, just that he is unable to believe it, incapable of believing it. Perhaps by using the word "cannot" in this ambiguous way, without further explanation, he may conceal from himself the difference which there is between "not being able to afford to" and simply not having it in one's power. But if he adds "and what is more, I *won't* believe it," he gives himself away. He would be wiser to say just "I can't believe it," and stop at that.

Why is it that a man cannot afford to believe a proposition p? There are several possible answers. The most obvious answer, and no doubt often the true one, is just that from an emotional point of view he cannot afford it. His existing emotional attitudes and desires commit him, so to speak, to some other proposition q; and he is aware that if p were true, q would be false, or its probability would be greatly decreased. For example, q might be the proposition that Mr. A, a politician whom he greatly admires, is a thoroughly honest and highly intelligent man. When he is told, even by an informant whom he admits to be generally reliable, or reads, even in the columns of *The*

*Times* newspaper, that Mr. A has said or done something very dishonest or very stupid, he cannot afford to believe it and he *will* not believe it.

Sometimes what he is emotionally committed to is not just one proposition, but a highly organised system of propositions, a theory or doctrine of some kind, for instance the Marxist interpretation of history. And then he cannot afford to believe any proposition which would falsify or weaken that system. For example, he cannot afford to believe that many of the people who went on Crusades in the Middle Ages were moved by motives of simple Christian piety. He cannot afford to believe this proposition, and he refuses to believe it.

But when someone cannot afford to believe a proposition p, his motives may be more respectable than these. Misguidedly or not, he may think it is his *duty* to believe a proposition q, which would be rendered false or less probable if p were true. Again, he may think it his duty to go on believing q as firmly as he did before, in spite of the adverse evidence which has just been brought to his notice. Then, taking the moral attitude he does, he cannot *morally* afford to believe the proposition p. When he says "I cannot believe p" (adding, perhaps, "and I won't believe it") this is rather like saying that one *cannot* go to London to-day, because one has promised to have tea with one's next door neighbour this afternoon, or to take one's Australian cousin round the colleges of Oxford. This moral justification which one gives for saying one cannot go may of course be fictitious. But the fiction only works because such moral justifications for the "cannot" are often perfectly genuine.

I shall have more to say later about the conception of a duty to believe. The point at present is merely to elucidate the sense of "cannot believe" in which it means "cannot afford to." It is possible that someone cannot afford this on moral grounds, i.e., because of the (second-order) belief which he has that there are certain propositions which he is morally obliged to believe, and not merely because of his emotional commitments.

Finally, there is still another sort of inability to believe which does not fall under any of the heads so far mentioned. Here, it is not that one has strong evidence to the contrary (*rational* inability to believe) nor yet that one cannot afford to believe the proposition, either because of emotional commitments or on moral grounds. What the "cannot believe" indicates may be just intellectual inertia. The man is simply unable to make the intellectual readjustments which would be required if he did accept the proposition. He would have to reconsider many of his present beliefs if he did, modifying some of them and abandoning others. Perhaps he would be willing to make these changes if he could. But the task is too much for him. He just lacks the necessary intellectual power, the mental flexibility which would be needed.

We may now consider some implications of this whole group of phrases, of which "cannot believe" is one. Others are "can believe," "easy to believe," "difficult to believe," "almost impossible to believe"; and also "will not believe" and "quite willing to believe." Taken together, these phrases suggest that belief is, normally, something voluntary; that we can decide voluntarily what to believe and what not to believe.

"Cannot believe," taken by itself, might of course appear to suggest the contrary. But as we have seen, the "cannot" often means "cannot afford to," and this has the implication that it *is* in one's power to believe the proposition if one chooses. Only, as it happens, one makes the opposite choice, because of the emotionally disagreeable results of believing, or sometimes because one would have a feeling of moral guilt if one did believe the proposition. It is true that there are cases where "cannot believe" does just mean literally what it says, namely that it just is not in the man's power to believe the proposition. But it looks as if these cases were regarded as exceptional; as if the normal and ordinary state of things were that we *can* believe whatever we choose to believe. This suggestion that belief is normally something voluntary is strengthened when we recall what was said earlier. Inability to believe seems to be regarded as the upper limit of a scale of increasing difficulty. The word "difficult," in its various degrees, is only applicable to things which are in our power. It *is* in our power to achieve them, though only with an effort—small, great, or very great, as the case may be. And finally, the suggestion that belief is normally something voluntary is strengthened still further when we consider such expressions as "I *won't* believe that," "I just *refuse* to believe it."

Accordingly, it is not at all surprising to find that some people use moral obligation words in connection with believing, as I have already remarked. If or to the extent that believing is something under our voluntary control, it does at any rate make sense to say that X ought, is morally bound, to believe a proposition p, and ought not to believe q or has no moral right to believe it; though there might still, of course, be exceptional cases where he could not help believing q or could not help withholding belief from p. (Cf. "He could not help breaking his promise, because the train was an hour late.")

The consequences of this doctrine that there is sometimes a moral obligation to believe are of course pretty horrifying. The religious wars of the 16th and 17th centuries were based on just such a theory. High-principled persecutors, religious or political (and some persecutors *are* high-principled) would justify their actions by saying that X is morally bound to believe a proposition p; and if he does not believe it, or even believe its contradictory not-p, this "misbelief" of his can only be due to moral wickedness, or badness of will. It is in the man's power to believe p if he chooses, and he has a moral obligation to believe it. He prefers not to do his duty. Surely he deserves to be punished for this moral delinquency; and the more important the proposition is which he refuses to believe, the more drastic the punishment should be.

But though the doctrine does have these terrifying implications, it might of course be true for all that. Moreover, someone might argue, I suppose, that although there is a *prima facie* duty to punish misbelievers, or suppress them by force, there is a conflicting *prima facie* duty which always, in practice, outweighs it; namely, the duty to preserve peace both within our own community, and between one community and another.

There is no doubt that some people do use moral obligation words in connection with beliefs. They say that X *ought* to believe a proposition p; and not just in the intellectually-normative sense of the word "ought," meaning that if he were to believe p, he would be believing reasonably, but in the moral sense of "ought." They really do think that X has a moral duty to believe p, or to go on believing it when he is inclined to give up his belief. What has led them to such an extraordinary opinion? Let us consider some examples.

You may remember the story about the Dean of a certain college interviewing an undergraduate who had climbed into the college at 2 a.m. that morning. The undergraduate gave some very unconvincing explanation; he had not realised that his watch was 2½ hours slow. The Dean replied "Of course I am bound to believe you; and now I am going to fine you £5." But when the Dean said "I am bound (morally obliged) to believe you," with the implication that he had actually carried out this moral duty of believing, it would seem that his remark was highly elliptical. He meant "I am morally obliged to *say the words* 'I believe you,' and I hereby do say them"; or again, "I am morally obliged *not* to use words expressive of doubt or disbelief about your story, and I hereby refrain from using them." A solicitor might say the same sort of thing to a client whom he has undertaken to defend. "Of course I am bound to believe what you tell me." He may say this, although he has the gravest doubts of his client's veracity. The moral duty which he acknowledges and carries out is just the duty to say the words "I believe you" or to refrain from saying words which would express disbelief or doubt.

It may be true, sometimes, that one really does have a moral duty to utter words expressive of belief, or to refrain from uttering words expressive of doubt. It may also sometimes be our duty to *act as if* we believed a proposition, or to act in other ways as if we believed it, for uttering words to someone is itself a kind of action. I find a rather disreputable looking individual wandering about the garden by night. He says he was looking for the back door because he wanted to ask the way to the London road. I take him to the front gate and show him which way he should go, though all the time I strongly suspect that his intention was to burgle the house.

But though we may sometimes have a moral obligation to express belief or to act as if we believed—things which certainly are under our voluntary control—it will not of course follow from this that we ever have a moral obligation to *believe* (or not to believe, as the case may be). And it will not follow that believing itself is under our voluntary control, merely because the outward signs of it are.

Let us now consider a more plausible example, where it does look as if belief itself, not merely the outward signs of it, might be a matter of moral obligation. I am thinking of a situation which quite often occurs in Victorian novels, and I suppose it must have occurred quite often in real life at that time, though it is not so common in our present degenerate period. It would seem that 19th century ladies acknowledged a moral obligation to believe that their husbands or fiancés were impeccably virtuous. When testimony, even quite strong testimony, was put before them to the contrary, they thought it their moral duty to persist in their belief all the same; to *go on* believing, as firmly as before, that their husbands or fiancés were impeccably virtuous, in spite of this adverse evidence. And it would seem that many of them succeeded in carrying out this duty, amidst universal applause. They might perhaps have some inclination to consider the adverse evidence on its merits. But this inclination must be resisted and overcome. Granted that one has a moral duty to believe p, one has a consequent duty to disbelieve q where the truth of q, if it were true, would be evidence against the truth of p; and not only where q, if true, would be *conclusive* evidence against the proposition which it is one's duty to believe, but also when it would be strong or fairly strong evidence against, even though not conclusive.

Sometimes, it would seem, this duty of believing (and of not believing) was supposed to extend still further. It was held that there was a moral obligation to believe that all the members of one's family were persons of the highest excellence, or at least of great excellence; and an obligation to go on believing this, come what may; and a consequent obligation to *dis*-believe evidence to the contrary—always, or at least nearly always, for just occasionally the adverse evidence might be so overwhelming that it would be beyond the power of even the most high-principled person to resist it.

What are we to make of this doctrine? I suspect that it is still quite widely held, though not perhaps in quite such an uncompromising form, and nowadays it is not so often stated explicitly. It looks rather like saying that in some cases one has a moral obligation to be prejudiced or biased, and a moral obligation to persist in one's prejudice even when one is inclined to adopt a more reasonable and "objective" attitude. We should all agree that such a persistence in one's prejudice might sometimes be excusable, and indeed that it might be a psychological consequence of something highly admirable, namely an affectionate disposition. But can we really suppose that there is ever a moral duty to be prejudiced, and to persist in one's prejudice when one is confronted with strong evidence against the proposition one believes? That, surely, is what the doctrine comes to. It says that you have a duty to believe a proposition p, and a consequent duty to go on believing p as firmly as before, even when you are presented with strong evidence to the contrary; and from this, in turn, it follows that you have a duty to reject or disbelieve the adverse evidence. When presented with this adverse evidence, you may no doubt have an inclination to give up believing p, or at any rate to believe it with less confidence than you did before. But in these special cases (the doctrine says) you have a moral duty to resist such inclinations; and you *can* resist them, if you try hard enough.

We must now consider a question which is sure to have occurred to you already. *Can* one really make oneself believe something, or make oneself go on believing it, just by an effort of will—by a great effort in this case, where the adverse evidence is strong, and by a smaller effort in others? Indeed, are our beliefs really under our voluntary control at all? Hume, you will remember, thought it quite obvious that they are not. It seemed to him evident that it is *not* in our power to believe whatever we please.[1]

It is true that we do sometimes use volitional words in describing the acquisition of beliefs ("I decided that p", "I made up my mind that p"). But we must not allow ourselves to be confused by the fact that something rather like preferring or choosing does quite often occur as a stage in the process by which a belief is formed, especially when we acquire our belief in a reasonable manner, after careful consideration of the evidence *pro* and *con.* Believing a proposition is, I think, a disposition and not an occurrence or "mental act", though the disposition is not necessarily a very long-lived one and may only last a few seconds. (For a few seconds I believed that the sound was made by an aeroplane. Then I ceased to believe this, and believed instead that the sound came from a racing motor car with a defective silencer.) But although believing p is a disposition, and not an occurrence, there is a characteristic sort of mental occurrence which we may sometimes notice when we are in process of *acquiring* such a disposition. I am going to call this occurrence "assenting" to the proposition. Similarly, when once a belief-disposition has established itself, one of the many different ways in which it may manifest itself thereafter is by subsequent acts of assenting or assent-occurrences. Now when our belief is a reasonable one, this assenting, and especially the initial assent, has a *preferential* character. For some time we were in a state of indecision, sitting on the fence as it were. We considered various alternative propositions p, q, and r, together with the evidence for and against each of them. But finally, as a result of this weighing of evidence, we prefer or "plump for" p, because this is the alternative which our evidence, taken as a whole, appears to us to favour. We no longer sit on the fence as we were doing before, but come down on one side. We decide for p in *preference* to q and r.

Now because of this preferential element in it, assent may

[1] *Treatise.* Appendix. Everyman edition, vol. 2, pp. 313–314.

look rather like voluntary choice. But the appearance is deceptive. It is not a free choice at all, but a forced one. If you are in a reasonable frame of mind (as we are assuming that you are in this case) you cannot help preferring the proposition which the evidence favours, much as you may wish you could. I mean, you cannot help preferring the proposition which *your* evidence favours, the evidence *you* are at the moment attending to, though the evidence which other people have may of course be different. It is no good refusing to assent to p in such circumstances, though of course you may *say* to other people, or even to yourself, "I refuse to assent to it." It just is not in your power to avoid assenting to the proposition which the evidence (your evidence) favours, or to assent instead to some other proposition when the evidence (your evidence) is manifestly unfavourable to it.

Thus we come back to the question raised before. Can one make oneself believe something, or make oneself go on believing it, just by an effort of will? How would one set about performing this duty—if it is indeed a duty? It seems to me pretty clear that one cannot do it directly, by just making a voluntary effort here and now. Nevertheless, there is some sense in the expressions "I won't believe q," "I will believe p," or "I will go on believing p as before, in spite of all." Indirectly, though not directly, and over a period of time, though not instantaneously, one *can* voluntarily control one's beliefs—at any rate up to a point. If so, it does at any rate make sense (whether or not it is true) to suggest that there are some propositions which we have a moral duty to believe and others which we have a moral duty to disbelieve.

Beliefs can be gradually cultivated, though they cannot be instantaneously produced, or abolished, at will. They can also be preserved when one is in danger of losing them. Doubts or inclinations to disbelieve, occasioned by adverse evidence, cannot be abolished instantaneously by a mere *fiat* of will here and now. But we have it in our power to weaken our doubts little by little, until at last they fade away and are felt no longer. This is a thing one can do (usually) if one tries hard enough and long enough, and thereby one can voluntarily restore or revive a belief which one was in danger of losing. So again it does make sense, whether or not it is true, to say that one sometimes has a moral duty to take steps to preserve one's belief in spite of strong adverse evidence. The prerequisite that "ought implies can" is after all fulfilled. And when someone who intends to carry out this duty says "I *will* go on believing p," "I *refuse* to give up believing it," he should be understood to mean that he has resolved to take these steps, and to persist in his gradual belief-restoring procedure until the cure is complete. We must now consider how he is to set about it.

The crucial point here is that the direction of our attention is to a large extent in our own power. One can voluntarily avert one's attention from the adverse evidence; one can refuse to consider it whenever it comes into one's mind. Or if this is too difficult at first (it becomes easier in time) one can at least weaken the effect of the adverse evidence by directing one's attention to the general truth that testimony is often erroneous, or to the possibility that there may be some alternative explanation of the events reported. Again, one can fix one's attention upon the evidence which favours the proposition one wants to believe or to go on believing, as well as averting one's attention from the adverse evidence. There is almost sure to be some favourable evidence, and there may well be a good deal. Make the most of it. Dwell on it in thought as much as you can.

By such systematic and voluntary direction of the attention, continued over a sufficiently long period, one may manage, in time, to do what is demanded. By degrees, though not immediately, one will probably get back into the state where one again believes the proposition p without any doubts or qualms. "I must be loyal to X not only in my actions but in my inmost thoughts." That is the obligation which these Victorian ladies were supposed to undertake.[2] "Being loyal to him in one's

[2] If I recollect rightly, it is formulated in this way by one of Trollope's heroines.

inmost thoughts" consisted, I suggest, in a habit of directing one's attention appropriately, by attending carefully and repeatedly to all the evidence which is creditable to X, and averting one's attention from all the evidence which is discreditable to him. By such methods one gets back into the state where the *only* evidence before one's mind is favourable to the proposition one wishes to believe. When that state is reached, and so long as it is maintained, there is no difficulty in believing the proposition as firmly as one did before, when the adverse evidence had not yet come to one's notice.

This, I suspect, is what these Victorian ladies did, and were so highly approved of for doing. This was how they managed to carry out the rather difficult duty, which public opinion imposed on them, of believing—or continuing to believe —in spite of adverse evidence. Of course, if the adverse evidence was *very* strong, the voluntary effort required for directing one's attention continually in the appropriate manner might be very great. But then the moral approval one received for fulfilling one's duty was correspondingly higher.

I said just now that by this voluntary and systematic direction of attention they got themselves into a state where the only evidence *before their minds* was favourable to the proposition which they "ought" to believe. What their unconscious or sub-conscious state of mind might be, is another question. One might suspect, perhaps, that the memory of the adverse evidence, which they so carefully and diligently dismissed from consciousness, was not got rid of altogether; that it was still retained unconsciously (all the more so because strong emotions were attached to it) and still had its effect upon them. If you could have examined their dreams, or their slips of the tongue or the pen, or other things they said and did when they were "off their guard," you might have found that Mrs. X's unconscious beliefs about Mr. X were rather different from her conscious ones, and even opposed to them.

There is, however, another method of voluntarily cultivating beliefs, and perhaps these Victorian ladies practised it too. Probably it has had its practitioners in all ages, since the dawn of human history. This method is not concerned with the evidence for or against the proposition one wishes to believe or go on believing. And if it is effective it gets one into a state where one no longer bothers about evidence at all.

Here again the essential point is the voluntary direction of attention. But now we just fix our attention on the proposition itself. We dwell on it in thought, and bring it before our mind repeatedly. We also consider repeatedly the consequences which the proposition entails, and the further consequences which it makes probable. This may be summed up by saying that one fixes one's attention repeatedly on what it would be like if the proposition were true. If one is good at imaging, one may also find it helpful to *imagine* in as much detail as possible the kind of situation there would be if the proposition were true. Images, for some people at least, have a more powerful emotional effect than words have. So if we can succeed in "cashing" the proposition with images, emotional attitudes will tend to be aroused with regard to it. Thereby we shall come to take the proposition more seriously. By cashing it with images, we shall come to "realise what it means" in a way we did not before. It will cease to be a mere verbal formula, as perhaps it was at first, or was in danger of becoming. This is one of the points which Newman is making when he distinguishes between "Real Assent" and "Notional Assent," if I understand him rightly[3].

This procedure of dwelling upon the proposition in thought may be supplemented by Behavioristic methods. Whenever an opportunity arises, you make a point of acting as if the proposition were true, and you get yourself into the habit of acting in that manner. You even go out of your way to *make* opportunities of acting as if the proposition were true. For example, you go out of your way to be seen in X's company when you could easily have avoided it. You go out of your

---

[3] *Grammar of Assent*, ch. 4. The word "real," I think, is used by this classically-minded writer, in its Latin sense of "thingish" (cf. the legal phrase "Real Property").

way to attend minor meetings of the Party, though you would have got into no trouble if you had stayed at home. By this procedure you commit yourself, as it were, to the proposition which you wish to believe. Pascal recommends somewhere that if a man's religious faith is weak, he should "Use holy water and order masses to be said."

By such methods—by dwelling upon a proposition continually and repeatedly, by considering again and again what it would be like if it were true and imaging in detail what it would be like (if you can), by acting as if the proposition were true on all occasions to which its truth or falsity is relevant, and by increasing the number of these occasions whenever possible—by such means you will gradually get into a state of believing the proposition. You will wake up one fine day and find that you do believe it. Or if you believed it already, by these methods you will get into a state where you believe it almost unshakeably; a state in which you no longer have to bother about adverse evidence, or indeed about favourable evidence either. You may still be perfectly ready to discuss the evidence, adverse as well as favourable, showing due respect to those who disagree with you. You may even write whole books on the subject. But all this will be done with a certain inner reservation, as it were. The discussion of the evidence will not make any real difference to you. Your belief will still remain as it was, whichever way the discussion goes. Of course, the state you have got into is one of non-reasonable belief, just because it is independent of the evidence (which will not necessarily prevent the proposition believed from being true). But the point at present is that it *is* a state of belief, and of very firm belief too; and that it is brought into existence by your own voluntary efforts, or *mutatis mutandis* restored by your own voluntary efforts when you were in danger of losing it. Everyone admits, of course, that such a state can be produced in us *in*voluntarily, by what is called "Social Conditioning" (the process which Hume in the *Treatise* calls "education"). But it was worth while to point out that it can be produced voluntarily too, though only with considerable effort and trouble, continued over a long period of time.

I conclude from these considerations that when William James talked about "the will to believe," there was after all some sense in what he said, though the name is not a very good one, and the process should rather be described as the voluntary cultivation of belief. It would seem too that there is some sense in saying "I *won't* believe q", "I *will* believe p" or "I *will* go on believing it, in spite of everything". Moreover, when we say "it is difficult or very difficult for me (or for X) to believe this", it is easy, or quite easy, for me to believe that" these words really do sometimes have the literal and volitional sense which they have in other contexts. It is true that these volitional words—"won't", "will", "difficult", "easy"— have no application to a momentary act of assent. The most one can voluntarily do there is to say the words "I assent to p" or otherwise behave as if one were assenting to it, for instance by signing one's name on the dotted line at the foot of the page. But these volitional words do apply to beliefs, in the sense in which a belief is a persistent state or disposition. This state can be acquired or abolished, strengthened or weakened, by a longish course of voluntary effort, though not by a mere momentary *fiat* of will here and now. Moreover, it is conceivable that when someone says "I cannot possibly bring myself to believe p", he is mistaken. Perhaps he could and would acquire this belief if he tried hard enough and long enough, and used the psychological techniques (directing attention etc.) which I have described. Similarly, a man may be mistaken when he says "I cannot go on believing p as I did". Perhaps he could and would restore his belief by means of these methods, if he tried hard enough and long enough. Of course, when he says he cannot bring himself to believe the proposition p, or to go on believing it as he used to, he may be saying that the evidence which he has, or the new evidence he has just acquired, makes it unreasonable for him to believe the proposition. If so, he will no doubt refuse to use the belief-inducing techniques which I have described. But this refusal is a voluntary choice too. He resolves to go on being reasonable, to continue to regulate his beliefs in accordance with the strength of the evidence available to him.

But what about the doctrine that there is sometimes a *moral obligation* to believe things? If what I have said is correct, and there is such a thing as "voluntary belief", in the sense I have explained, it is not just absurd to maintain that there are some propositions which it is our moral duty to believe; as it would be, if Hume had been right in thinking that belief is wholly involuntary. It is true that this duty, if it is one, should rather be described as a duty to direct our attention in certain ways and to continue doing so, a process which may be expected to *result* in belief, or in the restoration of a belief we might otherwise have lost. But to say "X has a duty to believe p" (or to go on believing it) would be a natural enough abbreviation for "he has a duty to take steps which will result in his believing p" (or in his continuing to believe it).

Nevertheless, the doctrine that there is sometimes a moral obligation to believe may still be false, even though it is not absurd. Even though it is often in our power to cultivate beliefs by a course of voluntary effort, it does not follow from this that we ever have a moral obligation to make such efforts. Even in the sphere of outward conduct there are surely many actions which are morally indifferent. They are neither actions which we are morally bound to do, nor actions which we are morally bound to refrain from. And the voluntary cultivation of beliefs, or the voluntary strengthening of beliefs we already have, might likewise be morally indifferent activities. If they are, it is something to be thankful for. We have already noticed the horrifying consequences which follow from the doctrine that there is a moral obligation to believe.

But surely it *is* sometimes a man's duty to direct his attention in this way rather than that, and to continue doing so? Of course it may be. It is the professional duty of a plumber's apprentice, at least in his working hours, to direct his thoughts to the properties of lead, and to do so repeatedly, until these properties are thoroughly familiar to him. It is the professional duty of a classical schoolmaster to consider intently and frequently the anomalous behaviour of certain Greek and Latin verbs. Again, if you have promised to give a message to someone by word of mouth, it may be your duty to go over the contents of the message on the way, and to do so several times, so that you will not have forgotten it by the time you arrive. Moreover, if, or to the extent that, the direction of our thoughts in this way rather than that has an effect on other people for good or harm, in a telepathic manner, to that extent the notion of moral obligation applies to it.

But in so far as the direction of our attention is relevant to the formation of beliefs or to the strengthening or weakening of beliefs which we already have, I think we should be very reluctant to admit that the notion of moral obligation applies to it. My grounds for saying so are themselves in part moral or quasi-moral ones. It seems to me that we are all far too much addicted to blaming people as it is. If we are to be allowed, or even encouraged, to blame them for the way they direct their thoughts, as well as for their actions, there will be a perfect orgy of moral indignation and condemnation, and charity will almost disappear from the world.

Let us consider the example of the Victorian ladies which I discussed before. Surely it is clear that they did *not* have a duty to cultivate these beliefs about the virtues of their husbands or fiancés. They did *not* have a duty to suppress their doubts on the matter by systematically averting their attention from the adverse evidence. To do so may well have been excusable, but surely it was not morally obligatory. Still less did they have a duty to adopt the second procedure I mentioned, by which one gets oneself into a state of believing which is indifferent to evidence altogether—a non-rational state of unquestioning and undoubting acceptance.

One might even be inclined to say that they had a duty to do precisely the opposite, a duty to consider the evidence both *pro* and *con*, with the result that they would give up their beliefs (or hold them with less confidence, as the case may be) if the adverse evidence was strong enough. And *a fortiori*, one might be inclined to say, they not only had no duty to adopt, but actually had a duty to avoid, the second procedure, which results in a non-rational state of undoubting acceptance, a state in which one is indifferent to evidence altogether. In short, we might be inclined to say that there is a moral duty to be *reasonable* in one's believing, or as reasonable as one can; a duty to consider impartially all the evidence one can lay hands upon, regardless of one's likes or dislikes, and to believe in accordance with the evidence. It would follow from this that we might often have a duty to revise or abandon one of our beliefs when new evidence was brought to our notice; and also, I suppose, that we have a duty to suspend judgement when the evidence is evenly balanced, or too slight in quantity to justify a reasonable belief either way.

But if we do say these things, I think we go too far the other way; too far in the opposite direction from those moralists by whom these Victorian ladies were victimised. I think we are confusing the moral "ought" with the prudential "ought."

Reasonable belief, and therefore the impartial consideration of evidence, *is* something which is to one's long-term advantage, however distressing it may sometimes be in the short run. If we say that a man *ought* to believe only that proposition which the evidence favours, that he *ought* to consider the evidence impartially, this is like saying that a man with a decayed tooth ought to go to the dentist; it is to his long-term advantage to go, though it is unpleasant or inconvenient at the moment. Or again, it is like saying that Smith ought to get up at 7:30 tomorrow morning, because he will miss his train if he does not get up by then. (We may suppose that he is going on a holiday, and missing his train will harm nobody but himself.)

Or perhaps one should put it this way, as I think Professor Braithwaite would: what is for our long-term advantage, though often unpleasant in the short run, is the *general policy* of forming one's beliefs in accordance with the balance of the evidence. Why is this policy to be recommended on prudential grounds?

Because it is for our advantage that the propositions we believe should be true, or that as many of them as possible should be true. This is obviously advantageous on practical grounds. True beliefs are better guides to action than false ones. But I think we also have some desire for truth for its own sake. Even when it makes no practical difference, we prefer to believe truly rather than falsely. We only need beliefs at all as a substitute for knowledge where knowledge is not available, or not at present available. (This still remains so even if you think that knowledge is just a special sort of belief; only you will then say that beliefs which do not qualify as knowledge are a substitute for those which do.) False beliefs are poor substitutes for knowledge, though it must be admitted that sometimes we cannot acquire true ones without holding false ones first, and then testing them and finding them to be false.

Now by adopting the policy of forming our beliefs reasonably, the policy of believing in accordance with the evidence and revising or abandoning our beliefs, in the light of new evidence, we do not of course ensure that *all* the propositions we believe will be true, or even that any of them will be *certainly* true. But when we reflect on the meaning of the word "evidence," we see that the policy of believing in accordance with the evidence is the only one which will ensure that the propositions we believe are more *likely* to be true than false. For when we say that such and such facts or experiences are evidence for a proposition p, we just mean that they make it likely in some degree to be true. And so in preferring a proposition for which the evidence is stronger to a proposition for which the evidence is weaker, we are *ipso facto* preferring the one which is more likely to be true. The statement that one is more likely to believe truly if one believes reasonably (that is, in accordance with the evidence) is an analytic statement which follows from the meanings of the expressions "evidence for" and "likely to be true."

Thus, if it is to our long-term advantage to believe truly rather than falsely, it is also to our long-term advantage to adopt and to stick to the policy of believing reasonably. I conclude, then, that there are very good grounds for applying

the *prudential* "ought" to the process of forming beliefs, though
there are no good grounds for applying the *moral* "ought" to it.

Thus, if I am right, it is misleading to speak of the "Ethics
of Belief." But there *is* such a thing as the Economics of Belief,
if one may use the word "Economics" in a wide and old-
fashioned sense to mean "the theory of prudence," the theory
of those activities, both mental and physical, which conduce
to our long-term advantage.

## PRIVATE LANGUAGES

### JUDITH JARVIS THOMSON[1]

There is a thesis which has been argued for by certain Wittgensteinians, namely that there can be no such thing as a private
language. This thesis is often referred to as, and we are given
to understand that it is, both important and original. I hope
to show that it is, properly understood, something very familiar
and rather tired. But the philosophers who argue for it are no
more to be confused with Wittgenstein than the Platonists are
to be confused with Plato; so to show this is not to cast discredit
on Wittgenstein himself. On the contrary, the disservice was
done by those who credited the thesis to him. If nothing else,
they failed utterly to take seriously his claim that he held no
opinions and put forward no theses in philosophy.

### I

Norman Malcolm[2] says "By a 'private' language is meant
one that not merely is not but *cannot* be understood by anyone
other than the speaker." This characterization is presumably

Reprinted from *American Philosophical Quarterly* (Vol. I, No. 1,
January 1964) by permission of the editor and Judith Jarvis Thomson.

    [1] My thanks to James F. Thomson for very helpful comments and
criticisms.

    [2] "Wittgenstein's *Philosophical Investigations*," *Philosophical Review*,
vol. 63 (1954). All further references to Malcolm are to this article.

suggested by *Investigations* #243, where Wittgenstein asks if we can imagine a language of which he says, "Another person cannot understand the language." And a little later on, Malcolm tells us that the "cannot" here is to be a logical "cannot": A private language is one of which it is not merely the case that it is not understood by anyone other than the speaker, but more that it is logically impossible that it should be understood by anyone other than the speaker. The thesis then—and I'll call it Malcolm's form of the thesis, or more briefly Malcolm's thesis—is that there can be no such thing as a language which is private in this sense.

Now what is remarkable is that some philosophers[3] who have understood the thesis in this way nevertheless take it to be relevant to discuss the question whether or not a man who grew up alone on a deserted island could have invented a language for his own use. But why should a man's growing up alone make the language he invents (if he can invent a language) of necessity unintelligible to the anthropologists who discover him? And if what is in question is the possibility of a language which is of necessity unintelligible to anyone else but its speaker, then having shown that a man who grew up alone couldn't have such a language you would still have to do the job of showing that a man who grew up in company couldn't have such a language. Which, if you were to look at the nature of the arguments which have actually been produced *for* Malcolm's thesis, would be to do exactly the same thing in both cases; i.e., the supposed proof of Malcolm's thesis calls for no assumptions whatever about how the supposed speaker of the private language grew up.

[3] E.g., Ayer in "Can There be a Private Language?" *Aristotelian Society Proceedings Supplementary Volume* 28. A. J. Ayer says the thesis is, there can be no language which is of necessity unintelligible to anyone but its speaker, and then, oddly enough, thinks he has refuted this thesis by proving (if he has proved even these) the quite irrelevant points (1) that there can be a language which is and always has been as a matter of fact unintelligible to anyone but its speaker, and (2) that sensation-reports are not of necessity unintelligible to anyone but their maker.

    Cf. also R. Rhees in "Can There be a Private Language?" op. cit.

It may be objected that Malcolm doesn't *own* the private language thesis, and that there is this or that other thesis (turning on this or that other definition of the expression "private language") which is the *real* private language thesis, and that I should have been dealing with them instead. I'm not going to take time to canvass these other possible theses, for (though I shall not defend this) it seems to me so plain that either they would rule out that English is a language or they rest on the (so far as I can see) utterly unjustified assumption that a man who grew up alone couldn't exhibit behavior which would justify us in saying of him: "Now he is following this rule." So I shall be dealing in what follows strictly with Malcolm's thesis—i.e., the thesis that there can be no private language, where a private language would be one which it was logically impossible for anyone but its speaker to understand.

## II

But in fact not much has yet been made clear about what the denial of the possibility of a private language amounts to. For the question arises: What could there be about or in a language in virtue of which it would be logically impossible for anyone else but its speaker to understand it?

Wittgenstein says (#258): "Let us imagine the following case. I want to keep a diary about the recurrence of a certain sensation. To this end I associate it with the sign 'E' and write this sign in a calendar for every day on which I have the sensation." Now what would make "E" such that it was logically impossible for anyone but LW to know what it meant? For suppose that we were to watch LW very carefully every day for several years, and suppose we were to notice the following regularities in his use of the word "E": Generally when he does write "E" in his diary he has held his cheek and furrowed his brow, he has gingerly touched his tongue to a tooth (and then winced), he has looked into his mouth in a mirror, . . . and he has phoned the dentist. Why are we not entitled to say that by "E" LW means "toothache" or "I have a toothache today"?

Malcolm cites a passage from *Investigations* #243: "E" would be a word in (or itself a small self-contained) private language if it referred to "what can only be known to" LW, to an "immediate private sensation" of his. Now as we described LW's use of the sign "E" it certainly looks as if we do know what the sensation is which he uses "E" to report on; so what we must take to be meant here is this: If in using "E" to report on the having of a sensation LW is referring to that sensation, *and* if it is the case that no matter how much cheek-clutching and dentist-phoning LW does it is logically impossible that we should know what sensation it is that he refers to by "E," then it is logically impossible that we should know what he means by "E." LW's use of the sign "E" would then be a small self-contained private language.

*Who* says that when we use sensation-terms (such as "pain," "toothache," etc.), we are referring to our sensations, and that it is impossible that you should know what sensation it is that I refer to when I use these terms of myself? The sceptic about other minds does. Smith alone (he says) can *know* what it is he's feeling when he thrashes about like that, or even if he's feeling anything at all.

So the point, then, is this: If the sceptic about other minds is right, then no matter what we observe of LW's behavior, it is logically impossible that we should know what sensation it is that he is feeling, and in particular, what sensation it is that he is referring to by the use of "E." So then it is logically impossible that we should know what he means by "E."

It is worth remarking that if the sceptic about other minds were right, then not only would "E" be a word in (or the whole of) a private language, but so also would *all* the sensation terms. We would each of us be speaking private languages in using the words "toothache," "pain," "hunger," and the rest. And this is as it should be. For one thing which is plain is that the point of raising these questions in this part of the *Investigations* is not to discredit the possibility that you or I should invent a special kind of language, but rather to bring out what queer things would have to be said about our ordinary language if the sceptic about other minds were right.

## III

One last point remains to be cleared up. As I said, the sceptic says that it is logically impossible that anyone but Smith should *know* what Smith is feeling, and it may be argued that this still leaves open the possibility that the rest of us should be entitled on occasion to claim that it is *probable* that he is (say) in pain, or hungry. We should distinguish, then, between Weak Scepticism about other minds, which is the view that we can never know what is in the mind of another, but that we may have good reason for thinking that he is feeling this or that; and Strong Scepticism about other minds, which is the view that we can never know what is in the mind of another, and more, that we are never in a position even to have good reason for thinking he is feeling this or that—that any claim we make about what Smith is feeling can at best be a mere guess. Now it is certainly arguable that Weak Scepticism is not a consistent doctrine—there are very familiar arguments which purport to show that where there can be no knowledge there can be no probability either—and thus that a Weak Sceptic must, to avoid self-contradiction, grow into a Strong Sceptic. I am not going to consider these arguments. I want only to point out that with each degree of Scepticism goes a different strength of "private" in the expression "private language." With Weak Scepticism goes the view that we can never know what LW means by "E" but that it is conceivable we should have good reason for thinking he means (say) "toothache," and with Strong Scepticism goes the view that we can never know what LW means by "E" and that it is not conceivable that we should have any good reason for thinking he means "toothache" or anything else—any view we have as to what "E" means can at best be a mere guess.

Now I think that what Malcolm means to be denying is the possibility of any strongly private language—i.e., any language in which it is logically impossible we should have any ground at all for supposing we understand. (In fact I think that he would not regard Weak Scepticism as even a consistent view to take, and thus as not interestingly to be distinguished from Strong Scepticism.) I shall not cite the passages which make me think this. It is not necessary, for it would plainly be *harder* to show that there can be no weakly private language than it would be to show that there can be no strongly private language. For by my definitions, if you have proved that there can be no strongly private language, then you would have still to do something more to prove that there can be no weakly private language, whereas proving that there can be no weakly private language calls for proving that which would already make a strongly private language impossible. And this can in any case be seen independently. If I can and could have no reason to think I knew what was meant by "E," then this would surely be a better ground for doubting that "E" was a word in a language than if, while I could never know that I was right, I could at all events form a reasonable conjecture to the effect that it means "toothache." So in attributing to Malcolm the thesis that there can be no strongly private language I do him no injustice: I give him the easier rather than the harder task.

## IV

The thesis, then, is this: There can be no such thing as a language in which it is logically impossible that anyone else but its speaker should have any good reason at all for thinking he understands. And now why should we suppose that this is true?

There seem to me to be three steps in the argument. The first is this: If a sign which a man uses[4] is to be a word in a language, his use of it must be governed by a rule or set of rules; and this means that it must be possible for him to use

[4] Sometimes the private language argument runs: And what could be the use, the role of the words in a private language? Well, why not simply to keep a record for one's own amusement? And then it seems to me that if this is to be ruled out, the argument will have to proceed as I describe it in what follows.

the sign correctly or incorrectly—i.e., on the one hand to follow the rule or act in accordance with it, or on the other hand, to violate or disobey or break it. For R is not a rule unless it is possible either to follow or violate it.

Straightaway, however, the difficulties rush in. What could *the* or *a* rule governing the use of the words "table" or "pain" or "revolution" be? Indeed it is not only the Wittgensteinians who rely heavily on the notion of a linguistic rule which one could follow or violate, and it is worth bringing out that thus far at all events nothing whatever has been done in the way of making this notion clear. For let us notice that something familiar from Carnap's writings, what he called Semantical Rules, will not do what is wanted here. For example, there is the Semantical Rule that says the sentence "The moon is round" means that or is true if and only if the moon is round; but this isn't anything you could follow or violate because it doesn't say anything about your doing anything. The rules of inference in the more familiar logical systems do at all events say "You may do thus and so"—e.g., the *modus ponens* rule. But what would count as a violation of a rule which says only "You may do thus and so"? What would even count as an instance of following such a rule? Not just doing the thing, for the rule didn't enjoin it on me to do it, but said only that I might do it. It would be a joke to say "I'm only following the rules" as I sit smoking in a carriage marked "Smoking Permitted."

I gather that there are some systems of logic which do contain rules which prohibit—rules which say "You may not do thus and so." These rules could of course be both followed and violated, but it can scarcely be supposed that the linguistic rules meant by the philosophers I have in mind could *all* be of this sort. It would follow that a sign could be a word in a language so long as there was a prohibition against its use.

Malcolm gives an example of a purported linguistic rule: "I will call this feeling 'pain' and will thereafter call the *same* thing 'pain' whenever it occurs." As this sounds more like the adoption of a policy than a rule which I hereby subscribe to, let us rewrite it in the form of a rule—and also replace "table" for "pain" so as not to prejudge any issues about private languages: Call this object "table" and thereafter call the same sort of thing "table" whenever—but now whenever what? Whenever you see one? It sounds mad; who would subscribe to a rule which enjoined it on him that every time he sees a table he make some remark about it? But then what should be filled in here? Even "whenever you want to refer to one" would be mad, for why shouldn't I allow myself just to use the word "that" and point to the thing when I want to refer to it? And very much worse still, *what* would I be accepting if that were what I should always do? I am to *call* things "tables," and just what is it to do this? I might say to you "Call Henry," and then if you are obliging you'll call out "Henry!"; but suppose I point to myself and say "Call me Ishmael"—is it so clear what it is I am requesting you to do? Must you ever actually *say* the word "Ishmael"? I'm not saying we don't say this sort of thing, but just that the notion of a linguistic rule is at least as much in need of an explanation as any of the things philosophers make use of it *to* explain.

But these difficulties may be set aside here, for they are not difficulties peculiar to the private language thesis. Let us set out the form of a linguistic rule for a name "K" of a kind of thing—leaving it open that words which play a different role should be governed by linguistic rules of different forms—as follows: You may call anything of kind X "K" and you may not call "K" anything which is not of kind X. And let us, for the sake of bringing out the rest of the argument, just *pretend* that there are no difficulties with it—we shall pretend that "call" is transparent, and that we need not worry about the fact that one couldn't either follow or violate the first conjunct of the rule. At all events, to subscribe to it is not to commit oneself to always doing something, or to always doing something in this or that kind of situation.

It is to be remarked about rules of this form (and this is an important fact about them from the point of view of the private language argument) that they involve mention of a sign,

"K," *and* of a kind of thing, the X's. What the rule says is that X's and only X's are to be called "K's" and "X" of course can be any expression whatever that stands for a kind of thing.

The first step of the argument, then, can be restated in this way: If a sign "K" which a man uses is to be a name of a kind of thing in a language, his use of it must be governed by a rule of the form, X's and only X's are to be called "K's."

## V

The second step of the private language argument has been thought to be self-evident (so it seems to me) by everyone who has written on this subject at all; and the fact that it is not self-evident is worth bringing out because what it says *is* peculiar to this argument. What it says is this: A man's use of a sign is not governed by a rule unless it is not merely possible that he should violate the rule but more, that he should violate it unwittingly. That is, it must be possible that he should think he is following the rule and not in fact be following it; from the fact that he thinks he is following the rule, it must not follow that he really is following it. And it is said that this is essential to the concept of a rule. (Cf. Malcolm, p. 532). Wittgenstein's #202 is generally appealed to here: "to *think* one is obeying a rule is not to obey a rule."

At first sight this second step does look to be self-evident. It seems so clear: After all, if from the fact that I think x-ing is following rule R it follows that it is following rule R, I am then free to do anything or nothing. That "rule" doesn't point in any direction. No restriction is imposed on what I do. R is not a rule but a mere "impression of a rule." (Cf. Malcolm, pp. 536, 537.) Now indeed, a "rule" which rules out nothing isn't a rule. But *does* it follow from the fact that if I think that x-ing is following rule R it is following rule R, that rule R rules out nothing? For why should it not be the case that I think of some activities that if I were to perform them, I would be violating rule R? And then it would certainly seem that if, thinking this of an activity, y-ing, I then y, I *am* violating rule

R. The adoption of rule R does seem to impose this restriction on me: I must not y, thinking that to y is to violate rule R.

All this is too abstract. So consider the rule "Always decide to do what you think at the time it would be most fun to do." Note, not "Always *do* what etc., etc.," for I might think I was following this rule, and not really be following it—e.g., all unknown to me I am paralyzed, and so I am not doing what I think I am doing. Rather, "Always *decide* to do etc., etc." Is there anything in the concept "rule" which rules it out that this should be a rule? Indeed, it even appears that this rule satisfies the first condition on rules, namely that a thing isn't a rule unless I can either follow or violate it. For I could surely, out of some moral compunction, say, decide not to do what I think at the time it would be most fun to do.

It might be objected that it is not at all plain how a man could adopt this rule while not adopting the rule "Always *do* what etc., etc." "All I resolve on is to decide in that way. What I actually do is another matter entirely; I adopt no rule to govern that." This is very odd indeed. "I just do the deciding—which has nothing whatever to do with what I actually *do*." But a man might not have anything nearly so strong as this in mind. One can almost hear a philosopher say to himself, "Now it is not possible to know for certain whether or not one really will be able to bring off what one decides to do. At some times it seems very likely indeed, at other times not. But still, I shouldn't commit myself to anything unless I am absolutely certain I can bring it off. Hence I should adopt 'Always decide,' and not 'Always do.'" (It is reported of Prichard that he would never say "I promise," but only "I fully intend.") Now one might argue that if this is what's behind it, then this man's rule "Always decide" is the same as another man's "Always do"; these are not distinct rules. (Prichard's "I fully intend" was as good as a promise, and was taken for that by his friends.) At all events this calls for an argument—that this is so (*if* it is) is not something that follows from the concept "rule."

Or again, Mummy writes "Whenever you feel the least bit

gloomy, think of your Mummy. (It will cheer you up.)" Could
I think I was following this rule and not be? (Of course it may
be said that it is not possible—knowingly at all events—to violate
this rule, so that it does not satisfy the first condition on rules
which was set out in step one of the argument. But then surely
the possibility of something like this should rather show either
that step one of the argument is not true for all rules, *or* that,
while one must be able to violate a rule if it is to be a rule,
it is not required that one be able to violate it knowingly. And
in fact things are really even worse than this. For notice that
one can't even violate this rule unwittingly unless one has, in
a sense, forgotten the rule. And now what rules—however
private—can't be "violated" in that way? How much help *is*
all this abstract talk about rules anyway?)

To say S is not a rule unless I can think I am following S
and not in fact be, is to set out a condition on rules which would
rule it out that rules of the sort I mention here—rules which
could in a perfectly ordinary, garden-variety sense be called
private rules—are rules. But that they should be ruled out as
not really rules is surely by no means self-evident.

But let us turn to linguistic rules in particular. The form
of a linguistic rule for a kind-name "K" was to be this: You
may call anything of kind X "K" and you may not call "K"
anything which is not of kind X. So the requirement is this:
If the sign "K" which a man uses is to be a kind-name in a
language, it must be possible for him to think he is following
a rule of this form and not in fact be. Now I think it would
plainly not satisfy that he might make a slip of the tongue: to
be confronted with something which is not X, and to mean to
say "It's L" or "It's M," and for "It's K" to come out instead.
For one thing, one might wish to say that if his utterance of
"It's K" was a slip of the tongue, then he did not *call* the
thing of which he said it a K, for this is not what he meant to
say of it. For another, it is not plain that following a rule of
this kind requires that a man should actually say anything.
But more important, since it is always possible that a man
should make a slip of the tongue or pen, there would be no

sign which a man might use which would be such that his use of it would fail to meet this condition. However private you imagine his use of it, he could think he was saying or writing it and not in fact be. (And moreover, looking ahead to the third step of the argument, that he had made a slip of the tongue or pen could be independently established.[5]) But then if the mistake is not to lie in his thinking he is calling a thing by some other name than "K" and its being "K" that in fact comes out, it must be that the mistake is to lie in his belief that the thing in question is an X when in fact it is not (or vice versa) : he calls it "K" thinking it is an X when it is not an X, thus unwittingly violating the prohibition against calling anything which is not of kind X "K." And so the requirement in the case of linguistic rules for kind-names is the following: If a sign "K" which a man uses is to be a kind-name in a language, then it must be possible that he should call a thing a "K" thinking it is an X when it is not an X, where it is the X's and only the X's which (in his use) are to be called "K's."

This certainly *sounds* a reasonable thing to say. But in the first place it is not so far as I can see a consequence of the concept "rule" itself, and in the second place I do not see how it should even be examined for correctness or incorrectness until the notion "call" is made clearer to us than has anywhere been done.

But before turning to the third step of the argument there are three further points which should be made:

(1) The Wittgensteinians I refer to—and many other philosophers besides—are in agreement on this, that it is *not* possible that a man should think he is in pain and not be in pain. And it might appear that one who says the following three things contradicts himself—namely (a) I can't think I'm in pain and not be in pain, (b) if a sign "K" which a man uses is to be a kind-name in a language, then it must be possible for him to

---

[5] Unless the sign is "private" too, which is a possibility that no one has remarked on—and this because it has not been noticed that the notion "private language" as Malcolm defines it does not require that the terms of the language be names of sensations. Cf. Section VII below.

call a thing a "K" thinking it is of the kind to be called "K"
and that it nevertheless not be, and (c) that "pain" is in fact
a word in the English language. In defense of the Wittgensteinians, who do say all these three things, we should bring out
that one may say them all without being guilty of an inconsistency. For one thing, it could be said that "pain" just isn't a
kind-name—and the Wittgensteinians of course do say this.
"Pain" is not the name of a kind of thing (a kind of sensation)
but rather something that "replaces pain-behavior." But more
important, it could be said that it is not required for "pain" to
be a kind-name that a man should be able to think he is in
pain and not be, as one can think this is alcohol (from its
being a colorless liquid) and it not be (cf. Malcolm, pp. 555,
556). It is only required that he should be able to think that
the sensation he now has is of the kind of which he, years
ago, decided that sensations of that kind and only sensations of
that kind are to be called "pains," and yet that it should not
be. (Here "X" in the rule is replaced by "sensation of the
same kind as that one.") And this, it might be said, is, for
all that has so far been argued at any rate, surely possible—for
he might have forgotten just which sensation it was of which
he had said to himself (or been told): Sensations of the same
kind as this one are to be called "pains." And also the Wittgensteinians could (though they don't) insist that though "pain"
is not a kind-name it is all the same a word in the language
in virtue of (among other things) its meeting conditions analogous to that which we set out for kind-names—perhaps that
a man's use of, e.g., the sentence "I'm in pain" is only a use
of a *sentence* in a language if it is possible that he should say
"I'm in pain" thinking he is in (roughly) a *situation* (which
includes his behavior as well as what is happening to him) of
the kind in which he may say "I'm in pain" and only in which
he may say "I'm in pain," and he is not. And a man could make
a mistake in this way if he had forgotten just which situation it
was of which he had said to himself (or been told): In situations of this kind you may say "I'm in pain." (Malcolm does
say [p. 541] that the verbal utterance "I'm in pain," like crying,

is in some sense "incorrigible," which if I understand it at all would mean that this condition is not met for the statement "I'm in pain." And it is no wonder Malcolm does this, for he is here trying to derive yet another thesis from the *Investigations*—this one from Wittgenstein's suggestion as to *one* possible answer to the question, how do human beings learn the meaning of the names of sensations. Cf. #244. [And it should be noticed that Wittgenstein nowhere else says anything about "pain" or "I'm in pain" replacing pain-behavior—he says only such things as that these are "tied to" the natural expressions of pain.] But then of course it is equally no wonder that Malcolm has trouble making out how the sentence "I'm in pain" can all the same be used to report on a matter of fact, i.e., be true or false.)

(2) The second point which should be made comes directly out of the first. We said that (for all that has so far been said) one can think something is of the kind to be called a "pain" and it not be; and in exactly the same way it is (for all that has so far been said) possible to think a thing to be of the kind to be called a "decision to do what one thinks at the time it would be most fun to do," or a "gloomy feeling" or "thought of Mummy," and that it not actually be one. But this does not show that it is possible to think one is following the two non-linguistic rules I mentioned above and not be; it does not show the two rules do after all satisfy this second condition on rules. For the two rules did not enjoin it on me that I should or should not, may or may not, *call* anything anything, but only that I form a certain kind of decision, think a certain thought. And it is not to be understood that one who grants "It is not possible to think one is in pain and not be" should also insist "But it is possible to think one is making a certain decision, feeling gloomy, thinking of Mummy, and not be."

And lastly, (3), it may be thought that this condition which a man's use of a sign "K" must satisfy if it is to be a kind-name in a language *already* rules it out that a private language should be a language, and we should bring out that it does not. Let us go back to LW who invented the sign "E" to report on the recurrence of a certain kind of sensation. Wittgenstein said (#258): "Let us imagine the following case. I want to keep a diary about the recurrence of a certain sensation. To this end I associate it with a sign 'E' and write this sign in a calendar for every day on which I have the sensation." And it may be asked: How does the sign *get* associated with a kind of sensation? Presumably LW gives himself a "private ostensive definition." He fixes his attention on a sensation, and says to himself: You may call this sensation and any others of the same kind as this one "E." Same kind? *What* kind? Supposedly "sensation of the same kind as *this* one" is to stand for a kind of sensation, but how do I get it to do that? Just by fixing my attention on this sensation? For there to be a kind of sensation (kind of thing in general) there must be limits as to what is or isn't of that kind; and how should I get limits to the kind marked out by simply fixing my attention on one given sensation? But if I don't demarcate a kind of sensation, then the rule I recite to myself is mere words—my future conduct is not directed in any way.

The question, "How do I demarcate a kind of sensation?" is a very respectable philosophical question. But of course it is only a special case of the very respectable philosophical question, "How do I demarcate a kind of *thing*?" And we may ask: Just why is there supposed to be any more difficulty about a private ostensive definition of a newly invented sensation-word than there is about a public ostensive definition of a newly invented thing word? *Why* any more trouble about demarcating a kind of sensation than about demarcating a kind of *thing*? Suppose I were to set about introducing by an ostensive definition a new name for a shade of red or blue I would like to single out or (for a particularly relevant example) for a kind of squiggle I would like to single out. I write a capital letter E on a bit of paper, and I say, that and any others of the same kind are to be called "E's." Have I demarcated a kind of squiggle? Well, what other marks would also be of the same kind? Would an italicized capital E be of the same kind? Or one with a long middle bar? Suppose when asked I said, "Yes they are of the same kind," or, "No, they are not of the same kind." Need I have had them specifically in my mind when I introduced the kind-name "E" in order for it to be the case that I was indeed picking out a kind of squiggle? Surely not.[6] Or better, if anything of this sort *were* necessary if I were to have demarcated a kind of thing, then it could have been present when I demarcated a kind of sensation—i.e., if I could have had other squiggles in mind as also of the same kind, then I could have had other sensations in mind as also of the same kind.

Indeed, private ostensive definition of a newly-invented sensation-word *is* supposed to be in a worse position than public ostensive definition of a newly-invented thing-word. But then something else will be required to show that it is worse than just this, that it is a matter of fixing one's attention on a sensation and saying of it: Any sensation of this kind is to be called "E" or "K" or "pain." It would have to be shown why its having been a *sensation* (an "immediate private sensation") that I fastened my attention on made it impossible that I should in this way demarcate a kind, whereas its having been a thing that I fastened my attention on did not make it impossible that I should in this way demarcate a kind. And in fact the third step of the argument can be regarded as an attempt to make just this very point.

# VI

Now this is where we have come so far. The thesis that there can be no private language is the thesis that there can be no language which it is logically impossible that anyone but the speaker should understand. And the argument for this thesis has so far proceeded in the following way: (1) It was said that if

---

[6] Does the child have to write "dog" just exactly as you do? Anything within a certain range will do. Of course in picking out for him a class of "dog"-inscriptions, you weren't picking out a new class of thing (you were taught what the class is just as he is now). All the same, you pick out a class for him in writing "dog," which he may learn from one sample alone. Why should I not be able to form a new class—of squiggles—and pick it out for you in the same way?

a sign which a man uses is to count as a word in a language, his use of it must be governed by a rule—here specifically, if a sign which a man uses is to count as a kind-name in a language, his use of it must be governed by a rule of the following sort: You may call anything of a kind X "K," and you may not call anything "K" which is not of kind X. (2) If a sign which a man uses is to be governed by a rule of this sort it must be possible that he should call a thing a "K" thinking it is of the kind to be called a "K" and it not be.

The third step of the argument is this: There is no such thing as a man's thinking a thing is of the kind to be called "K" and it not being so unless it is logically possible that it be *found out* that it is not so. And in the positive: There is no such thing as a man's thinking a thing is not of the kind to be called "K" and it being so unless it is logically possible that it be *found out* that it is so.

Since it is so plain when this third step is set out baldly like this what it is all going to amount to, it is worth stressing that this third step of the argument is required if the desired conclusion is to come out of it. That it is involved in the argument as actually set out might be denied, for it is nowhere set out explicitly. (Though I think it would be difficult to deny this. Consider, for example, Malcolm's queries: "Now how is it to be decided whether I have used the word consistently? What will be the difference between my having used it consistently and its *seeming* to me that I have? Or has this distinction vanished?" Of course one doesn't know for certain what a philosopher is appealing to when his argument for a thesis proceeds by the method of rhetorical questions, but it seems to me that unless Malcolm is taking it that, where it is not possible to "decide" whether I have used the word consistently the distinction between my having used it consistently and its seeming to me that I have *has* vanished, then this passage is simply incomprehensible. But we may in fact appeal to a more explicit passage, which follows shortly after: "My impression that I follow a rule does not confirm that I follow the rule, unless there can be something that will prove my impression correct." And then follows Wittgenstein's ironic comparison with the man who assures himself that what was said in his copy of the morning paper was true by buying several more copies of the same paper.[7]) But whether or not it could be denied that this claim was in fact being made by those who have argued against the possibility of a private language, we should stress this: That *without* this claim, the argument simply stops dead in its tracks, since nothing that has so far been said rules out the possibility of a private language. LW might say: "Indeed, there must *be* a difference between my sensation's being of the kind I had decided to call 'E' and its seeming so to me if 'E' is to be a kind-name of a sensation; but why should it follow from the fact that my sensations are strongly private that there is no such difference?" It might be said: "Well, how is it to be established that the sensation is or is not of the required kind?" And now if the argument is to proceed, there must be something which rules it out that LW should quite acceptably reply: Perhaps it can't be found out that my sensation is or is not of the required kind, but all the same it may be that it is.

And what rules this out is what I have called the third step, which simply amounts to the denial that there is any such thing as a thing's being or not being of the kind to be called "K" or "E" over and above its seeming to a man that it is unless it *is* logically possible that it be found out that it is or is not of that kind. I say, "Logically possible that it be found out"—for I think it cannot be supposed that what used to be called the "technical" possibility of finding out is required. (Remember how careful the Positivists were in regard to all these distinctions?) For if more than the mere logical possibility is required, then far more is going to be ruled out than just private

[7] Cf. Mr. R. Rhees (op. cit.): "And if every use of the mark is also a definition—if there is no way of discovering that I am wrong, in fact no sense in suggesting that I might be wrong—then it does not matter what mark I use or when I use it." Unless I am muddled as to syntax, the "in fact" does a job here which might equally well have been done by "or, which amounts to the same."

languages—e.g., it would be ruled out that "ace" was a kind-name in English on the ground that I have just destroyed a playing card without looking at it, and so it is not any longer as a matter of fact possible to find out whether or not it was an ace. But of course you would always need a stronger premise than just that something *is* the case, e.g., "I destroyed a playing card without looking at it," in order to get as a conclusion that it is not logically possible that something should be the case, e.g., "It is not logically possible that we should find out whether or not the card was an Ace." (Or rather, to be more precise, there is no familiar rule of inference which will take you from a contingent premise to the conclusion "It is logically impossible that . . ."—except the rule of inference which allows you to derive a necessary truth from *any* proposition whatever. And then of course you would have already to know independently that the conclusion "It is logically impossible that . . ." *is* a necessary truth.) As far as the playing card is concerned, it is surely logically possible that, e.g., someone else had looked at it before I destroyed it.

In fact I think (though I shall not try to show this here) that only a private language will fail to meet this condition. Any kind-name "P" such that there is one occasion on which it is not logically possible to find out whether or not "P" applies to a thing must necessarily be a private kind-name—i.e., one such that it is not logically possible to find out on any occasion of its use whether or not "P" does apply to a thing.

But what we should show is that this *is* true of private kind-names; what we should show is that if "E" is a word in or the whole of a private language, then it is not anywhere at any time for any person logically possible to find out that "E" applies or is true. And thus that, whether or not anything else does, at all events every sign in a private language *does* fail to meet the condition for being a kind-name in a language laid down in this third step of the argument.

To bring this out we have to fill in a certain vagueness in the statement of the condition. I put the condition in the words "unless it is logically possible that it be found out that a given

thing is or is not of the relevant kind," and the question arises
what "finding out" is to mean here. Must it be logically possible
to establish conclusively that the thing is or is not of the relevant kind? Or would it be enough that it was logically possible
that one should have or obtain good reason for thinking the
thing was or was not of the relevant kind? (Malcolm does use
the word "prove" here—I quoted the passage above—but in
fact the Wittgensteinians use the word "prove" and the related
word "criterion" in so relaxed a manner that it is not really
fair that we should take the appearance of this word as proof
that it is "proof" that is meant.) It seems to me that it is very
likely that it is the former that is required—as we might call it,
strong finding out. For one thing it appears to me that the two
possibilities would not be regarded as distinct—we have already
mentioned the familiar arguments purporting to show that there
can be no probabilities where there can be no knowledge. (Cf.
above on the distinction between Weak and Strong Scepticism.)
But more important, it is not plain how a private language
would be ruled out if it were not strong finding out that is required. For consider LW again: Could it not happen that he
should think his present sensation was of the kind to be called
"E"—and then later think "Oh what a fool I am. Now I remember what the sensation was which struck me that afternoon
last May. And I was wrong just now in thinking the one I just
had was of that kind—it wasn't like it at all." It could of course
be said: This appealing to further impressions shows nothing
unless it produces an impression "which is actually correct"
(cf. Malcolm, pp. 533, 534; on memories). But to take this line
suggests that it *is* conclusive or strong finding out which is
required—either because good reasons are not enough, or because where there can be no strong finding out there can be no
good reasons either. A case could *perhaps* be made for saying:
This that happens later is not a reason for thinking that his
former impression was false, but just itself the impression that
his former impression was false. A good reason for thinking the
former impression was false would be enough—strong finding
out is not necessary—but the impression that you were or were

not mistaken cannot amount to a reason for thinking it so. However, this is not at all clear; and it may in fact be absurd.

I am inclined to think that the finding out which is mentioned in the third step must be a conclusive or strong finding out if private languages are to be ruled out. But let us leave all this open. At all events, the possibility LW may later have the impression he was mistaken is not to count as the possibility that he should find out he was mistaken.

People have raised the question in connection with the denial of the possibility of a private language just why "corrigibility by others" should be required if the sign a man uses is to be a word in a language. So far as I can see it is not especially corrigibility by others that is being required, but rather just corrigibility. Corrigibility by others comes in in this way. The Strong Sceptic about other minds says that no amount of observation of LW's behavior could give us any reason whatever for thinking we knew what sensations he was having at any time—thus we are not in a position to find out whether or not he makes a mistake in thinking the sensation he now has is of a kind which he formerly had. But then similarly no amount of observation of LW's behavior by LW himself could give *him* any reason for thinking he knew what sensations he was having at any time—and in particular, no behavioral traces (such as a photograph of himself he had taken the day he was first struck by the sensation he wished to record) could give him any more reason for thinking he knows what he then felt than it could give us reason for thinking we know what he then felt. So what makes it impossible for us to correct his use of the sign "E" goes halfway to making it impossible for him to correct his use of the sign "E"—and if there were that which would make his use corrigible by us, it would also make his use corrigible by him. But it is supposed by hypothesis that there isn't that which would do this. Now add to the strong privacy of the sensations whatever it is that you need to make out in addition that LW's later impressions that he was or wasn't mistaken can't count as LW's finding out that he was, and you now have it that no one can find out whether or not he is now mistaken.

A private language, then, will fail to meet this condition, so long as we are given either an appropriate account of "finding out" (i.e., strong finding out) or an appropriate account of "later memory impressions" (i.e., that they could not count as finding out).

Well, is this third step of the argument true? I shall not bother to bring out the things that can be said in defense of it, or the things that can be said against it, for it will be plain what sorts of things they are the moment we conjoin the three steps of the argument to form one general principle, which is what I want to say the denial of the possibility of private languages amounts to. The general principle is this: A sign "K" which a man uses is not a kind-name in a language unless (by 1) he has identified a kind of thing to be called "K," which will only be the case (by 2) if it is possible for him to call a thing a "K" thinking it is of that kind when it is not, which will only be the case (by 3) if it is possible to find out whether the thing is or is not of that kind. Or in sum: A sign "K" is not a kind-name in a man's language unless it is possible to find out whether or not a thing is of the kind associated with "K" (over and above its seeming or not seeming to him to be so)—or more simply still, a sign "K" is not a kind-name in a man's language unless it is possible to find out whether or not a thing is a K.

And it is plain that this is nothing more than a revised formulation of something very familiar indeed, namely the Principle of Verification.[8] We are no longer to say that what purports to be a kind-name "K" has meaning if and only if it is possible to find out whether or not a thing is a K. But we are instead to say that what purports to be a kind-name "K" is a

---

[8] That there is *a* connection between the private language argument and verification has already been suggested by Ayer (op. cit.) and Strawson (reference given below). The connection is also noticed by Carl Wellman, in "Wittgenstein and the Egocentric Predicament," *Mind*, vol. 68 (1959), April number—though this article seems to me to underestimate not only Wittgenstein, but also the force of the private language argument.

kind-name in a man's language only if it is possible to find out whether or not a thing is a K. Strong finding out goes with what used to be called Strong Verificationism; weak finding out goes with what used to be called Weak Verificationism. And the change, then, amounts to this: from "if and only if" to "only if"; and from "is meaningless" to "is not a kind-name in a man's language." Perhaps the reasons why this might not be thought to be much of an improvement will not need to be set forth.

Since the denial of the possibility of a private language is surely a denial of the possibility of a pure sense-datum language—since the thesis we are concerned with is often appealed to in order to discredit phenomenalism—it may seem strange to suggest that the private language thesis is really a mere restatement of verificationism. After all, in recent philosophical history, verificationism has been taken to lead directly *to* phenomenalism. But we have only to reflect that there were physicalists as well as phenomenalists who rested their case on verificationism. Verificationism does not lead by itself either to one or to the other; your choice between them rested not on the question whether or not you adopted the Principle of Verification, but rather on the question what kinds of ascriptions you took it to be possible to verify. And on this matter, our Wittgensteinians are at one with the physicalists.

## VII

It may be asked, how can it be that the thesis we are considering really amounts to something quite general, like a revised formulation of the Principle of Verification, when all that was at stake was a private language—a language which a man invents to report on his own sensations, or the language which we would be using in reporting on our sensations if the sceptic about other minds were right.

In fact, if we take seriously Malcolm's definition of the expression "private language," then it is not merely our use of sensation-terms which (if the sceptic about minds were right) would count as private languages, but many other things as well. Malcolm said that a private language would be (if there could be such a thing) "one that not merely is not but [of necessity] *cannot* be understood by anyone other than the speaker." I now give a recipe for constructing hypothetical languages which would be private in Malcolm's sense. Take any classical metaphysical problem on which there is such a thing as a Sceptical View. Now take the range of statements of which it is the relevant Sceptical View that we can never know whether or not any statement in that range is true. And now *if* the sceptic's view were correct, then what we might call the relevant term or kind of term or form of term will be such that if a man uses that term or kind of term or form of term, he speaks a (at least partly) private language. Consider the metaphysical problem about the existence of material objects. And now suppose that the sceptic about material objects were right —i.e., that it is not possible that any of us should know of any term purporting to stand for a material object whether or not it really applies to anything. So, in particular, we are supposing that it is not possible that anyone should know of the word "table" whether or not it really applies to anything. We are supposing that although it can *seem* to us as if this really is a table, it is not possible that anyone should *know* that it is one (Weak Scepticism), nor even possible that anyone should have good reason for thinking it is one (Strong Scepticism). Now suppose some man—let us arbitrarily call him Moore—insists that *he does* know of many things that they are (and not merely appear to be) tables. "Here's one, for example," he says, pointing. But now what shall we take Moore to be saying here? That it looks as if he's pointing to a table, that generally when he uses these words there appears to be a table in the vicinity, is no proof (Weak Scepticism), or even good reason (Strong Scepticism), for thinking that he *is* pointing to a table, that generally when he uses these words there *is* a table in the vicinity. So how should we know—suppose ourselves to have good reason for thinking we know—what he means to be saying is here when he says "Here's a table"?

All that is needed for turning a class of sentences "S" into

sentences of a private language is that whatever it is which is
a way of finding out whether or not sentences of kind S are true
should be made logically irrelevant to the truth of sentences
of kind S. *Instantly* it is not possible that we should know
whether or not any sentences of kind S are true; and *instantly*
if any man uses sentences of kind S it is not possible that we
should know what he means by them.

Indeed it is surprising that those who have tried to
derive the thesis we have been considering from the *Investigations* have failed to notice this possibility of generalizing the
notion "private language."[9] Particularly in view of the fact that,
as Malcolm notes, Wittgenstein explicitly suggests (cf. e.g., p.
180) that the relation between reports about the behavior of
another and reports about the contents of the mind of another
is analogous to the relation between reports about one's sense-
impressions and reports about physical objects.

## VIII

So the thesis we have been considering amounts to no more
than a restatement of the Principle of Verification. But of course
it then amounts to no less than this. Whatever can be said both
for and against the one can be said both for and against the
other. The only trouble is: The arguments on both sides are
excessively familiar.

But it is worth bringing out explicitly that two objections
in particular which were made to the Principle of Verification
can also be made to Malcolm's restatement of it.

(1) Is this principle really of any use to us? How is it to

---

[9] P. F. Strawson (critical notice of Wittgenstein's *Philosophical
Investigations, Mind*, Vol. 53 (1954), January number) explicitly suggests
that the notion "private language" may be generalized: i.e., that the
terms need not stand for sensations, but may also stand "for things like
colours or material objects or animals." But in fact he is concerned with
a quite different notion of "private language": on Mr. Strawson's view
(cf. pp. 84–85) a private language is one which merely is not, and never
has been, understood by anyone but its speaker.

be decided if an expression *does* satisfy the principle? Suppose a man were to claim to be able to see a new color—for want of a word he calls it "K." He says: "I can't explain to you what it is any more than I can explain to a man who is color-blind what redness is. You just have to be able to see which things are K and which are not. And if you can't, you're just color-blind to K-ness." Well, in fact we don't see any difference between the things he calls "K" and the things he says are not K; the things he calls "K" all look black to us, but many black things, he says, are not K. Is his word "K" a kind-name in a language, or are his utterances in which "K" appears mere noises? The principle tells us "K" is a kind-name in his language only if it is possible to find out whether or not a thing is K. Only if it is possible that *we* should find this out, for *his* memory impressions aren't going to count here. *Is* it possible that we should find out, i.e., come to be able to see which things are K and which are not? One is inclined to say: It is possible only if "K" *is* a kind-name in his language, and not a mere noise. So we come full circle.

(2) Connected with this is a second objection. The principle, it will be remembered, was this: A sign "K" is not a kind-name in a man's language unless it is possible to find out whether or not a thing is K; and let us call this condition on a man's use of a sign "C." What we might then ask is: 'Is "C" a kind-name in a language? Well, it is a kind-name in a man's language if it is possible to find out whether or not he so uses "C" that it is possible to find out whether or not a sign in a given use does satisfy this condition. Does "K" in the preceding example satisfy it—over and above its perhaps seeming to its user that it does? Do "table" and "chair" satisfy it—over and above its seeming to some non-sceptic that they do? (And this difficulty becomes especially acute if it is strong finding out that is required.) How should I find out whether or not they do— which is not merely to be a matter of my asking myself whether or not it seems to me that they do? And it should be stressed that unless this is possible for some man, then if the new principle is

true, "C" is not a kind-name in anyone's language. In which
case, what should we take the principle to be saying? One is
always inclined to suspect that this kind of question—what
happens when we apply the principle to itself?—is something of
a game, for can we not learn something important from the principle anyway? All the same, if a thesis is to be defended, then
embarrassing difficulties have to be faced.

## IX

In conclusion, I would just like to say this about the new
form of the Principle of Verification, that it seems to me very
clear that Wittgenstein himself would never for one moment
have subscribed to it. It is astonishing that a man who repeatedly
insisted that he put forward no theses in philosophy should constantly be credited with having proved this or that thesis, from
the private language thesis to the dreary sorts of things that get
called "Wittgenstein's Theory of Meaning," or "Wittgenstein's
Theory of Meaning As Use."

There is a vast difference between proposing that we ask
a certain question in order to get clearer about the nature of a
certain kind of claim, and declaring that if this question does
not receive the sort of answer one might have expected, or has
no answer at all, then claims of the kind in question are
spurious, or meaningless, or not really in the language.

Wittgenstein does say to the Solipsist: You have made a
*grammatical* movement, which you interpret as a quasi-scientific
discovery. And yet he adds (#401): "But there is an objection
to my saying that you have made a 'grammatical' movement.
What you have primarily discovered is a new way of looking
at things. As if you had invented a new way of painting; or,
again, a new metre, or a new kind of song." No doubt hints
of this sort are obscure; no doubt it is not clear what it is
that we are to do with them. But that is no reason for thinking
that we are free to disregard them, or for thinking that they are
(perhaps) mere poetic embellishments on what is really a quite

straightforward theory about the necessary conditions for meaningfulness or for being-in-a-language.

## CAUSES AND OBJECTS OF SOME FEELINGS AND PSYCHOLOGICAL REACTIONS

### D. F. PEARS

The problem is this. There are many statements that a person can make about his own feelings and psychological reactions which seem to be causal or at least partly causal, and yet which seem to be incorrigible, or at least not corrigible in the light of parallel negative instances, as Hume's account of causation requires that they should be. For example:

'I was pleased by the publication of my letter.'

In this case it is arguable that I must know what pleased me, or at least that, if I am mistaken, this will not be established by my indifference when newspapers have rejected other letters of mine: and yet the statement seems to be partly causal. The same might be said of other statements which mention feelings that usually last longer, such as:

'His behaviour made me angry.'
and 'I am depressed by my lack of money'.

There are also statements that raise this problem at the opposite end of the scale, where the psychological reaction is almost too brief and superficial to be classified as a feeling. For example:

'I was amused by his remark.'
and 'The explosion made me jump'.

Reprinted from *Ratio* (Vol. 4, No. 2, December 1962) by permission of the editor and D. F. Pears.

This last example may look rather out of place in the list, but I think that it usually implies that there was a psychological reaction, namely surprise or shock.

These statements seem to force us to make a difficult choice between three alternatives. Either they are not causal: or they are corrigible in the Humean way; or Hume's account of causation is not universally true. Ought we to accept one of these three alternatives? Or should we look for a fourth solution, perhaps a compromise?

Before this problem is discussed, it needs to be made more precise, in two ways. First, it must be separated from another problem, the problem whether the person's knowledge of the truth of these statements is immediate. And secondly, the the type of corrigibility that is in question must be specified.

First, it is well known that statements of this kind have been said to possess the following peculiarity: the person himself does not come to make them by considering evidence; he does not use observation and inference; for him, at least, they are not hypotheses but immediate. This is obviously a very plausible thesis, and some version of it is almost certainly true of typical utterances of the statements that I have listed. But I am not going to discuss this thesis. For although the question whether a person makes a certain kind of statement immediately is connected with the question whether that statement is incorrigible, the two questions are not identical, and can be separated. For many ordinary causal statements are made immediately and yet they are corrigible, indeed corrigible in the Humean way. Therefore I shall separate the two questions, ignore the question of immediacy, and discuss only the question of corrigibility.

But at this point the second preliminary question has to be answered. What feature of the listed statements is supposed to be incorrigible, and what sort of correction is being ruled out? I shall not be concerned with the question whether the description of the feeling or psychological reaction is incorrigible, though that is an interesting question. I shall restrict myself to the question whether it might be incorrect for a person to say that it was his lack of money that depressed him, or that it was someone's behaviour that made him angry, etc. Also I shall not be concerned with cases where the incorrectness is the result of untruthfulness, but only with cases where it is the result of a mistake made by the person himself. Given the previous restriction, this means that the mistakes in question will be mistaken identifications made by the person himself, mistaken identifications of what depressed him, what made him angry, etc.

But even this question is rather wider than the question that I want to ask. For it covers some borderline cases of mistaken identifications, which raise special difficulties irrelevant to my problem. This comes about in the following way. Someone might know what it was that depressed him, in that he could produce a sufficiently individuating true description of what, in fact, it was. Then it might be the case that there was another description, which he also believed to be true of it, although, in fact, unlike the first, it was not. In this situation he might produce the second description instead of the first. Suppose that he did this, and suppose that he did it not merely because he expressed something that he really knew in the wrong words— which would be the sort of mistake that he could instantly correct for himself. Then he would have mistakenly identified what depressed him, and the mistake would be substantial. Yet *ex hypothesi* he would know what depressed him, since he could also produce the first, true description of it. Would this put him in a position to correct his substantial mistake? It might, since, on reflection, he might realize that the two descriptions did not apply to the same thing, and he might opt for the first. Alternatively, there might be some other outcome. It would depend on the nature of the particular case. There are all sorts of interesting complications in these borderline examples, but I want to avoid them, because they are irrelevant to my problem. So I shall confine myself to the extreme case in which there is a substantially mistaken identification and no knowledge in reserve that might lead the person to correct his mistake. My question is whether it is possible for a person to make this kind of mistake about what depressed him, what made him angry, etc.

From now on, when I ask whether one of the statements on my list is corrigible or might be mistaken, this will always be the kind of mistake that I mean.

The problem that I have posed is how, if at all, we should choose between three alternatives: that the statements listed are not causal; that they are liable to the kind of mistake that is revealed by parallel negative instances—e.g. by similar situations in which I am not angry; and that Hume's account of causation is not universally true. I shall begin by examining some of the ways in which others have dealt with this problem, or with part of it.

It is clear from what Miss Anscombe says in her book *Intention* that her view about all the statements on my list except the last one would be that they report that something is both the cause and the object of the feeling in question.[1] But does she think that, in so far as they report causes, they are immune from mistakes? It is difficult to tell. Her rejection of Hume's account of causation for such cases suggest that she does think this, since the main point of Hume's account is that causal statements are liable to mistakes revealed by parallel negative instances, and it does not seem likely that her view is that they are liable to mistakes revealed in some other way. On the other hand, she does not allow that such causal connections are known,[2] and according to her usage the verb 'to know' is admissible only if there is some possibility of mistake.[3] So it may be that her rejection of Hume's account of causation is only the rejection of another thesis which she perhaps ascribes to Hume, the thesis that causal statements are always based on inferences.[4] In any case, even if she were right in rejecting Hume's main point, that causal statements are always vulnerable to parallel negative instances, it would not be enough to do this. For if

---

[1] *Intention*, p. 16, cf. Wittgenstein, *Philosophical Investigations*, §476.

[2] loc. cit., p. 15.

[3] loc. cit., p. 14.

[4] Hume explicitly rejects this thesis in §§12 and 13 of Part III of the First Book of the Treatise.

there are causal statements that are not liable to this kind of correction, we shall need to understand why this is so: we shall need to know what the other peculiaries of these causal statements are, and how much they still retain in common with Humean examples. We cannot just accept a large unexplained gap between two types of causal statements. So this solution is, at best, incomplete.

Is it, then, possible to defend the first of the three solutions that I mentioned, the one that denies that the statements are causal? If they are not causal, what are they? The most plausible suggestion is that they report the object of the feeling or reaction, that and nothing more. Mr. Williams, in his article on *Pleasure and Belief*,[5] makes this suggestion about one group of cases, statements beginning 'I am pleased by—', 'I am pleased that—' and 'I am pleased because—'. His article also contains a theory about the nature of the connection between being pleased and its objects,[6] and an attempt to extend the theory to cover certain causal statements.[7] I shall examine this theory later. At the moment I am only concerned with his denial that statements in the group that he examines are causal. The point that I want to make about it is this: even if it is true that none of the statements in his group are causal (I shall argue later that it is not true), this is certainly not true of some of my other examples. For instance, the statement that I am depressed by my lack of money is obviously partly causal. Moreover, one of his reasons for denying that the statements in his group are causal is that they are immune from mistakes.[8] But I shall argue later that some of my other examples are not immune from mistakes, and that perhaps even the statements in his group are not immune from mistakes. (Here, as always, I mean mistakes of the kind specified above.)

Ought we, then, to adopt the only remaining solution of

[5] Proceedings of the Aristotelian Society, Supplementary Volume XXXIII, 1959, p. 59.

[6] loc. cit., p. 61 ff.

[7] loc. cit., p. 65.

[8] loc. cit., pp. 65–8.

the three that I mentioned, and say that the statements on my list are liable to the kind of mistake that is revealed by parallel negative instances? But this alternative will not work for all the examples. For there does not seem to be any possibility of mistake about the fact that I was amused by his remark. And where there is some possibility of mistake, as I shall argue that there is about depression, it seems that the mistake would not always be revealed by parallel negative instances.

So it seems certain that we cannot solve the problem by simply choosing one of the three alternatives and applying it to all the statements on my list. It also seems probable that those statements lies on the intersection of two different conceptual schemes, the conceptual scheme of ordinary causation, and the conceptual scheme of feeling and object. This is the possibility that I shall explore.

There are two reasons whey it is likely that this possibility is realized. First, a statement that something is the object of a feeling does not seem to be reducible to a causal statement. Secondly, in all the examples given, the high degree of certainty that the person himself would have, whether or not it amounts to immunity from mistake, always seems to depend on the identification of the object of the feeling. I shall now expand these two points.

First, suppose that we say that the object of a feeling or reaction is what it is about. This will hardly do as a definition, since other prepositions and even entirely different forms of words are capable of conveying the idea of being about something in this particular sense. But it does roughly demarcate the concept of the object of a feeling or reaction. Given this explanation of the concept, it is immediately clear that, although the object of a feeling or reaction may cause it, and although one and the same statement may imply that it is both the object and the cause, nevertheless the statement that it is the object is not reducible to a causal statement. My reason for saying this is not that object-statements, unlike causal statements, are immune from mistakes: for I shall argue later that at least some object-statements are not immune from mistakes. It is simply that there is an obvious divergence between the meanings of the two types of statement. For instance, someone might say that his depression was caused by too much aspirin, and this would not mean that he was depressed about his excessive consumption of aspirin. Or, to take a non-physiological example, depression is sometimes the sequel to a period of excessive excitement, but, if someone gives this as the cause of his depression, he will not mean that this is what he is depressed about.

It might be objected, at this point, that a general argument for the irreducibility of object-statements to causal statements ought not to be based on the solitary example of depression. For depression belongs to the class of feelings or reactions that need not have an object, although presumably, they always have causes: i.e., a person can be depressed without being depressed about anything in particular, although his depression will have a cause. And it might be thought that this is the only reason why object-statements cannot be reduced to causal statements in this case. But this is not so. For if we take an example from the other class of feelings and reactions, which must have an object, for instance being pleased, we still get the same result: i.e., we still find that, if a person says that something is the cause of his being pleased, he will not mean that he is pleased about it; for example, he may be asked why he is pleased about some trifling thing, and he may reply that it is because he is in a good mood, itself produced by a satisfying meal or an enjoyable opera, and yet this reply will not mean that he is pleased about any of these other things. So it seems that object-statements are not reducible to causal statements, because causal statements do not imply object-statements. (In spite of this it may be the case that object-statements imply causal statements: i.e., it may be that, if something is the object of a feeling, it follows that it, or at least some thought or belief about it, is the cause of the feeling. I shall examine this possibility later.)

The second point that I was going to expand is the suggestion that the high degree of certainty that the person himself would have about the statements on my list would depend on the identification of the object of his feeling or reaction. The argument for this is that, if we consider a feeling like depression, and if we take cases where the person does not know what he is depressed about, perhaps because there is nothing in particular that he is depressed about, or perhaps because, though there is, he does not know what it is, then he will not be so certain what made him depressed. That is, if we subtract the identification of the object, then his certainty about any residual causal statement will be diminished.

It might be objected that the argument is weak because this subtraction is not possible with the class of feelings and reactions that must have an object. For example, the concept of amusement does not allow the minimal knowledge that I am just amused: and perhaps the concept of being pleased does not allow the minimal knowledge that I am just pleased. But in at least some of these cases it is possible to take a related concept, for instance being in a good mood instead of being pleased, and to make the same point about the residual causal statement in this case. And perhaps this is enough for the argument. The only example on the list that looks as if it might be a counter-example to the suggestion that is being defended, is the last one, 'The explosion made me jump.' For at first sight it does not look as if this statement implies that there is a psychological reaction about an object at all, and so it seems that the person's certainty about it cannot depend on his identification of an object. In fact, this is how Miss Anscombe interprets a similar example in her book, welcoming the conclusion that it is a purely causal statement which refutes Hume's account of causation.[9] But this is unconvincing if it means that the example refutes the thesis that all purely causal statements are liable to the kind of mistake that is revealed by parallel negative instances. For if the statement simply reported a reflex movement, it would be vulnerable to parallel negative instances; and if, on the other hand, we regard it as immune from parallel negative instances, and so credit the person himself with a high degree of certainty about it, it seems that this can only be because it

9 *Intention*, pp. 15–16.

carries the implication that the explosion was the object of his reaction of shock.

So it seems likely that the statements on my list are grouped around the point of intersection of the conceptual scheme of ordinary causation and the conceptual scheme of feeling and object. What effect would this have on their analysis? This is a large and complex question. Perhaps the simplest way of approaching it is to begin by describing the conceptual scheme of feeling and object. So what I shall do next is to offer, without much argument, a general picture of the logic of object-statements. Then I shall try to defend this picture by dealing with two objections to it. And finally, I shall offer a solution of the problem stated at the beginning. These three tasks will occupy the remainder of this paper.

The first of them can be completed more quickly than the other two. For the important question about the logic of object-statements is whether the person himself can make a mistaken identification, and the general lines of the answer to this question are fairly clear. Two, at least, of my examples are not liable to mistakes in the identification of the object, 'I was amused by his remark' and 'The explosion made me jump.' For suppose that someone tried to persuade me that the object of my amusement was really something else. For instance, he might point out that a great many factors had predisposed me to laugh at a not very amusing remark, and that among those factors were other excellent jokes made by the same speaker, which had, in fact, greatly amused me. Then he would necessarily fail, because this sort of mistake is not allowed for by the concept of amusement. The most that could be conceded to him would be that the object of my amusement played an unusually small part in causing it, but this would not debar it from being its object. Similarly, if the statement about the explosion implies that I was startled, I cannot have made a mistake in identifying it as the object of my reaction, although it may have played an unusually small part in causing it.

But these two statements seem to lie at one end of a spectrum whose other end is quite different. For at least one of my examples is liable to a mistake in the identification of the object. Someone who says 'I am depressed by my lack of money' might well be led to change this identification of the object of his depression. For instance, he might be contemplating a journey when he made the statement, and he might later be brought to admit that what he was really depressed about was some aspect of his relationship with the people whom he was going to visit. If this happened, he would see that the thing that he had originally given as the object of his feeling was a kind of symbol, representing but concealing its real object. Perhaps it is also possible to be mistaken in identifying what one is angry about, or even what one is pleased about. But I do not want at the moment to extend this thesis towards the middle of the spectrum. I simply want to use the concept of depression to fix its extreme point.

How would it be established that someone has mistakenly identified the object of his depression? There seem to be three different ways, which are sometimes used together, and sometimes separately. First, the person might cease to feel depressed about the stated object as soon as his attention was drawn to the rival object, about which he would immediately begin to feel depressed. Of course, in this situation he might say that one bout of depression had been replaced by another. But he would not have to say this, as he would have to say the parallel thing about amusement. For in certain circumstances he would use a different criterion of identity for bouts of depression and he would say that he had discovered that the bout of depression which, according to the first statement, had one object, really had another.

The second way in which the mistake might be established is quite different. The person might come to realize that the stated object of his depression was not a sufficiently important part of its cause, and that something else, which might well be its object (unlike the excessive excitement in the earlier example), was a much more important part of its cause. And he might come to realize this in an ordinary Humean way: for instance, he might remember that he had not felt depressed on other occasions when he was even more short of money, and that he had felt depressed on other occasions when he was about to visit those people.

The third thing that might establish that a mistake had been made is behaviour. For example, either the person himself or other people might notice that he kept postponing the date of his departure and that this decreased his depression, and that he went on spending money on other things without increasing it. This method of correction is related to the second one, but differs from it in that the observations are confined to the history of the particular case, and do not range over other parallel cases in the person's life. I shall not discuss this way of establishing that an identification of an object is mistaken, but only the first and second ways.

It is sometimes said that the second way can never be used alone, as the first way can: or at least that, though it may be used alone in psycho-analytic case histories, it never is in everyday life. But this seems to be incorrect. For if the possibility of mistake and the relevance of Humean evidence are admitted, there cannot be any good reason for maintaining that Humean evidence alone, however strong, is never sufficient to establish a mistake. However, this kind of evidence is often very inconclusive, since the causation of human feelings is so complex that it is very often impossible to be sure that there is no relevant difference between the particular case that is under scrutiny and the parallel negative instances that are cited.

Much more ought to be said in defence of the thesis that a person can make a mistaken identification of the object of his depression and of other similar feelings. For example, an account is needed of the way in which his behaviour might lead him to admit that he had made such a mistake. And something should be said about the possibility that he might be forced back to an intermediate position, in which he knew that he was depressed, but did not know what he was depressed about.

But that will have to do as a general picture. And now my second task is to defend it by dealing with two objections to it. The first objection is simply that it is false that there are any

mistaken identifications of the objects of feelings and psychological reactions except in psycho-analytic case-histories. And
the second objection is that, even if my description of the logic
of object-statements is correct, it is inadequate: for we need to
understand the nature of the connection between feeling and
object, and, in particular, we need to know why mistakes are
possible at one end of the spectrum, but not at the other.

First consider the objection that mistaken identifications of
objects do not occur outside psycho-analytic case-histories. What
lies behind this objection is the notion that psycho-analytic accounts of such mistaken identification are either false, or else
contain conceptual innovations that are so extreme that the use
of ordinary words is illegitimate. I shall counter this objection
by trying to show that our ordinary conceptual scheme really
does allow that objects may be mistakenly identified, though
perhaps it would not allow some of the more extreme examples
that occur in psycho-analytic case-histories—but here it is by
now difficult to draw a line between ordinary and technical concepts—and though it certainly does not presuppose any psycho-
analytic theory about the nature of the difference between
appearance and reality, or about the nature of the screen that
divides them.

First, it is worth reiterating that the mistakes in question
are in one way fairly extreme: for they are to be made by the
person himself, and there is going to be no knowledge in reserve
that might lead him to correct them on reflection. But in another way they are not so extreme as they might appear at first.
For his original identification of the object need not be totally
mistaken, and perhaps never would be. There are various
reasons for this. One is that there is a very weak sense of the
word 'about', according to which, if a person is depressed, he
is depressed about everything that he thinks about in a depressed
way. This is what people mean when they say that they are
depressed about everything. I call this sense of the word 'about'
weak because it is very non-selective: it does not pick out one
thing that is thought about in a depressed way rather than
another. But though it is a weak sense, it is an important one:

for, as we shall see later, it is a much larger part of the normal meaning of the word 'about' when it is used with phrases from the other end of the spectrum, like 'being pleased' and 'being amused'. Anyway, in this weak sense of the word it would almost certainly be true that the person was depressed about the object that he stated first, even if he later admitted that he was really depressed about something else, this time using a more selective sense of the word. So here is one reason for not regarding the original identification as totally mistaken.

Another, related reason is that, even when the word 'about' picks out one thing that is thought about in a depressed way rather than another, it might be that it did not pick out the most important thing. In such a case, if the person corrected his original identification and made a more judicious selection from the possible factors, much more might be left unretracted. For it might still be true that he was depressed about what he originally said that he was depressed about, in a sense of that word that is selective, but insufficiently selective.

These variations in the selectivity of the word 'about' give a certain flexibility to the concept of 'the object'. Consequently, there is no need to insist that a person's original identification of the object of a feeling or psychological reaction must be totally mistaken if it is mistaken at all. This may remove one ground of objection to the thesis that I am defending. For objection to it is sometimes based on the false assumption that, if mistakes are possible at all, total mistakes must be possible, as they are with analogous statements about physical objects— for instance, it is possible to be totally mistaken about the direction in which an arrow is pointing. But if this analogy has a bad effect on philosophers who find it too attractive, it has an equally bad effect on those who are too averse from it. In general, it is unnecessary to assume that analogies between psychological reports in the first person and statements about physical objects are either total or null, so that there is no need to get exasperated by this artificial dilemma.

In spite of this palliation the thesis might still be found objectionable, and the interpretation of the example that I gave just now and of others like it might be challenged. For it might be argued that nobody could be ignorant even of the most highly selected object of his depression, and that what is interpreted as lack of knowledge is really self-deception. It would be admitted that a person might turn his depression loose on other things, allowing himself to dwell on them in a gloomy and destructive way: or—to take a more familiar example, where thought is more closely connected with action—it would be admitted that he might allow his anger to colour his thinking about perfectly innocent things. But it would be argued that, if he appeared not to know the true object of his feeling, this could only be because he was deceiving himself.

Here it ought to be reiterated that the impossibility of lack of knowledge that is being alleged is supposed to be conceptual, and the conceptual scheme that is in question is non-technical. Given this, is the objection valid? Is self-deception the extreme limit of what is possible here, or is it on the borderline between knowledge and lack of knowledge? The question is made difficult by the complexity of the concept of self-deception. For self-deception sometimes involves a kind of partial, intermittent lack of knowledge: the person half realizes at times what the object of his feeling is, but he suppresses the fact, or allows it to slide from his mind, or at least from the centre of his attention. But in other cases the lack of knowledge is complete and uninterrupted, because he simply will not raise the question whether the object of his feeling might really be something different from what he takes it to be, or, if he does raise it, he will not reach the correct answer, that it is. Now do all examples of the sort that I cited belong to one of these two kinds of self-deception? Certainly they do not all belong to the first kind, where the correct answer to the question is actually suppressed, and the suppression is close to being a deliberate action. And this is important, because people who make the objection that is being examined are usually thinking of this kind of self-deception.

But the line between the second kind of self-deception and simple lack of knowledge is exceedingly hard to draw. Some genuine surprise at the correct answer seems to be necessary in order to establish simple lack of knowledge, and certainly it sometimes occurs. But is it sufficient? Would it not have been possible for the person to have reached the correct answer if he had really tried? So is not the lack of knowledge still to some extent self-induced? In many cases it will be hard to tell, because the whole idea of making the best possible use of one's available psychological resources in such matters is an extremely vague one. But in some cases the statement, that one could have reached the correct answer if one had really tried, surely degenerates into a form of encouragement or blame. In any case, this kind of self-deception is not an alternative to uninterrupted lack of knowledge, but, rather, uninterrupted lack of knowledge maintained by a certain mechanism. So the objection could not be sustained by an appeal to it.

Another form which the objection might take is this. It might be argued that this so-called lack of knowledge of the object of a feeling, which, as I said at the beginning, is a necessary condition of the kind of mistake that I am investigating, appears to exist only when the question that the person is required to answer is very specific. For instance, he is able to say what he is depressed about, but unable to answer the more specific question, what aspect of that thing he is depressed about. But, it might be argued, this inability should not be called lack of knowledge of the object of the feeling, but, rather, lack of knowledge of the precise aspect of the object that arouses the feeling, and this is something entirely different.

I think that there is some force in this form of the objection, but not enough to make its point. There is some force in it, because, if we move in the direction of greater specificity, we often find something which should not be called the object of the feeling or reaction, but, rather, an aspect of the object. For instance, it is sometimes possible to give an undoubtedly correct account of the precise elements in a joke that made another person find it so amusing, although he himself could not give such an account, because it was too recondite, involving an analysis of the associations of certain words that produced their effect on him without his realizing how they produced it. But

this would not show that he did not know the precise object of
his amusement: for here we, the theorists, would have crossed
the line that divides identifications of objects from identifications of those aspects of them that explain the ways in which
people feel about them or react to them.

However, I do not think that the objection makes its point.
For often the aspect of a thing that arouses a feeling can be
regarded as its precise object. And, if we confine ourselves to
such cases, it is not enough for the objector to say that lack of
knowledge at a more specific level is always compensated by
knowledge at a less specific level: for instance, it is not enough
for him to say that, if a person does not know exactly what
aspect of a conversation depressed him, this is compensated by
his knowledge that at least it was the conversation that depressed him. For the thesis I am defending is that it is possible
to make mistaken identifications of objects without any reserve
of knowledge that might enable one to correct them: and, if
such mistaken identifications of objects occur at any level of
specificity, that is enough to establish the thesis; the fact, if it is
a fact, that a less-specific level the person can identify the object,
is irrelevant. The objector might as well argue that mistakes
about the apparent colours of physical objects are impossible,
and, when he is confronted by counter-examples, fall back on
the defence that there will always be a less specific colour-word
about which there will be no mistake. In any case, it is not true
that a person can always give a correct generic identification
of the object of his depression.

According to the second objection that has to be answered,
even if my description of the logic of object-statements is correct, it is inadequate: for we need to understand the nature of
the connection between feeling and object, and in particular, we
need to know why mistakes are possible at one end of the spectrum, but not at the other.

Let us begin with the question about the nature of the
connection. Obviously it is no good just calling it 'intentional,'
since that leaves everything unexplained. What we need is a
detailed, explanatory description of it. Perhaps the best way to

discover such a description would be to begin by looking at statements like 'I was pleased by the publication of my letter' and 'I was amused by his remark', since statements at this end of the spectrum seem to exhibit the connection in its purest form. Now the second of these two statements is, as I said earlier, quite immune from mistakes in the identification of the object: for it is clear that I could not be completely mistaken about the object of my amusement, and it does not even seem to be possible that, if I considered the matter more selectively, I would realize that its preponderant object was really something else. About being pleased, however, I am not so sure: for though there are many cases, like the one that I mentioned earlier, where the statement that I am pleased about something resists all attempts to undermine it by extraneous explanations, there seem to be other cases where this concept lies closer to the concept of a good mood; for instance, if what I say is not that I am pleased about something momentarily, but that I continue to be pleased about it—a steady state—then a mistaken identification of the object does seem to be possible. So perhaps the report of amusement occupies the extreme limit of the spectrum in this direction, and would be the best example to start with.

What, then, is the nature of the connection between amusement and its object? I shall approach this question like an auctioneer, beginning the bidding at a low point, in order to see how much it is necessary to raise it later. First, if I am amused about something, it is clearly necessary, even if it is not sufficient, that I should hear it with amusement, think about it with amusement, etc. That is, it is necessary that I should be amused about it in the weak sense of the word 'about' that I introduced earlier. But how ought we to characterize this element in the connection between amusement and its object? Mr. Williams' theory is that being pleased is a mode of attention.[10] Perhaps this theory could be generalized to cover amusement and other feelings and psychological reactions. For it seems to be a successful characterization of the connection marked by the

[10] loc. cit., pp. 70–1.

weak sense of the word 'about', since it brings out the fact that, even if feelings and reactions are effects, they are not separate effects, but colour one's perception of the object and determine the tone of one's thoughts about it.

But is this opening bid sufficiently high? Certainly it gives a necessary element in the connection between feeling and object, but is it all that is involved? Even for the concept of amusement it does not seem to be all that is involved. For when someone says that he is amused about a remark, he means more than that his statement is true in the weak sense of the word 'about'. He also means that the remark caused his amusement. (In other cases, as I pointed out earlier, it may not be the object itself but rather some thought or belief about it that causes the feeling or reaction.) It may not be so obvious that this causal implication is carried by the report of amusement as it is that it is carried by the report of depression. Nevertheless it is a fact that it is carried by the report of amusement. For, if it were not, that report would mean no more than that he merely happened to feel amused when he heard or thought about the remark. But this would understate its meaning. So here we have the problem that was posed at the beginning of this paper: an object-statement that is immune from mistakes implies a causal statement, which must, therefore, itself be immune from mistakes.

If we consider statements that lie further along the spectrum, it is more obvious that my opening bid is not sufficiently high. For when the implied causal statement can be mistaken it makes a much more noticeable addition to the meaning of the statement: i.e. it adds something much more conspicuous to the minimal connection signified by the weak sense of the word 'about.' Thus this addition is very obvious in the case of depression which lies at the far end of the spectrum. But even when a person says that he is pleased about something the addition ought sometimes to be fairly noticeable: for, if what was suggested just now is correct, in cases where this statement refers to a steady state it can be mistaken. But mistakes are not possible with the weak sense of the word 'about'. Therefore when a mistake is possible, it is clear that more is meant by the statement. And since one method of correction is to show that the stated object is not the cause of the feeling, or at least not a sufficiently important part of its cause, it is evident that the extra element in its meaning is partly causal.

I must emphasize that it is not necessary to use this particular argument. For the causal implication can be demonstrated in all these cases without appeal to the possibility of mistake. Where this appeal can be made, it merely helps to make the point clear. Incidentally, it ought also to make it clear that being pleased is sometimes more than a mode of attention. For Mr. Williams intended the word 'mode' to denote something that could not conceivably belong to anything but the person's attention to a particular thing, as, for instance, the care with which he attends to it cannot conceivably be concerned with anything else (which explains why his theory exactly fits my weak sense of the word 'about'). But, if so, it is probable that the word 'mode' cannot properly be applied to all cases of being pleased about something, since, when this feeling is a steady state, it seems that it might be concerned with something other than what the person is attending to with pleasure.

If even a person's statement that he is amused about a remark carries a causal implication, this confronts us inescapably with the problem that was posed at the beginning of this paper: How can the implied causal statement be known to be true unmistakably? For this problem can be evaded only when it can be shown that the identification of the object is liable to be mistaken. When it is not, as it is not in this case, it is impossible to evade the problem. Nor is it any good saying that hearing the remark or thinking about it cannot be regarded as causes of the person's amusement because his amusement cannot be separated from these events. For it is only necessary to describe his amusement in a more abstract, general way that makes no references to these events, and then it can be regarded as their contingent effect. I shall try to solve this problem in the last part of this paper.

I think that Mr. Williams was aware of the possibility that

being pleased about something might carry a causal implication. For he also puts forward another theory, which is related to the first one but different from it. He also says that being pleased is a mode of having one's attention drawn to something.[11] This is avowedly an attempt to do justice to the fact that being pleased is something that happens to one, like an effect, rather than something that one does, and to admit the causal implication without losing the immunity from mistake. Suppose that we substitute being amused for being pleased, in order to get a more convincing case of immunity from mistake. Then does this new theory work? It seems not. For, in general, it is possible to give a mistaken answer to the question, what drew one's attention to something. And, in any case, amusement colours the way in which one is brought to listen to it, so that the theory puts the causation in the wrong place.

The account that I have been giving of the connection between feeling and object, though it is fairly detailed, is still insufficiently explanatory. It says that object-statements imply causal statements at both ends of the spectrum and that this raises the familiar problem only at the end where object-statements are incorrigible. But it does not explain why the two ends of the spectrum differ in this way. Why should there be two such very different kinds of object-statements? This is puzzling.

If what is puzzling is the strangeness of the facts of human psychology, I do not see how this can be mitigated. But if it is the apparent isolation of the factor, corrigibility and incorrigibility, that varies along the spectrum, something can be done to mitigate it. For that variable is not really as isolated as it appears to be. Other connected things vary with it, and the connection can be explained. So the philosopher's task is not restricted to placing different statements at various points along the spectrum of corrigibility and incorrigibility.

The most important of the connected variables was mentioned at the beginning of this paper. It is duration. Depression lasts longer than amusement, and this gives it a stronger claim

[11] loc. cit., pp. 64–5.

to be called a feeling, whereas amusement is more of a reaction. It is a fact that there are such variations in duration, and this fact is then made part of the logic of the concepts that lie at various points along the spectrum. Some feelings or reactions are momentary, like amusement, and these tend to be individuated together with their objects. For there is simply no question whether the amusement that someone is feeling at this particular moment might be identical with an earlier feeling of amusement which had, or seemed to have, a different object. Contrast the other end of the spectrum, where a feeling like depression or anxiety is persistent, so that the person himself at the time when he is feeling it can sometimes individuate it in a minimal way that involves no reference to its object (i.e. it can be free floating). In such cases one can ask oneself questions of identity that are in many ways analogous to questions of identity about physical objects. For instance, is the anxiety that I am feeling today still yesterday's anxiety about a task that I rashly undertook? And the answer to this question can even be tested. The analogy with things in the external world, which is part of the concept of the introspection, may not be perfect, but it certainly exists.

But what is the connection between duration and corrigibility? Perhaps it is something like this. Amusement, which is a momentary reaction, is never free floating: the person himself can always claim to identify its object; and the same is true of nearly all momentary reactions and feelings. This, in itself, would not be enough to lead us to regard the connection with the object as unmistakable in such cases. An additional inducement is provided by the fact that a momentary feeling or reaction does not get any chance to collect other things on other occasions which the person would then be equally ready to identify as its object. Contrast a persistent feeling, like depression, which does collect other things in this way. Now these other things are candidates for the position of the object of the feeling or reaction. Therefore a momentary feeling or reaction, unlike a persistent one, lacks alternative candidates for this position. However, this still does not really explain why we should

regard a person's identification of the object of his momentary
feeling or reaction as unmistakable. For why should it not be
possible for him to make a mistaken identification of the object,
and to retract it without being able to produce an alternative
candidate? Perhaps the final step in the explanation is to appeal
again to the fact mentioned just now, that momentary feelings
and reactions are never free floating: i.e. the person himself is
never unable to make a claim to identify the object. For this
fact conditions the logic of such concepts by inducing us not to
regard it as an open possibility that he should retract his original claim to identify the object, and not produce an alternative
candidate, but to leave the position unoccupied. That is, the
first candidate cannot vacate the position, because it is impossible either to find another candidate or to leave the position
empty.

This explanation is rough and insecure, and it may well
be open to the charge of circularity. For it is exceedingly difficult to isolate the facts that underlie the logic of concepts. There
is always the besetting danger that the concepts that need to be
explained might themselves colour the supposedly independent
facts that are adduced in explanation.

Finally, there is my third task, to deal with the problem
posed at the beginning of this paper: How can an object-statement that is immune from mistakes imply a causal statement?
Perhaps it would be more accurate to call this the residue of the
problem posed at the beginning, since it has now been both
narrowed and sharpened: narrowed because it is only when the
object-statement really is immune from mistakes that the problem persists, and sharpened, because something has been done to
explain the component elements in the meaning of such object-
statements.

But why not just abandon Hume at this point, and so
dissolve the problem? I said at the beginning that this would
be inadequate, since some explanation of the non-Humean sense
of the word 'cause' would have to be given: for otherwise both
its points of difference from the ordinary sense of the word, and
its points of resemblance would be left obscure. But that was

really an understatement. For, if the word 'cause' here does not at least mean 'sufficient condition' or 'sufficient condition in similar circumstances', what can it mean? And, if it does mean this, how can it be invulnerable to parallel negative instances? Here it is no use saying that the fact that a person is amused about a remark in the weak sense of the word 'about' is exceedingly strong evidence that the remark caused his amusement: for, if this were so, it still ought to be conceivable that the causal statement should be mistaken, and mistaken not just because he had misheard the remark, but because, although he heard it as it was made and was amused about it in the weak sense of that word, nevertheless it did not cause his amusement. But this does not seem to be conceivable.

But what sort of inconceivability is this? I have said all along that a mistaken identification of the object is not allowed for by the concept of amusement. But it might still be the case that this particular inconceivability has a very firm contingent fact as its basis. After all, it is unlikely that the inconceivability was generated spontaneously out of nothing. And now that we have dissected the concept of being amused about something into two component elements, being amused about it in the weak sense of the word 'about' and having one's amusement caused by it, we do not have to look far for the contingent fact that could serve as the basis of the inconceivability. For it is plausible to suggest that it is the contingent fact that at one end of the spectrum the thing to which the feeling or reaction is linked by the connection signified by the weak sense of 'about' is always its cause. If this suggestion is correct, then, though the possibility of a mistaken identification of the object is not allowed for by the conceptual scheme at this end of the spectrum, it still exists in the substructure of this conceptual scheme. We avert our eyes from it because the concepts would be radically changed if it were realized, and in particular because the change would be a change in human nature, and the sort of change that is well known to make us uneasy. For though the possibility of a mistaken identification of the object at this end of the spectrum is not contained in our conceptual scheme, it

lies only just outside it. Perhaps we could say that the possibility
of this possibility is contained in it.

If this suggestion is correct, we ought to be able to describe
a contingency that would split the concept of being amused about
something into its two components. I shall end by describing two
such contingencies, both of which would upset our conceptual
scheme, but in slightly different ways. The first contingency is
this. It might have been the case that when a person said that he
was amused about something, it could be demonstrated quite
often that this was only true in the weak sense of the word
'about.' The demonstration would take the usual form of pointing
out that something else that happened to him previously was the
kind of thing that was sufficient to cause his amusement and that
the thing about which he said he was amused was not the kind of
thing that was sufficient to cause his amusement. There might
be a special difficulty in establishing this for amusement, but
that would not affect the general validity of such a speculation
about this end of the spectrum. It is, of course, an essential
feature of this speculation that the thing that is offered as the
real object is something that the person himself has ex-
perienced.

It is no objection to this speculation to say that the
contingency is not admitted by the concept of amusement. It
certainly is not admitted by our full concept of amusement, but
the point is that it is admitted by the attenuated concept that
merely uses the weak sense of the word 'about'. If it were
realized, it would be upsetting in the following way. Amusement
would have to become a persistent feeling like depression,
colouring our reactions to many things for long periods at a
time. So telling someone a joke would be a serious step to
take. Also the reasons that people gave for their amusement
would be regarded as rationalizations far more often than they
are now (or, at least, half-rationalizations; for this concept
admits degrees).

However, it is arguable that, though individual concepts
might have been shifted to the other end of the spectrum in this
way, it would not be possible for this to have happened to all

concepts, because steady psychological states pre-suppose momentary psychological reactions. If this is so, the part of the spectrum to which momentary reactions belong could not have been obliterated altogether, unless the rest of it had ceased to exist too. It is also arguable that, even if we confine ourselves to a single concept, like amusement, it would not be possible that everybody's first spontaneous identifications of objects should always be mistaken: for, as things are now, most of these identifications are intelligible, reasons can be given for them, and some kind of systematization of the laughable seems to be possible, and these extremely important facts constitute an immovable obstacle that stands in the way of a progressive extension of the concept of a rationalization, which anyway could not cover the whole area because it is logically dependent on the concept of a true reason. So the speculation, in the form in which I am putting it forward, is restricted in two ways: it does not apply to all concepts at this end of the spectrum, and it does not apply to all cases, or even to the majority of cases of any one concept. It is also worth emphasizing that it does not presuppose a breakdown of the general connection between amusement and laughter.

It is, perhaps, also worth emphasizing that these two restrictions on the speculation are very different in strength. For it is possible to imagine the situation in which the first would be removed: all that would be necessary is a radical change of human psychology—momentary reactions would cease to occur. Admittedly, if we tried to assess the conceptual effects of such a change, we should be putting out into a less easily charted sea, but there would be no difficulty in describing the change itself. But, if we tried to circumvent the second restriction by imagining an alteration in the facts, we should encounter an insuperable difficulty. For we should have to suppose the facts altered in such a way that there would be no such thing as understanding why people found some things amusing and not others. But, since the intelligibility of such reactions depends on their regularity and on the possibility of systematizing them, we could get rid of intelligibility only by getting rid of regularity. But, if there were no regularity in peoples' reactions of amusement, it would be impossible to assign them causes. And this would undermine the very concept of a reaction. So the obstacle here consists not only in the fact that rationalizations pre-suppose reasons, but also in the fact that all reasons of this kind are causes (though, of course, many causes are not even capable of functioning as reasons of this kind).

The second speculation includes the first, but goes beyond it. The additional element is this. Suppose that a drug, secretly administered, always made people feel amused about a number of things in the following hour, even if none of those things would have amused them had they not taken the drug. Suppose too that it is discovered that the drug works by producing a secretion in the blood stream, and that this same secretion is sometimes found for short periods in the blood of people who have not taken the drug, and that its effect is then the same. If all this happened, we should regard the reasons that both these classes of people gave for their amusement during these periods as rationalizations, in exactly the same way that we now regard the irrelevant reasons that people give for physically induced depression as rationalizations. What distinguishes this speculation from the first one is that the real cause does not also function as the real object. Consequently, the feeling of amusement, in this contingency, would not really have an object (except in the weak sense). In short, this second speculation, if it were realized, would completely assimilate amusement to depression. So it is not necessary to make the real cause of amusement physical, like the excessive consumption of aspirins in the earlier example of depression: it could equally well be made psychological, like the excessive excitement in the other earlier example.

This solution of the problem with which I began this paper is very sketchy. Much more ought to be said about the various stages in the assimilation of a concept like amusement to a concept like depression. I have imagined this assimilation occurring suddenly and completely: for in my speculation a feeling of amusement simply acquires an entirely different principle

of individuation, which is exactly like the principle of individuation of a bout of depression. But this probably seemed too
sudden, and the change ought to be broken down into its separate stages. What is needed here is really a proper investigation
of dispositions.

But some such solution ought to be correct. For the immunity from mistakes possessed by some of the statements that
I have been examining ought to be based on some statable contingent fact about human nature. Why should it be an ultimate
fact that statements as complex as these are immune from
mistakes (of the kind specified at the beginning)?

## OBSERVATION AND THE WILL

### BRIAN O'SHAUGHNESSY

The problem I am concerned with in this paper is that of
the observation of one's own actions. It is not that I am anxious to discover whether or not this is possible, for I am clear
in my own mind that in any straightforward sense it is not. It
is not even my primary concern to uncover the reasons why
that is so. Rather, my aim is to bring out these reasons in such
a manner as to reveal something of the significance of that fact.
You could say, therefore, that the main purpose of this paper is
to extract that significance.

### I

### Physical Action Is Like One World Intervening in Another World

The astonishing thing about action is that it is possible at
all. For, if a man is making a chair, you will find a physical
causal explanation of the movement of each piece of wood from

Reprinted from *The Journal of Philosophy* (Vol. LX, No. 14, July 4,
1963) by permission of the editor and Brian O'Shaughnessy.

its initial to its final setting; everything that happens is in accordance with law; but you will look throughout this world or universe forever in vain for an analogous physical explanation of their coming together in the form that they did, a form that mirrors human need and the human body itself (Try it). There is no naturalistic connection between gloves and hands or between the waxen beings of Madame Tussaud and the human originals; unlike, say, the relation that holds between a man and his shadow. Yet the chair is a material object. So action seems like a leak from another realm or world into this world, a leak or intervention—an intervention such as God would bring about were He able to effect change in the world without transgressing the laws of nature. It is true that this is not the usual conception of a miracle. But suppose there to be an apparently endless arm roaming the universe, which we call God's Arm, the most distant reaches of which are situated near the farthest known galaxies; suppose all of its parts seem to move in accordance with the laws of nature, but suppose nonetheless that any long-range prediction is impossible—except occasionally through prophecy and doctrine. Were this example to make any sense, and for physical reasons I doubt if it does, some people might feel an inclination to describe this as an example of one universe intruding into another.

By action we irreducibly alter the state of the universe; a form or pattern appears that was not there before, the existence of which does not seem to follow in any way from the physical state of the universe beforehand. This is creation. We are ultimate sources of change in the environment in a way a river or hurricane is not. A chair or table is a kind of gift to the universe as a whole, as if from another God, certainly from another creator. We alter the *status quo*. I brought that chair into existence, but we cannot ask which part of me brought it into existence or made it, nor can we say that all of me brought it into existence; I did it (all). If I am drawing a line, it is not originating within nature but from me, not from my body considered as natural object—for example, as emitter of sweat or light waves—but from my body as vehicle of another realm:

that of (my) reason and purpose. We stand within and without nature.

## I Cannot Observe My Own Actions Because They Belong to My World

What do I mean by saying that my present actions are of my world? I mean that, along with thoughts, feelings, and sensations, they stand to me and to me alone in the *bedrock* relation of being known as such for what they are and of depending upon me for their very being; they depend somewhat in the way the items of the "World of Science" depend upon Science as groundwork though not necessarily as origin. All items of my world present their face to me, and their face is their entire being—in all cases but one. Physical action faces Janus-wise in two directions, and it is just this dual character that constitutes the lifeline for this world, rescuing it from logical oblivion. So certainly I mean that I do not stand to my actions in the relation of observer, just as I do not adopt a perceptual or observational standpoint to tell that I am hot, hot all over, uncomfortable, and so forth. The greatest distance at which I can be placed from some of these is one merely of distraction; I can never be in a condition of ignorance for want of observation. Equally, my own actions are (in some cases) capable of being placed at the distance of distraction, but this is a distance of awareness and not of observation.

So, at the risk of uttering a tautology, I shall say that what at any moment I am doing is, so far as I am concerned, not a part of *the world* but of *my world*. If I am making something, then what I am doing is continuously "shed" as what I have done and becomes simply a part of the world; the pyramids that took decades to construct are as much a part of the landscape as mountains. What I am doing at any moment is for me at the juncture of my world and the world; at that point "inner" meets "outer," whereupon "inner" becomes objectified and is "shed" into the world as a thing.

Suppose you are engaged in an action like drawing a line or writing a letter, and suppose that you begin to wonder why it is that you cannot observe that action. Then I think one of the most natural answers to come too mind is as follows. It is the essential function of observation to apprise us of the world we inhabit, whereas this that I am doing is still of my world. This is not yet a part of nature, of the *status quo,* of what is, but is on the brink—on the brink of becoming so.

I shall now attempt to *typify* action and perception rather than to assert an essential truth demonstrated by logical analysis or revealed in every case, or a statistical truth borne out by the bulk of instances.

We could say that, were observation to be withdrawn from the world and directed onto my actions, involuted away from the world onto my world, then this would succeed in removing the relation between the world and my world which is the very foundation upon which rests the identity of both my world and my actions. My actions would lose all sense, and my world would lose its identity. So I would lose the world too.

We shall classify the actions of others as of the world. There is no comparable difficulty posed by the idea of observing the actions of others: such observation requires that we perceive the agent that acts and the field or object of action; there is no question of removing through the act of observation a relation between the agent and environment which founds the identity of his actions.

## II

I turn now to a discussion of certain somewhat primitive formative situations, in order to bring out the interdependence of physical action and perception. I stress that an assertion of such an interdependence is a typification of both, and that there are seeming departures from it at a more sophisticated level. Nonetheless such typification applies to and has significance for *all cases.*

Subsequently I examine the relation between these two fields in more detail and attempt to relate them to the central problem before us.

### The Ascription of Visual Powers Rests on Behavioral Foundations

The concepts of physical action and perception mutually require each other. While we can situate within some organisms the source of their own movement without ascribing to them perceptual power and without speaking of their "actions" —as in the case of the amoeba which merely "moves along" and "assimilates" food—the reverse is not possible. Thus we could not say of a shellfish that it could *see* simply because it changed color when pointed toward nearby red things; for, as photography reminds us, we attribute causal power to light, and we would do so in this case. The primitive behaviors of pursuit and flight relate movement with perception: we say that a crab or octopus *advances a limb because it sees* something moving or that a fish *flees because it saw* something large and unfamiliar.

These basic situations may not be linguistically basic in the manner of a teaching situation; at the same time they reveal at the level of formation the interdependence of the concepts of physical action and perception. I will now continue this task of *typification* by considering the formative situation in the case of human beings, and I hope to demonstrate the same interdependence. Most cases of so-called tactual perception essentially involve physical action; so I will turn to the sense of sight. I will spend some time at first emphasizing how rudimentary are its beginnings, for reasons which will shortly become clear.

How do we describe the visual field of an infant who has just been born? As a two-dimensional blur of lights and colors? No, this is an adult's literary image striving to convey the nature of an infant's so-called "experience" through the agency of special adult experiences. No, we say first of all that he can see, and we mean that his eyes and nervous system are normal and functioning, as they say, and we might even test for this with an encephalograph. Or else we say he can see because he reacts to bright lights, and we leave it at that.

But at this point we might be inclined to argue that *he can see at this moment because his eyes are open,* for after all clearly the light is bothering him *at this moment;* and it might be pointed out in support of this view that we would not say this if his eyes were shut. No, we would not say this if his eyes were shut—though if the light were bright enough we might; nonetheless we normally have very little occasion to say of a newly born infant that "he can see because his eyes are open" or that "he can see at this moment because his eyes are open." That his eyes are open is nowhere near so special a consideration here as it becomes later on. We think of it as opening up the door to seeing, as if the naked eyes presented us with the spectacle of *seeing itself* upon the very surface of the eyes. The constant temptation, here, is to have recourse to the word 'seeing' in lieu of the now unavailable word 'looking' and to say that "at this moment he is seeing" or "he is seeing all of the time." But we must resist that. It strands us in puzzlement over the possible object of such seeing. We more or less have to content ourselves with the assertion that he can see. Even if we would sometimes say, "He can see because his eyes are open," which I suppose we might just say of an infant if an operation had remedied a defect, I do not think we could say: "He can see now because the light is on and it is no longer dark." So much for the various meanings of 'He can see', which seem to be either physiological or rudimentary in the extreme.

These meanings are further clarified by noticing the fact that we do not speak of *what he sees.* We do not say he can see the sky if his eyes are directed toward it; if his eyes are directed at a light and he screws them up we say it shows he can see, and we say it is because the light bothers him, but I do not think we say that he can or cannot see that light. If instruments tell us that his eyes are focused an inch or two ahead of him we say that he sees "two of everything," but we cannot infer that he might now go on to see "one of anything—or everything." There is no such thing as describing "what we would see if we were to have his visual field for an instant."

We can learn from the above how little a thing is the "pure" sense of sight, how little we ascribe in the absence of physical action—physical action which is, in turn, little more than a mass of movements like those of a tree in the breeze in the absence of these apparently so attenuated senses.

In particular, we do not say that the infant sees that one thing is farther off than another. This does not entail that we should say that "it is all two-dimensional" or "all flat" or that he "fails to see depth." We simply do not apply any language (any expressions) of three-dimensional vision to him. But that does not mean we apply a language of two-dimensional vision, whatever that might be; and we should notice here that it makes no sense to say of someone that "his visual experience is literally at this moment of an entirely two-dimensional world." There is a tendency to think that if we legislate against speaking of three-dimensional vision then we are inevitably turning (back) toward two-dimensional vision, but our concept of two-dimensional vision is taken from the perception of surfaces, and the perception of surfaces is logically derivative from the perception of objects. In the case of the infant we cannot speak of what he sees. Therefore, if there is such a thing as a "direction of development," it is the reverse of what we have been accustomed to think. So we cannot say, "We see depth," since this has no intelligible alternative.

We would not say of an infant that "he can see his mother and the light she is carrying going farther away." But we would say this of a child who had achieved the basic physical mastery of his immediate environment, that is to say, of a child who reached for nearby objects and who crawled after more distant objects that he could see—without first of all reaching for them. If we said of such a child that "he can see that his mother and the light are going farther away" and were asked, "How do you know?", it would be perfectly in order to give a reply like "Because he could crawl after her."

## We Can See the Mutual Dependence of Action and Perception

Ascriptions of one kind of power imply parallel ascriptions of the other kind. They grow up together. For these reasons, I think we may say that action and perception as such as mutually dependent upon each other and present in each other's formation.

But surely the newly born can kick his legs *and* can see, and we ascribe these powers initially and in isolation of each other. Does not this disprove what I say? No, for two reasons. In the first place, as I have been at pains to show above, we ascribe the power to see without ascribing any object of visual perception; in other words, we ascribe something rudimentary and do not yet say that the infant can *perceive* anything. Added to this is the fact that the infant's "just kicking" is action without meaning: action that is "in itself" in a way no casual absent-minded example of doodling could ever manage to be in subsequent stages of development. That is to say, both the visual and active ascriptions are so rudimentary as to lift themselves more or less clear out of our ordinary concepts.

The second reason is this. Consider what enables us to say he can see and act. The main consideration is that he is an infant instance of a *kind of being* who is a conscious agent, recognizably a human being. If there were many macroscopic creatures of amoeba-like behavior and constitution, we might not so readily classify an infant example of an unknown species as conscious. Another factor is the presence of eyes; but it is important to remember that eyes are most unlike hands, with which we do things, and that a creature might have eyes situated in and indistinguishable from its skin. One might say that 'eye' is not necessarily a thing word.

It is not as if we could somehow become directly aware of the occurrence of visual experience within the newly born by looking at his eyes, or indirectly aware of it through certain signs, thereby circumventing the necessity of studying his behavior.

These reasons return us to the primacy of behavior. They are circular in that they depend upon the assumption that man, unlike the amoeba or periwinkle or chimpanzee, is a creature who is at the same time active and rationally conscious. I conclude that these are ineffective "exceptions" to my central thesis at this point: that action and perception find their way into the very heart and constitution of each other, that each is part of the very being of the other.

## Involuting Perception onto Action Tends to Deprive it of Meaning

It typifies promises that they are kept, since breaking a promise is breaking with an institution of trust and is therefore parasitic upon promise keeping. And engaging in action in a situation where perception plays no role is parasitic upon the situation where it does; if it is intentional behavior, it takes place in a climate created by action and perception, namely consciousness. And the reverse is true. I make these qualifications on the assumption that it makes sense to speak of consciousness "without perceptions" or "without actions"—which of course may not be so.

Part of what I wish to say of the relation between action and perception applies to all cases, but part strictly concerns only the basic situations we have been examining. These situations are logically prior to the cases of isolation in which action and perception occur independently of each other and for that reason are more revealing of the *nature* of action and perception, somewhat in the way speech rather than rumination more truly helps to typify and reveal what thinking is.

Of these cases of isolation we shall say, if they were typical or universal, action and perception would lose their identity, just as a man who always "wrote" his poems in his head but eventually ceased saying them would gradually cease to be a poet, despite the mercifulness of logic. And were perception never to be accompanied by physical action it would indeed be less than itself; someone totally paralyzed from birth would remain an "unmarked *tabula rasa.*" It may or may not be conceivable that, if he could move a little, one could construct for him a world composed of no more solid stuff than language. But we should remember that ordinarily we teach language to a child who has discovered both himself and the world of which he forms a part and that Helen Keller was *in the world* from the start, whereas this being seems merely to be poised as a potential person on its threshold.

So what I shall now say is meant to typify the relation between action and perception. It is not that action and perception are antithetical. Though this is true, it is misleading; they are inter-dependent and reveal each other, and isolated from each other they are nothing. My actions as such require a relation to the world which is given through the aid of perception if they are to have identity and meaning and if correlatively the world is to be real and discovered for me. (The link between personal identity and a meaningful active perceptual relation to the world is intimate.) Therefore to disengage perception from its normal role of *handmaid to action* and to involute it onto action itself, not as I say to put it to the services of action as an accomplice in actively helping to lay before the action its object and its field of action, would in general be to rob it of its relation to its environment and its object which helps to constitute its very identity. That is to say, looking at one's own actions is a logically derivative or secondary activity parasitic on the accomplice uses of perception. Watching one's arm as one throws a ball parasites upon the general situation of watching one's aim as one throws. But, further, to involute perception onto action from the standpoint of the *observer* would do more than parasite on other situations: not only is perception not a handmaid here; it plays an actually antithetical role, for what it seeks to discover through the use of the senses must be what can be seen, such as the path followed by a body, whereas what is revealed to action through the normal handmaid uses of perception is not visible. I mean the relation of hand and quest, for example. This attempt to situate one's actions in a perceptual field that is being put to uses that actually clash with the typifying basic uses is an attempt that must fail.

## What Does It Mean to Speak of the Meaning of Action?

I have just said that, without a relation to the world through perception, action would, as such, lose all meaning But what

does it mean to speak of the meaning of action? In the passage
that follows I attempt to answer that question. Further, since
intentional action is the logically primary case of action, I
wish to assert that all action has meaning as such, and I wish
to show that the exceptions to this generality are more apparent
than real.

If action were simply an event in the world, a phenomenon
in nature such as a fall of rain or the dilation of an artery,
something "in itself" whose relation to the rest of the world
was purely naturalistic, then perception would play no essential
role as stage setter, and we would not think of action, as we
now do, as something with *meaning*. We are, perhaps, insufficiently surprised at the fact that we ask, of an action that is
clearly visible: "*What* is it he is doing?" Such a question lines
the action up with portraits, arrows, hieroglyphics, and of
course in a sense with thoughts. There are, as I think Miss
Anscombe has pointed out, cases of intentional behavior in
which we say that a man is doing no more than one sees, namely,
that he is stroking his chin *simpliciter*. But it is important to
bear in mind with what ease, how with the slightest of alter-
ations or merely with an afterthought, this action can change
its identity in our eyes to "relaxing" or "posturing." I think
there is the permanent possibility of such re-description, and
we ought not to be surprised at this if we bear in mind how it
is possible for a skillful mimic to incorporate the slightest of
our gestures, and even perhaps *any of them*, in an accurate
satirical portrait—thereby re-describing them. Somewhat similarly we may ask of a group of marks on an Egyptian statue:
"What do they say?", and be informed that they are a purely
decorative use of the hieroglyphic symbols, saying nothing on
this occasion; but it would be entirely different to be told that
they were gashes it received in a fall. Now when we say a man
is stroking his chin *simpliciter* this is like the earlier answer
and entirely unlike the latter answer, for we are not classifying
it as an "in itself" item in the world. In this sense completely
unintentional behavior, such as absent-mindedly double de-
clutching, can be ascribed meaning.

### The Visual World of the Physical Agent Is Not that of the Observer

In this section I want to display in a little more detail the relation between action and perception, something of the nature of their interaction, and I shall contrast in certain respects the role played by perception when it is employed for the less typical requirements of observation. I think it becomes clear how this relates to our over-all problem of observing one's own actions.

Physical actions and perceptions are interdependent; yet it is possible to act without employing perception in the course of that action. We have seen, however, that this is not truly typical. Perception and action are typically intertwined in the sense that perception is a kind of stage setter for action, if you can imagine sets constantly changing with the changing dramatic line of the play. Perception reveals to the agent a world that is dynamic inasmuch as certain items in that world are goals or dangers in relation to which one is intentionally *acting:* this is perhaps the sense in which the orange that one is just about to pick seems to be saying: "Pick *me.*" It is a dynamically organized world in that it presents us with the spectacle of our there-and-then active purposes and goals and the actively chosen requisite avenues of launched behavior. Tintoretto displays a supreme example of such a dynamic world of activity and passion.

What of the observer? Well, whereas it is true that the world of the observer is one that is being actively questioned, in that I can characterize what I am looking at as—that which I hope will display phenomena of one particular kind, and it is possibly dynamic to that degree, it is nontheless the *world* that is doing all of the asserting—the expected and the unexpected. The relation of action and perception is, in this case, highly atypical, inasmuch as the perceived world of the observer is one that is going its own way, that is taking its own course, and that may or may not shed a certain requisite item for which we are scrounging, viz., facts of a particular kind. In that world we see not our purposes but our hopes or

needs or lacks. We could say that observation departs from
the generally and typically true maxim: To understand the
world it is necessary to change it. (I have in mind bird watching.)

  If I look at my hand moving toward an orange and try
to see this in the manner of an observer, then all I seem to see
is the hand and the orange, a world of discrete objects; certainly
nowhere do I see anything that is the actual intention to grasp
the orange. As observer I do not organize that hand and that
orange into a dynamic unity; they are not so linked and unified,
since as observer my role is that of attendant questioner. If it is
your hand, then sometimes I can see that it is heading for an
orange, in the sense that absolutely anybody can *tell* it is by
looking, and at other times I will *infer* that it is heading for
an orange; we must therefore notice that the relation between
"intending to grasp *x*" and *x* is not a relation that is visible.
Whereas if it is I who am reaching for an orange, then I can
describe that orange as—an orange; but it is also possible
for me at the very same time to describe it as—that for which
I am reaching; and this is an incorrigible description. Here
the link occurs at the level of description. So in such a case I
can say that I see my hand and the object for which it is
heading, and be offering an incorrigible description: it is
*something that I see.* These characterizations of what I see are
*altogether normal and everyday;* yet it is an incorrigible
description. I think this obvious fact is truly worthy of astonish-
ment. As intentions introduce the idea of incorrigibility apropos
the future, so they do also apropos the visible, which can be
described almost in the manner of an itinerary rather than a
map. It is as if we were forever freshly tracing out invisible
roads and times upon the forever-changing face of the visible—
an almost Heracleitian picture.

  It is not as if I saw the orange as orange and then, bearing
in mind what I am doing, as that for which I am reaching; it
is not as if some of the time I lived in a world of things, and
some of the time in a world of intentions. The idea of such a
world of things is a myth, designed for a species of Observer
Beings, a world calculated to stultify all action through the

extremity of its power to inspire apathy, the apathy of the catatonic, capable of turning all action to stone by a single look. The idea of such a world of intentions is equally mythical, as if somehow the world were to manage to look literally as Tintoretto has painted it, an expressive humanized world instantly absorbing and precipitating us headlong through tracts of space with no gap between intent and achievement. We cannot separate the world of objects and the world of intentions; they are One.

This dynamic concept of what is seen, that is to say, the possibility of describing the visible in terms of intentions formed in the light of one's anticipations of the environment, is entirely different for the agent and for the observer. As agent I characterize what I see as—the orange I am going to get, the hand with which I shall get it, the bowl in which is contained the orange I shall get, the part of the table across which I shall move. As observer I characterize these things as—the orange I am looking at to see if he takes it, the hand I am looking at to see if it moves and takes the orange, the path across which I expect the hand might move if it does take the orange. In one case I was looking at the orange I was about to take; in the other I was looking to see whether he would take the orange. In one case I describe what I am looking at in terms of my intentions; I already impose a form on the world. In the other case I describe what I am looking at in terms of what I am querying of the world and in terms of what I am ready to receive from it. We can see how it would be impossible to observe one's own actions.

Of course it is possible to replace all that I have said by some simple trenchant statements about the purposes of observation, the role of expectation in the case of the will, and the like. These I have deliberately avoided.


III


Here I discuss the suggestion that the difficulty in observing one's own actions resides in the difficulty in engaging in several simultaneous unrelated actions. After showing that this is not a problem of a trivial kind, I attempt to bring out the natural unity of perception and action and to show the impossibility of fulfilment of the longings of Narcissus.

## Does Involution Deprive Action of the Will or of Identity?

Does observation of one's own actions halt them through the diversion of one's will into another channel or through the reduction of that action to something less than itself?

To the extent that I observe my own action, to that same extent I withdraw my concern from whatever is the object, purpose, or aim of that action; to that extent my action loses its *raison d'être* and identity, and ceases to be, or becomes instead something (minimal) of which I am oblivious. It is then no longer intentional behavior.

Why, if I were to begin to succeed in observing my own action, should that action simultaneously begin to come to a halt, or at the least cease to be intentional? I am inclined to say that it is because both the action and I myself would thereby cease to be directed or oriented toward that aim or object of the action which helps to define it for what it is. And we should remember that if my action is oriented toward an object, then I am oriented toward that object. So I am inclined to say that the action ceases to be because it loses its object or goal—its very identity.

Let me express it this way. As I attempt observation of my own actions, either they begin to come to a standstill or else observation seems merely to skid over the surface of the action. Then did the action go out of existence through losing its object or through losing my will? Did it cease to be out of atrophy or through sheer diminution? Two different ways of going out of existence: as red on a white background may grow pink and finally white, or instead faint and finally invisible. Was I, that is to say, like one who slowly desists from what he is doing? Or was I like a walker who gradually came to a halt as he gradually forgot where he was going; or if he continued, now is to be described simply as "walking"? So, did my action simply come to a halt because I was doing something else, or did I lose sight of what it was that I was doing?

Now the difficulty *looks as if* it cannot consist either in my failing to be aware of or in my failing to be oriented toward the object of action; for were I to direct my observations not onto the action itself but actually onto the object of action, this too would interfere with that action—provided it was not integral to my purposes (But of course it need not be the *same kind* of interference). Why would it? It would not be because I was thereby failing to be oriented toward the object of my action, but rather that my orienting to it in the way of observation obstructed my orienting toward it in the way of, say, pursuit or appropriation. (Some might say that this means I failed to orient toward the object of action.) But why does this obstruct? Is it because I lose the goal or object of my action in transforming it into another kind? But at this point someone might suggest that there is no need to restrict what we are doing to observation, since its special function seems no longer relevant, and invite us to consider an example in which a man engages in two unrelated actions with the same object—tries, for example, simultaneously to catch and describe the path of a rapidly moving ball. By this time the difficulty seems merely to be that of engaging in two unrelated actions at the same time.

## Is the Difficulty One Merely of Doing Two Things Simultaneously?

Might it not be the case that the difficulty is one merely of doing two things simultaneously? But what is this "mere difficulty" that can apparently be accommodated with such ease? Of what nature is it? I believe that if we examine it we shall find it to be anything but a triviality.

Why is it that we cannot do two things at the same time? At first sight it seems that we can, provided they are not too absorbing or complex. Then is it that we have *so much* attention to distribute and no more; in other words is it a purely quantitative question? This would be the triviality. But it cannot be quantitative, since the *difficulty* in the case of complex unrelated intentional actions is a logical difficulty. No, it is a consequence of being a person, one person and not two, and the difficulty is with most illumination to be likened to the difficulty in engaging simultaneously in two contradictory activities. Just as I cannot be going north and south at the same time, so I cannot be reading a book and playing tennis at the same time. In the way in which one can be walking and talking one cannot be reading a book and playing tennis. Naturally if we dilute these activities anything becomes possible, and we can become like the chess player who plays a roomful of people "at the same time."

If the difficulty were quantitative then the miracle of a man who is absorbedly sculpting, painting, designing buildings, and composing poems all at the same moment would be like the miracle of the loaves and fishes. But instead of saying: "It is absolutely bewildering that he can simultaneously manage to do all of that," as if he were a Michelangelo, we should think of him as the most astonishingly splintered being in history, or not even as that. Michelangelo was one great unique person, but this being is a monster, a monster of ordered disorder, something that might occur in the myths, but not a human being—a Minotaur of the mind. When we say that human beings are One we are not making a statistical generalization: men like Michelangelo are not freakish departures from human nature but are glorious and undreamed-of realizations of it.

If the point seems elusive, consider how you would in fact react to the story that someone had been engaged in solving an extremely difficult mathematical problem while he was fighting for his life in a raging mountain torrent; consider what you would *say*. Contrast the use of eye, hand, and ear on the part of an operatic conductor. Again, we may describe a man who is dancing as he listens to music as a man engaged in listening to music—the dancing is subsumed under the heading of listening; whereas for a ballerina who listens as she dances, her listening may be subsumed under the heading of dancing. These seemingly wayward accompaniments of activities are subsumed under one heading and thereby unified. But nothing could unify two activities like painting and sculpting unless, tautologically, they were already unified like the hands of a pianist.

The difficulty is not quantitative. I believe it stems from the fact that, being one person, we can only really orient ourselves in one direction at a time. This is a tautology. I should want to pass from the word 'really' to the word 'completely' to the word 'wholly' and on to 'with all of one's being,' and feel that this progression had been worth while. We should consider such expressions as 'He is lost in that action' with seriousness.

I cannot be wholly given up to an activity and simultaneously "miles away"—another expression we ought to take seriously. I cannot think about two things at the same time or "mindedly" about one thing and absent-mindedly about the other, and any action that involves the mind to any great degree is liable to be incompatible with any other such action; what happens in my mind cannot be absent from my mind, whereas what happens in my foot can; habitual or trifling physical actions or movements can go on absent from my mind and unnoticed and therefore, of course, simultaneously. A man who is carrying on two entirely different animated conversations with his hands and mouth is, of logical necessity, a divided being and a freakish monster.

So we shall reject the word 'merely' and say that the "mere difficulty" is not a result of the finite amount of attention available to all of us, but is a direct consequence of the fact that, since each of us is no more than one person, we can be given up wholly to no more than one action at a time.

Is the difficulty in observing one's own actions identical with the difficulty we have been discussing? Is it any different from that of observing the actions of *others* while one is engaged simultaneously in some further activity? Can I be trying desperately to recall a name while I am listening with interest to your singing? Not properly, not really. But just as there are many dilute cases of simultaneous action in general, so there are many in this kind of situation; however, where one of the actions in question fully "engages me," it becomes a logical impossibility. Therefore, unless my intentional activity and your activity are unified under one heading, unless for example I were to be giving a description of your movement, we should have to say it was impossible. But *how could there be* such a unity in the case of my own actions? A unity preserving the concept of observation? I would need to construct a unity between my actions which I propose to observe and the act of observation of that action. Were there to be such a unity I would surely not be observing; I would, say, be looking in the course of something else. It seems that the only way we could escape this difficulty is to make the act that one observes one's own act of observing.

Is observing one's own actions a case that *necessarily* implies simultaneously engaging in two intentional actions that cannot be subsumed under the one heading? I think it is. And I think this is a decisive reason for saying that one could not get absorbed in either. But cannot one talk and at the same time paint or walk or drive, and cannot these activities be logically separate from talking? Yes, one can, and they are separate; but one cananot be wholly absorbed in any of these activities and absorbed simultaneously in talking. Then ought one not be able to observe one's own actions provided one is not absorbed either in the action or in the observing? Perhaps, but I think we *cannot* observe them, whether or not we are absorbed, and herein seems to lie an important difference.

### The Natural Unification of Many Actions and Many Perceptions

What unifies the various actions and perceptions, let us say in the case of the operatic conductor who watches closely, listens attentively, beats time precisely, controls the volume delicately, exhorts or encourages or controls with a dictatorial will of iron, all perhaps at the very same moment in time, is that they are all logically subordinated to the one activity of conducting at an operatic rehearsal. Without these activities and perceptions the activity of operatic conducting could not exist. By engaging in such multifarious activities the conductor engages in *one single activity* in which he may be completely absorbed and lost. But, unlike the musical purist, he is not thereby completely absorbed in listening to the music; unlike her admirers, he is not completely absorbed in watching the singer; and so on. Though their experiences are logically different, the pianist who is completely absorbed in the act of performing music will experience no less of it than the listening audience completely absorbed by his performance of it. The conductor's activity is not the sum total of his various component activities: for at any moment the object of his concentration is one thing— the opera seen from the musical side. These component activities are not the self-subsistent *atoms* out of which is constructed something that is, mysteriously, a one and not a many. He is not a kind of juggler, but he is a man engaged in a single rich and complex activity involving the greater part of himself—body, mind, feelings, and senses.

You can see that his activity is not the sum total of component activities if you consider that in watching the singer he watches not so much her face and form as her movements and expression; not so much her movements and expression as her movements and expression in relation to the music that animates them; and these in turn in relation to the drama that channels and contains them. So he watches not so much the singer as an aspect of the singer in relation to the needs at that moment of the music and drama. These component activities are unified and related to one another through their subordination to the over-all activity. For example, listening to the music and controlling the tempo and volume are clearly related to each other, and together they come as a kind of musical fabric into which is woven the sound of the singer. This is a kind of world-for-the-conductor constituted by these various items which exist in his eyes, in relation to one another and in relation to him, in a way which is completely determined by the over-all activity he has chosen to engage in.

## The Impossibility of Narcissism

The conductor cannot listen as *observer* to the music he makes, since he already listens to it from the standpoint of conductor. His listening is logically subordinated to that activity, of which it forms a part somewhat as the painter's looking forms part of the activity of painting: it is coordinated with the movements of his arms and is informed with his over-all purposes. Were he to listen as observer, his listening would no longer be logically subordinated to the activity of making music. That activity would be impoverished. One cannot be listening to the music one makes both from within the act and from without the act: one cannot simultaneously listen in two entirely different ways. This is the nature of the difficulty where the use of the sense in question forms a (let us assume essential) part of the activity in question.

And where it is neither an essential nor an inessential part of the action? Then, for a man to observe his own actions would be for that act of observation to fall *outside* the unity created within his action: the act of observation would not be a component part of the action under observation, nor would the action under observation be a component part of the act of observation of itself. We have two proposed actions, unified neither one within the other nor through any over-all action of which they are components. It may appear, then, that the difficulty consists merely in engaging in two simultaneous unrelated activities—which is not insurmountable in certain cases. But we have seen that this is no *mere* difficulty lacking in all significance: it is the difficulty of not being two people; to succeed absolutely in this quest would be to succeed simultaneously in becoming two people, the being who acts and the being who observes that action. Insofar as one approximates to this impossible ideal of the division of the self, one is approximating to the replacement of *oneself* by two selves, which I think we should have to call a dispersal or destruction of the self. So the dream of observing one's own actions is, in part, the dream of loss of the self through division and dispersal. We

should call this the absolute antithesis of the renaissance ideal
of *the complete man.*

All of this may be true, but there is more that needs to be
said concerning this ideal of self-observation. The two actions
that are unrelated in the way of whole and component are
related in another way, namely, in the way of act and object
(I do not mean act and thing). As I have already remarked,
the act of observation has to fall *outside* the unity created within
the action that is to be observed; so one has, as it were, to
overtake oneself—it is as if one had to encapsulate and engulf
this unity or world of one's action within the world or unity
created by the over-all activity of observation of it. One action
has to become subordinated to another, only not now as component activity but as object. It has to play the role, in this
topography, that is normally played by something in the
world.

One has to be divided into two selves, since the actions are
not unified, and, what is more, one self has of its very being
to appear as object in the eyes of the other: one has to be two
selves, and yet, in the very moment of their appearance, one
self has to be engaged in incorporating the other. I say "incorporating the other," because the very ground of the being of
the agent-self is that it is locked logically in the scrutiny of the
observer-self, whose being, in turn, is constructed upon the
ground of the observation of the agent-self. It is *the nature*
of one self to see and of the other to be seen. The relation of
observer and observed is an internal relation that unites and
defines these two selves. The moment this relation draws to a
close these two selves coalesce into oneself. This is to be contrasted with the situation of the Minotaur-Being. The very
quest of the self that destroys the self through division—the
quest of observation of one self in action—forces logically upon
the agent-self the role of object in relation to the observer-self.

Over all of this then might be pasted the label: The
Impossibility of Narcissism. The two internally related selves
are all that remains of oneself, assuming Narcissism to be
successful, but are in fact less separate than Siamese twins or

the dual beings on playing cards. One is therefore in no position to describe the agent-self and observer-self as true selves, as selves resulting from the fragmentation of oneself; one simply describes them as *what* results from the (almost) division of oneself.

We should infer the impossibility of observing one's own actions on two counts. In the first place, were the only objection to be one against simultaneity of action, we should speak of two distinct selves neither of which is oneself; so we would not have an example of oneself observing one's own actions. We would have an example of the Minotaur-Being. But our objections are based also on the consideration that observation of our own actions would situate them in the world in the eyes of the observer. So in the second place—and this diverges from the objection in terms of simultaneity of action—since these dual selves are internally related, it is a necessary proposition that the observer-self observe the actions of the agent-self; this seems too gross a departure from usage to be described as the observation by one self of the acts of another self.

In so far as one seems to observe one's own actions one ought to have the experience of the loss of the self through division into observer and agent. Agent in the world and observer in limbo—oneself dispersed. One's actions become a part of the world, and one observes them from an isolated world that has no point of juncture with the world. One observes one's own actions as the actions of another being in the world, and thereby one loses them and ceases to have any relation to the world. In the section that follows I will consider such a state of affairs.

## IV

Let us express this last statement in different terms.

If one is to observe anything one has to be "without" it, whereas if one is to do anything one has to be "within" it. Now, either we remain "within" the action we are attempting to observe, in which case we may have a completely empty and self-delusive experience of observation—comparable to Wittgenstein's example of the right hand attempting to pay the left hand money—or else we remain "without" in some fairly serious sense, and genuinely seem to observe the action. But, remaining "without," we lose the action as ours in gaining the observation; we lose any "withinness". The action becomes an event in the world, and we become dispersed and lost amongst the bric-à-brac of the world; we become of the world in our own eyes; we suffer the experience of loss of identity. (I say 'experience' because nobody can actually *lose* his identity.)

## Observing One's Actions and Experiencing a Loss of Agency and Self

A man whose behavior is dramatically out of keeping with his normal behavior is liable to suffer from an experience of loss of agency. (This suggests the existence of a positive experience of agency, which we might draw attention to as "the experience one becomes aware of when that experience of loss of agency suddenly departs".)

In what follows I describe an example of the experience of loss of agency which is dependent upon the experience at the moment of action of becoming a stranger to oneself. I do so because I wish to exhibit the links between the experiences of seeming to observe one's own actions, of loss of agency, and of loss of identity.

Let us take as our example the situation of engaging in a solitary extreme political gesture during the middle of an important piano recital. One is liable to feel: "Am I *really* doing this?" or "Is this *me* who is doing this?", and most significantly one is liable to have the experience of being a spectator of one's own actions. At 8:35 precisely, when all is still and the music is hushed and overwrought with feeling, one is to rise to one's feet and deliver a short speech at the top of one's voice. One's behavior may be completely rational. One may have chosen one's moment exactly and have the most impressive political justification for one's action. It is now

8:34.50 . . . 55 . . . 58 . . . one is getting to one's feet . . . 59
. . . and there is one's voice sounding distant and flat somewhere up near the roof of the auditorium! After a time, as the
hubbub slowly breaks out, that sound near the roof links up
with one's own mouth, one no longer "hears" the voice, it is
now echoing in one's ears, and one is *now* engaged in address-
ing these people. The sense of agency returns and with it the
sense of identity: one *is* the person who is in the center of
this turbulent scene, who has just created a disturbance.

At this point the voice is no longer something in the
world. It is now like a gate or window or aperture through
which one directly encounters these people. It is like the open
road whose only meaning is that it leads to Rome.

We need to notice that the experience of loss of agency
means that, between 8:34.59 and 8:35.01, "something" began
to sound up near the rafters, "a voice," the occurrence of which
is in some ways somewhat mysterious to one; one is not completely on the "inner," so to speak, with regard to its occurrence,
as one is on the "inner," later, with regard to that sound echoing
in one's ears (it is a kind of logical by-product). True, one
realizes all along that one is responsible, but one has for a
time no *awareness of creating.* Therefore one has no sense of
*how* the voice comes into existence. And this suggests that where
in more normal circumstances one does something, the will
provides us with an answer as to how we effect what we do
effect.

It might be said of this case that it provides us with a
genuine example of a person's witnessing his own actions.
Against that I would make several points. In the first place,
the description of the agent's experience is not necessarily the
decisive test for establishing that he has witnessed his own
actions. In the second place, the intimate relation between
viewing one's own actions as an observer and the (perhaps
momentary) loss of the sense of identity introduces a new
variable into the discussion. Who is it, one might ask, that is
supposed to be observing whose actions? This seems to me to
support the position I maintained earlier in this paper, namely,

that the ideal of observing one's own actions is an impossible ideal, on the grounds that, were one to suppose it to have been realized, one would have to suppose there were two different selves related in a way (internally) that would in fact make it impossible for us to describe them as selves, and also impossible for us to describe one self as observing the actions of the other self.

## The Experience Alone Never Establishes Observation of One's Actions

Before I pass on to the discussion of the inconclusiveness of the description of the experience, I must first clarify the important concept of being aware of what one is doing, since it occurs in that discussion.

We say on occasion that a man is not aware of some trivial action he is engaging in, and we imply that his attention is elsewhere. This is quite usual. But to say of a man that he is not aware of what he is doing is to say something more serious. It may be to ascribe to him a somnambulistic or drugged condition, a condition we would characterize as lack of consciousness in general, as an absence of awareness of his surroundings and actions and indeed of anything whatsoever (including, of course, that he is thus unaware). It may on the other hand be to ascribe to him a condition of "transport": a condition of such extremity of feeling—the absolute extremes of grief or joy, for example, or murderous and terrible rage— that he is unable to say afterward what actions he engaged in during that time. We cannot say that he was barely conscious, but we can surely say that he was barely conscious of his surroundings or of what he said or did. All he seemed to be conscious of was his joy or his grief or his extreme and horrifying hatred.

There is one further very important case, and this case concerns us: that in which a person seems to be experiencing no very strong feelings, is apparently awake and engaging in a complex activity, but an activity bizarre in the extreme, and cannot tell you what it is he is saying or doing. We would say he was not aware of what he was doing, and we would allow that statement, together with the bizarre nature of his activity, to speak for itself as a way of characterizing his condition. If this condition persisted for much of the time we might describe it as a kind of loss of the self.

I do not think we ever say that a man can tell us what actions he engaged in because he *observed* that he engaged in them. In the first place, were he to give a description of his experience of the kind I have depicted in the example of the public political gesture, we would not have any reason (on the basis of that alone) to say that he could tell us what he did because he observed it. For if we have decided that he was aware of what he was doing, then we have decided against such an account. And we have other, more decisive, tests for establishing that he was aware of what he was doing.

One of the most important tests here is the nature of his behavior. Thus, if he described his experiences as I have done, but spoke nonetheless with great verve and inventiveness, I think we would agree that he was a man who had been at all times aware of what he was doing. So the nature of his experience is by no means decisive, whereas behavior tends to be. Suppose even that the description he gave of his experience seemed *completely* that of an observer: suppose he made very accurate comments of the kind elocutionists make, noting how at this point the voice was flat, there reedy, now hasty and breathy, and so on. Still, if he knew that it was his own voice and if his behavior was full of inventiveness and humor, I think we would not hesitate to say that he was aware of what he was doing and we would let the other descriptions take care of themselves.

And what if he could not tell you what he said at the point where his voice was drowned by a storm of shouts? Well, here we move into an entirely different and very important consideration: Does he or does he not know that the voice he "heard" was his own? If he does, and if his behavior is marked by inventiveness and the like, it seems to me that these two criteria overrule all possible accounts of the experience.

No doubt there is a variety of intermediate cases here which we should take account of. If his behavior is bizarre and stereotyped, if he makes accurate elocutionist's comments, but if he knows that the voice he described was his own and if he can tell you all he said except for that time when his voice was drowned with shouts—then should we or should we not say that he was aware of what he was doing? Or should we say he was only partially aware? (For there are degrees.) Or is there no over-all characterization available for such a case? Well, I think we will say each of these depending upon the details of the situation and, in particular, upon how bizarre the behavior is. But I cannot ever see us allowing that he knows that and what he said and did, and attributing this knowledge to his having perceived his own actions. If he knows that he acted and how he acted, we are more or less forced to say he was aware of his own actions. No account of the experience will ever tip that balance. And if he was aware, he did not tell by perception.

But if his account is of "a voice," if he genuinely seems to have no idea that it was himself that was speaking, if his behavior is bizarre and his report that of an elocutionist, then perhaps we shall soon have to describe him as a man unaware of his own behavior in the sense I have drawn. And if, having given the elocutionist's account, he can tell us roughly what "the voice" actually said, should we not then say that he can do this because he could hear what it said? But what would be the point in saying such a thing? Is it that we do not want to be unfaithful to such an apparent entailment as: Since he knows what he said and since he was unaware of what he was doing, it follows that he must have found out what he said through some other method than "awareness"? But does it? Against such a view it might be said that he is not in a fit condition to be an observer of anything. It is no use saying at this point: Do you mean we have one of those interesting cases of knowledge without observation?—as if we were like mail sorters, dropping things in boxes. In any event, I doubt if we would bother to invoke the concept of knowledge in such a case. Or if we did, I doubt if we would ask how he knew what he said; each new logical constellation corresponds to a different state; each state is explicated in terms of a logical constellation; in a sense, each state is self-subsistent, requiring no such thing as a "justification." The distinctions we are drawing are antecedent to such a concept as that of knowledge.

And if we have the situation in which he cannot tell you what it is that he did and does not even know that he did anything, then undoubtedly he did not know what he was doing. But of course this case excludes the possibility of perception of his own actions.

Since we say that the experience of loss of agency that I at first detailed is compatible with complete awareness of what one was doing, we cannot identify the experience that accompanies the "recovery" of his voice with what we are normally referring to when we speak of an awareness of what one is doing. If we could, then in the more extreme case the experience of loss of agency ought to be overwhelming. That is to say, a man who reports that he heard a voice (his own) saying all kinds of things need not add to this a report of a sense of a loss of agency: on the contrary, he might claim that he felt deeply engaged in the activity of listening to that voice. We would say that he was unaware of what he was doing, and we would have no need to invoke the occurrence of an experience of the kind I have described.

Though certain cases may seem to suggest it, we are never in a position to say: It is because he is in a condition of loss of the self that he can observe his own actions. For whatever *seem to be* grounds for saying that he had more than merely a very strange experience and did actually *observe* his own actions—for example his ability to say what he did, together with the details elocutionists give and speakers ordinarily miss—are at the very same time grounds for saying that he was *aware*, at least in part, of what he was doing and, therefore, for saying that his condition of loss of self was only partial.

That is because the account of the experience is overruled. Therefore loss of the self could not engender observation of one's actions, because that which is requisite for such observation tends to return the self to the self.

### The Humean Experience

I have described the experience of a man who seems to observe his own actions and suffers at the same time the experience of loss of agency and loss of the self.

This is a man whose reason leads, as it were, in a direction of which the rest of him is ignorant or in which it is unwilling to go. He is in subjection to his reason, or rather in subjection to a reason that is split off from action or imagination or feeling, and he finds himself betrayed by it into a totally alien situation. It seems to him that he *finds himself* making a public gesture that in his eyes at that moment has the quality of exhibitionism; it seems to him that his avowed reasons for acting thus are not the reasons of this being who is acting thus, or else that his reasons for acting thus have nothing to do with the avowed reasons of that being who avowed reasons. In other words, if the avowed reasons are his, then the action is not, and if the action is his, the avowed reasons are not. It is the former case that I have described. Perhaps it is both.

The subsequent experience is almost Humean, in that there seems to be a conglomeration of sounds, sensations, and sights, but nothing that is *oneself!* All those faces are looking in the same direction, but one does not know that what they are looking at is oneself, for one has no awareness of one's own location. We see, here, a close interrelation between the sense if identity and the most primitive possible knowledge of one's position in space. We remember the genuinely primitive cry: "Where am I?", of a person coming out of deep unconsciousness, the sense of which is much closer to: "Who or what am I?" than to: "What room in what building is that ceiling a part of?" or even: "What has been happening?"

Common to all experiences of loss of agency is the sense of becoming a spectator of one's own actions. Common to all experiences of recovery is the sense of one's actions becoming so close to one, almost in the manner of one's own eyelids, that it is impossible for one to remain any longer a spectator of them; instead one seems to look through and beyond them, as if through glass or a frame. One is relating to the world.

The experiences of loss of agency and of becoming a spectator of one's own actions, when taken to their extreme limit, lead, not to the resolution of Narcissus' problem, but to a complete unawareness of what one is doing. In other words, one's actions are lost—for they become like the actions of another.

To conclude, let us ask why it is that the Humean experience of disintegration should go together with the experience of seeming to observe one's own actions. I shall make a brief comment on this very difficult question. The speaker who "heard a bizarre voice" came nearest to observing his own actions, but ceased thereby to be aware of what he was doing. Not to know what one is doing, in the case of a trivial act, is to have distributed one's attention elsewhere, but in this above case it is something entirely different. Here the expression 'not know what one is doing' is the specification of a *state*, the existence of which we may infer merely from his unawareness of *one* "minded" action, and here we may no longer speak of the distribution of attention. There are "minded" actions, such as the delivering of a speech, that one cannot engage in absent-mindedly. Onto what, then, is his mind or attention directed on such an occasion? Onto nothing else, and hence onto nothing. Given such a state, it makes no sense to attribute to him any kind of intentional action, and therefore we cannot speak of *his reasons* for such actions. At such a moment he is "out of his mind," but is nowhere else!

But was he not aware of attending to what "the voice" said? No, we would never say that. If he claims he was, we classify it as a delusion, for in reality he was engaged in a bizarre public gesture.

He is neither asleep nor unconscious, neither barely nor half nor partially conscious. But he is not *properly* conscious, and his state is a disturbance of consciousness: he is unaware of what he is doing, of what he is doing to those around him, probably of who they are, and the like. We would say that he was completely unaware of what was going on. These are not empirical claims, but are involved in the concept of being unaware of what one is doing. Now, it may or it may not be that we would say he is unaware of what he is doing, even when he displays a keenly observant attitude to all of his surroundings —but I doubt if we would. I doubt if there is any behavior on the part of a man who is gravely announcing that he is Perseus that would convince us he was both keenly aware of his surroundings and altogether unaware of what he was doing. So, it is at the least generally true that the account we give of what this man sees is one that greatly reduces the normal perceptual account, reduces it in awareness of situation and spatial lay-out and detail.

This man was unaware of what he was doing, and what he was doing could not be described as intentional. Nonetheless he was doing something. But if his state deteriorated, and his speech became senseless and finally became pure incoherence and formless babble, we would describe him as raving, and would desist from speaking of his being unaware of what he was doing. In the end we might describe him as barely conscious, as hardly aware of his surroundings—and all of this through the loss of the mind alone! What, then, does he see? It is no accident that it is like the case of the newly born infant. All we could do in order to try and answer this question would be to continue the above process of draining away awareness from what is seen, so that consciousness would fade—not through a withdrawal of attention, as in sleep—but through a loss of the identity of everything that is seen. Such descriptions would not, I think, fall far short of the Humean account. Intimations of this account were already felt in cases where we seemed, perhaps, close to observing our own actions.

## EMOTION AND THOUGHT

### IRVING THALBERG

Many emotions appear to be founded or based upon states of belief. If we hear that a cattleman is dismayed, anxious, or indignant about falling meat prices, have we any need to inquire whether the cattleman has thoughts concerning the price of beef? It seems perfectly obvious that he must not only imagine that the market value of beef is decreasing; he must be relatively sure of it, if that is what alarms, disquiets, or shocks him. Although it is so obvious that such emotions are founded upon some form of thought, it is not immediately clear what kind of dependency this is. And that is one reason I wish to examine the relation between a person's feelings, moods, inclinations or attitudes, and his convictions, doubts, or guesses. A more important reason for investigating this liaison between emotions and thought is that our pre-analytic view of it will neither accommodate nor show the impossibility of some baffling cases. Let me convey my perplexity by asking whether any of the following statements could be true of John, a dinner guest:

a. John is embarrassed that he is late for dinner, but he doubts that he is (late for dinner) ;

b. John is delighted that there will be champagne with dessert, but he merely conjectures that there will be;

c. John resents the hostess for having gossiped about him, but he is not at all sure that she has done so.

There seems to be a discord, if not an inconsistency, between John's feelings and opinions. Is it possible to feel

Reprinted from *American Philosophical Quarterly* (Vol. I, No. 1, January 1964) by permission of the editor and Irving Thalberg.

embarrassment over something which you believe not to have
happened? Why rejoice about a future event when you have
no assurance it will occur? Does it make sense to bear a grudge
against a person when you are uncertain that the person has
wronged you? One reply, which only deepens our puzzlement,
is that we have no difficulty at all with some descriptions of
closely analogous states of mind:

> a′. John is worried that he is late for dinner, but he
>     doubts that he is;
> b′. John hopes that there will be champagne with dessert,
>     but he merely conjectures that there will be;
> c′. John suspects the hostess of having gossiped about
>     him, but he is not at all sure that she has done so.

If a′–c′ describe possible *mélanges* of feeling and cognition,
why are we inclined to reject a–c as patently ridiculous? In
general terms, the problem I wish to raise concerning the relation between thought and emotion is this: Must we think
something whenever we have an emotion? And if so, must
each affective state be founded or based upon a particular type
of thought? The architectural metaphor has no importance in
my analysis, but I do find it less tendentious than some alternative phraseologies: "Must one's feelings be consistent with,
ruled or governed by, or in harmony with one's surmises, assumptions, convictions, and doubts?" These logical, political,
and musical idioms are quite as inadequate as the architectural
one to reveal any blatant or hidden nonsense in the examples
a–c. For if apprehensiveness is consistent with (ruled or governed by, in harmony with, built upon) doubt, why does embarrassment clash with disbelief? Similar questions may be
asked regarding the other pairs of cases.

These questions, as well as the standard replies to them,
are peculiar. This suggests that we must begin with a brief
inquiry into the concept of emotion. Then it will become
clearer how, and why each sort of emotion—shame, anxiety,
and so on—requires a particular cognitive consort. My analysis
of emotion is not meant to be taxonomically exhaustive. Only

those features of emotion will be discussed which seem important in determining the relation of feeling to thought.

## I. Objects of Emotion

For expository convenience I plan to stretch the label "emotion" to fit a heterogeneous assortment of reactions, moods, appetites, inclinations, aversions, desires, and attitudes, as well as emotions in the strict sense, like rage and disappointment. I mainly wish to exclude urges, impulses, decisions, intentions, resolutions, and similar dispositions to engage in some course of action. Consequently, to the extent that an emotion involves a proclivity to undertake overt action, as feeling vindictive includes a disposition to seek vengeance, I shall be silent about it.

In my discussion of thoughts, I shall concentrate upon opinions concerning matters of fact, as opposed to matters of value, which appear to be involved in emotions.[1] Thus, in examples a and a', I take it for granted that when John is embarrassed or worried that he is late for dinner, he thinks it is wrong, or at least embarrassing (worrisome) to arrive late for dinner. Surely John thinks one ought to be embarrassed (worried), or at least that it is normal to be ashamed (anxious) in the circumstances. I would find it odd for someone to be ashamed of a faultless performance, or to be worried about his good deeds. My reason for neglecting these normative beliefs is that their main function is to justify or excuse an emotion. By way of illustration, take a housewife who becomes infuriated when she is short-changed by the grocery clerk. She, or a bystander, might declare: "You have a right (it is perfectly natural) to get angry when you are short-changed." My analysis, in this case, would focus on the housewife's belief that the clerk actually cheated her; because this belief seems

[1] In "Emotions," *Proceedings of the Aristotelian Society*, vol. 58 (1956–57), pp. 290–300, Mr. E. Bedford clearly demonstrates the connection between feelings and evaluations. For applications to moral philosophy, see G. Ryle, "Conscience and Moral Convictions," *Analysis*, vol. 7 (1940) and I. Thalberg, "Remorse" (forthcoming in *Mind*).

more closely related to her current emotion, her outrage with
this clerk at this time, than her conviction that it is (generally)
infuriating to be short-changed.

Now let me introduce some distinctions which will be
crucial for an account of the relation between an emotion and
the state of thought upon which the emotion is founded. All
the emotions in my puzzling examples a–c, as well as the
straightforward a'–c', share one feature which is not possessed
by emotions like depression, euphoria, apathy, and the like:
In each instance, John is worked up *about* something—his tardi-
ness, the dessert wine, the hostess. As a contrast to his emotions, consider the following:

> d. I am depressed this morning as a result of having con-
> sumed eight gin-fizzes last night; I neither believe nor
> doubt that I had gin-fizzes to drink. My memory of the
> previous night is a blank, because of alcohol or defense
> mechanisms. So I do not even wonder if I hit the bottle
> last night.
>
> e. A young actress becomes euphoric when she learns that
> a maharajah wants to marry her. In fact, she becomes
> so ecstatic that she forgets all about the maharajah and
> his offer.
>
> f. An art collector falls into a state of total apathy as a
> result of doubts concerning the authenticity of his
> favorite Pre-Columbian vases; ultimately he loses his
> grip to the extent that he ceases to have any thoughts
> about his treasures and their origin.

In situation d, I am not gloomy *about* anything; to say
that I am depressed because I drank eight gin-fizzes last night
is only to specify the cause of my foul humor. How can I feel
rotten over my excesses, since I have no idea that I committed
them? With regard to situation e, it would be incorrect—and
linguistically odd—to say that the actress is euphoric about
the maharajah's proposal, or euphoric that the maharajah wants
her as a wife. How can she have any feelings about his offer,

when she no longer believes or doubts that he has proposed to her? The art collector in f cannot be said to feel apathy toward his vases, because this phrase suggests, for one thing, that his mood is directed toward his pottery rather than his family, his business activities, politics, or what not; it also implies that he has some opinions regarding the vases. *Ex hypothesi*, neither of these implications hold: A man in a state of total apathy does not respond—even with indifference—to anything; furthermore, as I described the art collector, he has ceased to think about the vases.

The difference between d–f and each of the previous cases is that depression, euphoria, and total apathy have no objects. I shall explain this phrase in a moment; but first I want to say something about the connection between emotion and thought in d–f. My gloom, in situation d, would have been the effect of a belief, in case I had recalled my debauchery. Since I had no thoughts about my carousing, my gloom happens not to be a result of my cognitive state. The actress' euphoria, in story e, happened to result from her antecedent belief that the maharajah wanted to marry her; still it is easy to imagine circumstances in which she becomes equally giddy without the concomitance of any beliefs; she might become euphoric as a result of severe fatigue before the movie-cameras. The same may be said of case f: The collector's apathy might have resulted from a cerebral lesion, rather than doubts concerning the authenticity of his treasures. So d–f illustrate situations in which emotions and thoughts *are* related as effect to cause; they also prove that it is not self-contradictory to suppose that *some* emotions are unaccompanied by (not founded on) thoughts. I shall attempt to show, in Section IV, that this holds only for emotions without objects.

I said that depression, euphoria, and total apathy "have no objects." Grammar partly explains my meaning: We can say of someone that he is depressed, euphoric, or apathetic *simpliciter*; and there is no use for phrases like "So-and-so is depressed (euphoric, apathetic) that (about, with, at, over, on

account of). . . ." Whereas, to start with b', c, c', we cannot
say "John hopes," "John simply resents," or "John suspects."
John must hope for something, or that something will or did
happen; he must bear a grudge against, or feel misgivings
toward, somebody. I need more than grammar to explain how
embarrassment, worry, and anticipatory pleasure have objects;
for it is quite correct to say, *tout court,* "John is embarrassed
(worried, delighted)." However, it is a grammatical fact that
there is a use for questions of the form, "What is he embarrassed (worried, delighted) about?" "Is he embarrassed
(worried, delighted) that (with, etc.) . . . ?" And this point
leads to a more adequate explanation, namely that it is always
germane to ask these questions if you are seeking an adequate
characterization of a man's affective state.

We have, then, emotions which cannot take objects (depression, free-floating anxiety); emotions which must take
objects (hope); and emotions which may be expected to have
objects (embarrassment). Among the emotions which are always directed toward something, we may distinguish two sub-
groups: Hate, aversion, love, admiration, appetite, and enjoyment must be focused on people, activities, events, things, or
on groups of people, activities, events, or things. An infantryman cannot simply feel hate; he must, for instance, detest his
sergeant or noncommissioned officers. A sybarite cannot simply
feel aversion; he must dislike sports or physical exertion. I shall
say that these emotions are directed toward *non-propositional*
objects, to differentiate them from other "necessarily transitive"
emotions whose objects may be characterized by means of
complete declarative sentences. Hope exemplifies the other sub-
class. I may hope (that) I have been appointed ambassador to
Bolivia, and I may hope for the appointment or the ambassador-
ship. Of the emotions which *may* take objects, we seem to have
a choice, in all cases, between propositional and non-propositional descriptions of their objects. Consider a unionist's feelings about the forthcoming strike. It is clearer to use the
propositional idiom, and say, "He is glad (afraid, sorry, angry,
dismayed) (that) there will be a strike"; but it is never incor-

rect to say, "He is pleased (worried, etc.) about the impending strike."[2]

Three points are worth noting in passing: (i) Object-expressions, propositional and non-propositional, do not always occupy the accusative position in a sentence which describes someone's emotion. A camper might say, "I shall come across a rattlesnake during my trip, which frightens me," rather than: "I am frightened that I shall come across a rattlesnake." Of course these sentences are not equivalent in meaning; the first one could be used to make a true statement only in case the speaker does meet a rattlesnake, whereas the camper may use the second sentence to give a correct description of his fear even if his trip does not include a confrontation with a rattler. (ii) Thus far, my characterization of the objects of emotion, and my distinction between propositional and non-propositional objects, are largely grammatical. Negatively, then, I have not attempted to say what sorts of things are designated by the expressions "his sergeant" and "there will be a strike," when

[2] Professor R. M. Chisholm makes use of the term "propositional object" in *Perceiving* (Ithaca, 1957), p. 142. It has been suggested to me (by Professor Mary Mothersill) that the objects of many emotions are best construed as possible or probable states of affairs. As I understand this view, it would have us say, of a prudent lathe-operator who buys accident-insurance, "He fears a possible (probable) injury," rather than "He fears an injury." In the *patois* of propositional objects, we should say, "He fears that he *might* be mutilated," or "He fears that he will probably be mutilated (that his chances of mutilation are such-and-such)," instead of "He fears that he will be mutilated." Is there any reason to adopt this analysis for fear and other anticipatory emotions? I think not. How can the object of the machinist's fear be a possible— or even a likely—injury? An *actual* mutilation will hurt; it will require hospital care; it will prevent the machinist from working; it will leave scars. If he suffers an actual mutilation, the additional fact that it was possible, or likely, will not make it any more painful, costly, time-consuming, or disfiguring. Further, imagine that the machinist retires without having suffered any actual injuries, although it was possible, or probable, that he would be injured. In other words, imagine that his injuries were merely possible or probable. Could he have feared these possible or probable, but nonactual, injuries? Did his possible or probable injuries hurt? Did they need medication? Did they keep him from working? Did they spoil his looks? If not, then probable or possible injuries were not what he feared when he bought insurance.

these expressions appear in the sentences, "The infantryman hates his sergeant," and "The unionist is glad (that) there will be a strike." (iii) I have not discovered any philosophical significance in the grammatical fact, noted above, that emotions like hate and enjoyment are always given non-propositional objects. Nevertheless it is a fact that we cannot specify a propositional object for the infantryman's loathing. Suppose, for example, that the sergeant has assigned our hero to Kitchen Police. We can say, "The soldier is furious (pleased, astonished) that the sergeant put him on K.P.," but not: "The soldier detests that the sergeant put him on K.P." And if we declare, "The soldier detests the sergeant because the sergeant put him on K.P.," we have not specified a propositional object of his loathing; rather, we have mentioned the fellow's grounds or reason for despising his sergeant.

## II. Grounds for Emotion

The last distinction, between the objects of and the grounds for an emotion, demands some comment. Let me confess, to begin with, that two of my initial examples, c and c′, are rather obviously mongrels: Does John feel resentment (misgivings) toward the hostess on the grounds that she gossiped about him? We can rid ourselves of an extra entity by saying: "He feels resentment about her having gossiped," and "He suspects that she has gossiped." In this sort of example, it is arbitrary to separate object and grounds. In other cases, the distinction is worse than arbitrary; it is logically untenable. Here is one illustration: The leader of a big-game expedition declares, "I'm frightened of cannibals because, after all, they do eat human flesh." There is an analytic connection between the phrases used to describe the objects of his fear (cannibals) and his reason for fearing them. Therefore no distinction is possible. Is the utterance of the safari leader too bizarre to prove that grounds are at times logically inseparable from objects of emotion? No, because his utterance does have a function which might not be served by the utterance, "I'm frightened of cannibals."

The latter might leave us wondering: "What is it about cannibals that scares him? Do their war cries, their weapons, or their magical rites terrify him?" When he says he is frightened of them on account of their taste for human flesh, he has given us the information we need.

So much for the problematic cases. Let me illustrate how the distinction between *objects* of emotion and *grounds* for emotion may be free of the logical difficulties I noted above. For this purpose, consider a government security agent who learns that Brown, a candidate for the diplomatic service, receives a number of Marxist periodicals. The investigator begins to suspect that Brown has subversive tendencies, because Brown subscribes to Marxist periodicals. However, the sleuth is not at all convinced that Brown is disloyal. Now plainly the security man does *not suspect* that Brown reads Marxist periodicals; his misgivings are directed toward Brown's loyalty, not Brown's reading habits; presumably the investigator is sure of Brown's reading habits, if that is why he suspects Brown of disloyalty. In this example, then, we must distinguish the object from the grounds. Perhaps I should append a *caveat:* To say, "The investigator has grounds (a reason) for suspecting Brown of subversive proclivities," is not to say that he has good grounds, epistemically or morally, to suspect Brown. The concept of "good grounds for emotion" will not be examined here.

We noted, in Section I, that some emotions, such as hate and enjoyment, must have objects. Do any require grounds as well? Surely I can like (or dislike) hillbilly songs "for no reason at all"; that is, I enjoy (abhor) them, but not because the tunes are catchy (simple-minded), or because the lyrics contain valuable information about American history (because the lyrics are stereotyped), and so forth. But can I desire revenge against my boss, or feel grateful toward him, and not desire revenge (feel gratitude) because of (for, on account of) anything he has done? Perhaps these are cases of "necessarily grounded" emotions; but the claim is very weak, since these examples do *not* involve a clear separation between the object of emotion and the grounds for emotion. The grounds disappear if, instead of saying, "I want to get revenge against my boss because he humiliated me," or "I'm grateful to him because he made me a junior partner of the firm," I say: "I want him to suffer the same humiliations he inflicted on me," or "I'm grateful that he made me a junior partner."

As long as it is clear that many emotions which must have objects need not have grounds, and that emotions which happen to have objects often do not have grounds, the distinction between object and grounds will advance our analysis of feeling and thought.

How are a man's thoughts connected with the object of, and the grounds for, his emotions? Let us start with a normal fellow, our cattle-breeder who believes that meat prices are falling, and who is indignant about it. From this description of him, it sounds as if the object of his indignation is his belief that meat prices are falling. But plainly this analysis of the object of his indignation will not work: For it is false to say, "He is indignant about his belief that meat prices are falling" or "He is indignant that he believes that meat prices are falling." His outrage is not directed toward himself or his own belief! He is furious about prices.

What is the connection between his belief and the object of his emotion? His belief is directed toward the same object as his outrage; he believes that livestock prices are falling and he is indignant that they are.

This view, that objects of a man's emotion are objects of his thoughts, provides an answer to some questions the reader might have about my ontological commitments when I speak of emotions and their objects. Are emotions and their objects like automobiles and their engines, like teams and their coaches, like husbands and their wives, like citizens and their rights, like desks and their dimensions, like adjectives and the attributes they stand for? Any satisfactory reply[3] to the question, "What

---

[3] Dr. Richard M. Gale has an excellent, up-to-date review of the literature on "intentional objects," entitled "Propositions, Judgments, Sentences, and Statements," in the forthcoming *Encyclopedia of Philosophy* (Crowell-Collier, Free Press, and Macmillan Co.). His own doctrine

is the cattleman thinking about when he believes that meat prices are falling?" will be an answer to the metaphysical puzzle, "What kind of thing or event is the cattleman angry about when he is indignant that meat prices are falling?" If this phraseology sounds overly Platonic or Cartesian, then suppose that the cattleman is talking with his barber; he makes a bitter and abusive speech about the price situation; the object of his emotion turns out to be "what the cattleman was talking about (discussing, alluding, or referring to) in the course of his diatribe."

I shall not be able to dodge some other metaphysical questions, but let me postpone them in order to describe the relation between the grounds for an emotion and the thoughts (convictions, doubts, conjectures) upon which an emotion is founded. I shall use the cattleman again, and suppose that the *reason* he is indignant about falling beef-prices is that the Secretary of Agriculture had assured livestock owners that meat prices would be high this year. The cattleman believes that the Secretary made this claim. Under the circumstances it is correct to say, "The cattleman is outraged that meat prices are dropping, because he believes that the Secretary of Agriculture assured. . . ." It would be pedantic to drive a logical wedge between the cattleman's belief and the grounds for his outrage. His belief is his reason for being angry. However, the belief upon which his emotion is *grounded* is not the belief upon which his emotion is *founded:* His indignation that prices are

---

is that we can believe or state what is not the case because verbs like "believe" and "state" "are used in such a way that there need not be anything *in rebus* answering to their grammatical accusatives"; he adds that "there is no need to introduce Platonic complexes, or anything else, to serve as the object" of thinking and asserting. I agree with this, but I wonder how we can—as we must—then provide for differences like the following: One girl is expecting a letter today, and another girl is expecting a telephone call; if neither of the girls receives what she expects, are we to say that they both have the same expectation, that they both expect nothing at all, or that they have no expectations? Shall we characterize the difference between their expectations in terms of the different descriptions they do or would give of what they expect ("a letter," "a telephone call") ? This sounds like the most economical solution.

falling is *founded* on his belief that prices are falling; his indignation that prices are falling is *grounded* on his belief that the Secretary gave assurances to livestock owners. Is this distinction between "grounded" and "founded" a pedantic one? No! For it enables us to talk of groundless hopes, suspicions, and resentments, without implying that such emotions are unaccompanied by assumptions, surmises, or convictions. Suppose that our investigator, mentioned above, has no reason to suspect that Brown is unpatriotic. It would be true to say, "His suspicion is not grounded on any belief, conjecture, or assumption," but this does not mean: "The investigator neither believes, supposes, takes it for granted, conjectures, or doubts that Brown is unpatriotic!"

### III. Are Objects of Emotion Causes of Emotion?

My metaphysical worries would be over if I could identify objects of emotion with causes of emotion. In fact many of the things we like, fear, long for, and so on, are causes of our enjoyment, our fright, and our longing. If a rhinoceros is bearing down on me, and I fly in terror of it, the rhinoceros is both the object and the cause of my fear of it; you could use the same declarative sentence to describe the propositional object of my fear and the state of affairs which makes me frightened: "The rhinoceros is chasing him." (To say that the approaching rhinoceros causes my fear is not to deny that other circumstances—the condition of my nervous system, previous experiences with wild animals, etc.—contribute to my terror.)

Is it always possible to rank the object of emotion as a cause of emotion? Unfortunately for our metaphysics, no. For suppose that I am in a state of terror as I cross New York's Central Park, and when sympathetic passersby ask me what is bothering me, I declare: "I am terrified that I shall be chased by a rhinoceros during my stroll." Call my fear unmanly, ridiculous, or peculiar; the fact remains that the propositional object of my fear is correctly described by the sentence, "I shall be chased by a rhinoceros during my stroll." Does this sentence describe the cause of my fear? Well, perhaps a rhinoceros is in the offing—one escaped from the zoo and made its way to Central Park. In these circumstances it is true to say that I shall be chased by a rhinoceros. Even so, how could the future chase produce my current fear? In this case it is, to say the least, implausible to maintain that the object of my fear also causes my fear. And the assimilation of object to cause fails utterly when Central Park is free of rhinoceri. The sentence, "I shall be chased by a rhinoceros," still describes the propositional object of my fear, but does not, *ex hypothesi*, describe a cause of my fear. I assume that only actual events, states of affairs, and things can cause other events, states of affairs, and things. No rhinoceros is in the cards. Therefore it is false to say that my fear is caused by a rhinoceros attack. So the object of my emotion (a rhinoceros attack) is not a cause of my emotion.

Let me generalize from this odd example: Whenever an emotion is directed toward a future event or state of affairs, or something yet to be born, and whenever an emotion is concerned with something that did not, does not, or will not occur or exist, the object of emotion is not a cause of emotion. If very strict nominalists grumble—heroically—that a person *cannot really* fear what does not exist, my reply is this. Such a method of controlling the population of superfluous entities has the consequence that nobody has ever really feared ghosts, goblins, demons, or other imaginary powers. I doubt that superstitious fears will be destroyed by this sort of verbal magic.

## IV. Are Thoughts Causes of Emotion?

Our initial problem was to explain how emotions are based on thoughts (beliefs, assumptions, speculations). The main requirement we set was that the analysis of the relation should show whether it is possible, e.g., for a man to be embarrassed that he is late for dinner, but doubt that he is late for dinner. Enough distinctions have been established to consider one hypothesis: An emotion is founded upon a thought if and only if the thought is a cause of the emotion. "Cause" must mean

"empirically necessary condition" rather than "empirically sufficient condition." Even if my conviction that the milkman beats
his horse sometimes makes me angry with the milkman, I may
at times be too distracted with my own cares to work up any
emotion about the milkman's cruelty, despite my belief that
he is mean to his animal.

According to this hypothesis, the puzzling cases a–c (on
the first page of this essay) would be at most causally impossible. I find some merit to the conclusion, but the analysis from
which it follows is seriously defective.

If a man's thoughts are only causal conditions of his emotion, then it is conceivable that, for any emotion he has, he
might have had precisely that emotion without the concur-
rence of any thoughts at all. On the causal analysis, people just
happen to be fairly sure that some event will occur when
they rejoice that it will occur. If their makeup or conditioning
were different, they might be in the same affective state although
they neither believe, doubt, nor imagine the event will occur.

Why do I resist this view? I admitted, in Section I, that
moods like depression, euphoria, and total apathy may be
caused by the subject's beliefs, doubts, or conjectures. Why
not say the same of embarrassment and other emotions? Because the latter group of emotions may have objects, whereas
depression, euphoria, total apathy, and free-floating anxiety—
as its title indicates—are not about anything.

Let me explain why this fact invalidates the hypothesis that
emotions with objects are effects of the convictions, doubts, or
conjectures upon which these emotions are founded. Take the
annoyance of a balletomane who thinks that no seats are left
for this evening's dance recital. It is irrelevant, for the time
being, to specify whether he simply takes it for granted that
seats are unavailable, whether he is convinced of it, whether
he merely conjectures that seats are unavailable, or whether
he doubts it. Whatever the nature of his thought, could it be the
cause of his annoyance that no seats are left? In so far as his
annoyance is a form of agitation, including physiological dis-
turbances and behavioral changes like fidgeting and inability

to concentrate, his annoyance resembles objectless emotions. So his agitation might be a result of his thought that seats are unavailable. However, will any examination of his pulse rate, blood pressure, galvanic responses, salivation, or his bodily motions disclose that he is annoyed over the lack of seats for tonight's performance? If not, then a study of his agitation will leave out an essential feature of his annoyance. It will not yield an answer to the question, always germane in such cases: "What is he annoyed about?"

Of course we shall get a quick answer if we interrogate him. His reply, "I'm annoyed that no tickets are left," indicates the propositional object of his chagrin. But his words also reveal that he has thoughts regarding the tickets. How does this prove that his thought cannot be a cause of his annoyance that tickets are gone? It seems to me that any time you claim one event or condition is a cause of another event or condition, you must be able to gather evidence of the effect which is logically independent of your evidence of its putative cause. According to this principle, you may claim, "There was a short circuit in the warehouse, which caused a fire in the warehouse," but not: "There were flames in the warehouse, which caused a fire in the warehouse." Evidence of a conflagration is not always evidence of a short circuit, but it is always evidence of flames. How does this principle apply to the particular hypothesis concerning the ballet enthusiast, "His thought that tickets are gone caused his annoyance that tickets are gone"? Well, it appears that if we prove he is vexed that tickets are gone, we also prove that he thinks (believes, conjectures, doubts) that tickets are gone; therefore we cannot claim that his emotion is the effect of his thought.

In the foregoing argument I took it for granted that only a man's verbal behavior will give us evidence regarding the object of his emotion. Will my conclusion, that emotions are not the effects of the thoughts upon which they are founded, hold without this methodological assumption? Since the behavior of chimpanzees and other speechless animals permits us to ascribe rage, fear, and dejection to them, perhaps verbal behavior is dispensible in the case of human beings. So consider, for purposes of the argument, some nonverbal responses and activities which might be evidence for saying that our ballet enthusiast is annoyed about the lack of tickets: An hour before curtain time, he approaches the box office, which is closed; his blood pressure rises, his face reddens, he bites his lip and stomps off toward the nearest cowboy film. Now we cannot grant that he *read* the sign on the box office, "Tonight's performance sold out," because this would automatically show he had thoughts regarding the lack of tickets. In the circumstances, what would entitle us to assert, "He is vexed that tickets are gone," rather than any or all of the following: "He is vexed that the box office is shut," "He is vexed that he made a fruitless visit to the box office," or "He is vexed"? It seems to me that any other clues about the object of his annoyance would also indicate that he had thoughts regarding the same object.

I would give a similar interpretation of the non-human cases on which this objection depends. Take a psychologist's rats: They are conditioned to display fear-reactions whenever they are placed in a compartment where they had received electric shocks. Now we put them in their chamber of horrors. They dash about, squealing pathetically, even though they are not being shocked this time. *If* their agitation entitles us to say, "Now they fear they will be shocked," then do we have to perform additional experiments before we can claim, "They think they will be shocked"? I do not claim that any psychologist would say, "The rats fear they will be shocked"; but if he did demonstrate this claim, it seems to me he would thereby demonstrate that his rats think they will be shocked. I conclude that the relation between thought and emotions which have objects is not a causal relation.[4]

_____

[4] The causal theory is not entirely made of straw; it is Hume's doctrine in the *Treatise*. See pages 368, 386, 415–426, 439–446, Selby-Bigge edition (Oxford, 1955). His kind of analysis of the relation between feeling and thought has been under intermittent attack, but I find the most current objections fairly weak. It is said that my belief that I in-

## V. Two Alternatives

What have we proved thus far? Only that emotions which have objects are logically tied to *some* form of thought about the same object. So there are two methods of resolving the odd cases I listed at the beginning of this paper:

1. We can declare that each sort of emotion which has an object is based (founded) upon a particular kind of thought, in the sense that the latter is a logically necessary condition of the former;[5]

2. We can hold that each sort of emotion is based upon some form of thought or other, i.e., thought is a

---

herited somebody's fortune cannot be a cause of my pleasure that I did, because: (i) I cannot be mistaken when I relate my pleasure to my belief; however, one can, in principle, be mistaken regarding the causes of any phenomenon; (ii) I never need to observe the concomitance of my belief and my pleasure, nor do I make use of inductive evidence of similar affective-cognitive couples in my past experience; but one always needs this sort of evidence when claiming that something is the cause of another thing; (iii) thoughts and many emotions are not processes, but causes and their effects are events having earlier and later spatio-temporal phases. Of course I accept the conclusion of these arguments, but I think that (i) confuses two distinct notions: a person's *de facto* or (perhaps) *de jure* incorrigibility when he makes some first-person psychological statements, and the logical status of assertions (by anyone) regarding someone's psychological condition; (ii) seems to me to embody a similar confusion, between the plausible claim that one does not utilize observational procedures in making some first-person psychological state-ments, and the dubious claim that inductive evidence is irrelevant to other people's assessment of the truth or falsity of one's first-person statements; (iii) seems to me to depend on a very restrictive notion of "cause and effect." For extremely persuasive developments of (i), (ii), (iii), and other arguments against the casual view, consult: B. A. O. Williams, "Pleasure and Belief," *Proceedings of the Aristotelian Society, Supplementary Volume* 33 (1959), pp. 57–59, reprinted in this volume; and J. Teichmann "Mental Cause and Effect," *Mind,* vol. 70 (1961), January number.

5 This is Bedford's view in "Emotions," cited above. Discussing the statement, "*A* resents what *B* did," Bedford writes: "*A*'s belief that *B* has done something that affects him adversely is . . . a necessary condition if the word 'resentment' is to be used at all" (p. 295); elsewhere he says, "The expression 'I hope that . . .' implies . . . a very vague estimate of probability . . ." (p. 293).

logically necessary condition of every emotion which
has an object, but it happens that people have some
kinds of emotion when they doubt, and other kinds
when they conjecture.

With regard to example

a. John is embarrassed that he is late for dinner, but he
doubts that he is (late for dinner),

a champion of the first analysis would assert that my imaginary
situation is logically impossible: My description of John's
mental state is self-contradictory. According to the second
view, the situation is unusual though possible; my description
of John is unlikely to be true, but it might be. Analysis 1 commits us to the view that the sentential function, "—— is embarrassed that . . ." means, *inter alia*, "—— believes that . . .";
"—— is worried that . . ." means, *inter alia*, "—— believes or
conjectures or doubts that . . ."; and so on for each item in
our emotion-vocabulary. Analysis 2 requires, for its intelligibility, some hint of an explanation for the observed concomitance of types of emotion and types of thought, if this correlation is not due to the meaning of emotion-words.

A number of considerations favor analysis 1. The argument I used against the hypotheses that there is only a causal
relation between emotion and thought applies here with equal
force. Any proof that John is embarrassed that he is late for
dinner seems to prove that John is convinced he is late, and
thus to falsify the conjunction, "John is embarrassed that he is
late for dinner, but doubts that he is late for dinner." If John
makes a sincere avowal, "I'm embarrassed that I'm late for
dinner," has he not expressed his conviction that he is late?
Plainly he has not manifested disbelief! Add to this evidence
various forms of non-linguistic behavior: his manner, his
gestures and carriage, his sheepish grin, his blushes. Isn't this
the picture of a man who believes he is late?

Now what if all this confirms the seemingly redundant
hypothesis, "John is embarrassed that he is late, and he believes
he is late"? Have we thereby refused the claim, "John is em-

barrassed that he is late, but he doubts he is late"? To save space, I wish to use shorthand names for the statements under examination:

> $E$ for the statement "John is embarrassed that he is late"
> $D$ for "John doubts he is late"
> $B$ for "John believes he is late"
> $B'$ for "John believes he is not late"
> *not-B* for "It is not the case that John believes is late"

If we use "&" as a name of the conjunction operator, then example a will read: $E$ & $D$. My problem is this: I admit that any proof of $E$ will count in favor of $B$. Therefore I must admit that nothing would ever prove that $E$ & $D$ is true.

I think the argument is faulty. It does not matter whether $E$ entails $B$, or whether the truth of $E$ makes $B$ very probable. It is not obvious to me that the truth of $B$ entails the falsity of $D$. I assume that $D$ is equivalent to $B'$ rather than *not-B*. If that is so, then the truth of $E$ & $B$ does not entail the falsity of $E$ & $B'$ ($E$ & $D$), although $E$ & $B$ does entail the falsity of $E$ & *not-B*. In other words, $E$, $B$ *and* $B'$ might all be true. That is, John might believe he is late and believe he is not late.

Is such a thing logically possible? I admit the following points: (i) John's belief that he is late is inconsistent with his belief that he is not late; (ii) consequently, to assert "John believes he is late and John believes he is not late" ($B$ & $B'$) is to assert that John has inconsistent beliefs. Notice, however, that (i) and (ii) do not show that the statement $B$ & $B'$ is an inconsistent statement.

At this juncture, a partisan of analysis 1. will reformulate his argument along the following lines: "Of course it would beg the question to say that nobody can (logically) hold inconsistent beliefs; so $B$ & $B'$ is not self-contradictory; however, what evidence could possibly show that $B$ and $B'$ are conjointly true? Whatever counts in favor of $B$ automatically discredits $B'$ to the same degree that it favors $B$, and *vice versa*." If I accept this last methodological premise, I would be guilty of unverifiable speculation if I said, "*E* is true, so *B* is (probably) true; but perhaps *B'* (i.e., *D*) is true as well."

It seems to me that this argument begs the same question in methodological disguise: Whatever entitles us to say that evidence for *B* counts against *B'*? Take some evidence for *B*: Another guest at the dinner-party asks John, "Do you believe you are late?" and John replies affirmatively. If this disconfirms *B'* *to the same degree* that it confirms *B*, then we must have assumed that a person cannot (logically) believe and disbelieve the same thing. And consider some evidence for *B'*: John's wife telephones him to ask whether he arrived on time, and he tells her: "It was a wild trip, but I believe that I'm not late." If we take this as a sincere avowal of his belief, his declaration will have equal weight against statement *B* only on the assumption that *B'* and *B* are logically incompatible.[6]

The upshot is that analysis 1 will exclude the imaginary situations a–c only if we take it for granted that nobody can (logically) hold inconsistent beliefs. It is not my purpose here either to vindicate or to give a counter-example to that difficult assumption. However, I should like to show that analysis 2 will take care of the odd cases without the disputed assumption. Let me explain this alternative analysis by reference to,

  b. John is delighted that there will be champagne with dessert, but he merely conjectures that there will be.

Why does this statement bother us, although its counterpart,

  b'. John hopes that there will be champagne with dessert, but he merely conjectures that there will be,

sounds quite plausible?

---

[6] The argument in this and the four preceding paragraphs owes whatever merit it possesses to comments I received from Professors Sue Larson (Stanford University) and Roderick M. Chisholm (Brown University). My main reason for supposing it is logically possible for people to have inconsistent beliefs is that people are urged and trained to be consistent and blamed when they appear to hold incompatible opinions. The fact that a man with inconsistent beliefs has, in most societies, very little chance of persuading others to adopt his opinions is a strong inducement for him to avoid self-contradiction.

A follower of the second view would explain that in b, John's emotion is somehow inappropriate to his state of thought; there is an incongruity between his conjecture and his delight. b′, on the other hand, ascribes an emotion to John which somehow fits his cognitive outlook. I suggest two interpretations of the claim that a conjecture is an inappropriate foundation for anticipatory pleasure, but an appropriate basis for hope. The verdict, "His emotion is inappropriate," may mean:

I. It is not normal for people to feel pleasure about a future event when they merely conjecture that it will occur. People do not, as a rule, feel that sort of emotion, or that degree of it, when they are only guessing; so on statistical grounds alone we wonder: "Perhaps John is secretly convinced that champagne will be served? Or if he is just guessing, then he is probably in a state of hope rather than anticipatory delight." Statistics will entitle us to assume that John's thoughts are consistent, i.e., that he does not believe or doubt that champagne is forthcoming at the same time that he conjectures that champagne is forthcoming. We can go on to account for the concomitant variation we observe in John's community between people's emotions and their states of thought, as well as their tendency to alter their beliefs when they notice inconsistencies among their opinions. I assume that the account would show the observed regularities to be the effect of brain processes, social conditioning, and so forth. If we have an adequate explanation of the regularities, it would also indicate how odd cases like b might result from cerebral lesions, childhood traumas, or insufficient training. There is no need to add the following: We might find quite different correlations between types of emotion and types of thought, when we compare groups which have diverse hereditary proclivities or dissimilar social institutions.

II. A man's emotions may be inappropriate—in kind or degree—to his state of thought in another respect. We might judge that John is unreasonable to feel anticipatory pleasure when he merely conjectures that there will be champagne. Is it reasonable for him to hope? At least it is not unreasonable.

The notion that our feelings can be reasonable or unreasonable, *vis-à-vis* our cognitive state, depends upon their similarity to many of our habitual and instinctive actions. It is reasonable for a pugilist to duck or to raise his guard when he believes his opponent is throwing an uppercut, and it is unwise of him to stiffen before the other man's punch. To be sure, the boxer does not decide to move out of range or to hold his position; but his movements are reasonable or unreasonable in the sense that they are effective means for him to achieve victory and to avoid a pummeling. Now compare emotions like anticipatory pleasure to the boxer's defensive activity. Emotions of this sort are also forms of readiness. In example b, John is prepared for champagne. Perhaps he is *set to drink* champagne as well, but we are not considering the conative aspects of emotion. How then may emotions, as states of readiness, acquire the labels "reasonable" and "unreasonable"? A man's emotions are reasonable when, in view of the man's beliefs, doubts, or conjectures, the form of readiness they involve is likely to be effective and necessary. When they involve inadequate or superfluous preparations, his feelings are unreasonable. In example b, John only guesses there will be champagne; consequently he must think that his delight is probably an otiose form of preparation. He is like a boxer who engages in elaborate dodging and protective maneuvers when he believes his challenger is staggering on the ropes.

Fear, as usual, is a perspicacious model for reasonable and unreasonable emotion. If your friend's train is several hours overdue, which leads you to believe it was derailed, it is reasonable for you to worry that his train was in a mishap. If the wreck is suddenly announced, you will be less shaken than if you had not prepared yourself. What if his train is not behind schedule at all, but you are struck by the thought that it crashed? Then you stir yourself up needlessly if you worry. Your anguish is unreasonable—not because it is unlikely to be "fulfilled," not because you will be "disappointed," but because your agonizing preparations are unlikely to serve their function in this case. Perhaps you cannot help worrying anyway, but that only proves you are not to blame for your unreasonable fears.

This comparison between emotions and preparatory activity only makes sense if we assume that both have a function in the life of a reasonable person. In saying that a man's actions or feelings are reasonable, we presuppose that he thinks rationally; when he is certain of something, it is more likely to be true than when he has a hunch about it, or doubts it; and we presuppose that he sets some value upon the ends that are to be achieved by preparatory activities and emotions. We assume, for instance, when the boxer *believes* his opponent is aiming an uppercut at him, an uppercut is more likely than when the boxer doubts or conjectures that his opponent is loosing an uppercut. We also take it for granted that our pugilist wants to defeat his opponent and to avoid his blows.

A satisfactory analysis of these assumptions, which are packed into the concept of reasonable and unreasonable emotion, would take us far beyond the topic of this paper, "How are a man's worries, hopes, resentments, and so on related to his states of thought?" In particular, the claim that a person's emotion is not just statistically odd, but unreasonable, raises problems about the justification of emotions. Evidently, to say of John in example b, "He is unreasonable to be delighted that there will be champagne, when he only has a hunch that champagne is on the way," is to suggest that his state of thought does not justify his emotion; he should not feel that way on the basis of a guess. I cannot undertake an account of these normative concepts here.[7]

---

[7] Aristotle seems to take the view that emotions can be appropriate, in the sense that they may serve important functions in the life of a reasonable man. See *Nicomachean Ethics* ii 1106b 15–25; also Mrs. Warnock and Professor Ewing, "The Justification of Emotions," *Proc. Arist. Soc. Suppl. Vol.* 31 (1957). The appropriateness relation is more evident when we consider conative states. Aristotle declares that intention or choice "cannot relate to impossibles, and if anyone said he chose them he would be thought silly; but there may be a wish even for impossibles" (op. cit., iii 1111b 20–25). Is it logically possible for a man to be "silly" in this way—to decide or intend to do something he believes he cannot

My thesis in this final section was that two analyses of the rapport between feelings and thought will do justice to the important distinctions made in the preliminary discussion of objects, grounds, and causes of emotion. In section IV we had to discard the view that a person's beliefs, doubts, and speculations are nothing but causes of his emotions; we rejected it, ultimately, because it was epistemologically vacuous, for we could discover no way to specify the object of someone's emotion without assuming that he had thoughts about the object. The remaining views may be reformulated quite simply:

1. A particular type of thought is a logically necessary condition of each type of emotion which has an object;

2. Some type of thought is a logically necessary condition of each type of emotion which has an object, and each type of emotion is appropriate to particular types of thought, inappropriate to others.

If we take 1 as an explication of phrases like "resignation is founded on certainty, pleasure is founded on belief," the relation between emotions and their cognitive cohorts is entirely logical. However, we can exclude the difficult cases a–c only by appealing to a disputable maxim, "A person cannot (logically) hold inconsistent beliefs." 2 makes the relation between emotion and thought partly logical, partly causal, and— if we say that "appropriate" means "reasonable" as well as "statistically normal"—partly normative. Analysis 2 seems more in keeping with a flexible, empirically oriented psychological theory of emotion. 1 would present us with fixed *a priori* relations between various forms of emotion and thought. Explication 2 of what it is for an emotion to be founded upon an appropriate type of thought does appeal to some obscure normative considerations. But this is not a compelling reason to discard 2. In fact, it may be illuminating to investigate further the similarities, (i) between admiring, disliking, resent-

---

do? Such a man would be unreasonable, of course, and statistically rare to boot. See my discussion of "Intending the Impossible," *Australasian Journal of Philosophy*, vol. 40 (1962), May number.

ing, or fearing something, and appraising or evaluating it; (ii) between moral justification or censure of someone's emotion, and the kind of assessment that is involved in judging someone's emotion appropriate or inappropriate to his beliefs, doubts, or conjectures.[8]

## PLEASURE AND BELIEF

### B. A. O. WILLIAMS

We can be as pleased by what we only believe to be the case and is not, as by what we know to be the case. Thus I may be pleased because (as I suppose) I have inherited a fortune, when I have not. This fact deserves consideration, in particular because it raises the question of the relation of pleasure to its objects; it is with this question that this paper will be principally concerned.

If anyone is tempted to think that the object of my pleasure—what I am pleased by, or at—is the *cause* of my pleasure, this type of case should discourage him. For the object of the pleasure in this case seems to be an inheritance, but this, since it does not exist, cannot be a cause (as it used to be said, *non entium non sunt effectus*). Yet the cause of the pleasure cannot be something else quite different from the supposed inheritance. For one thing, if I am persuaded that I have not in fact inherited a fortune, my pleasure will disappear and so must have been connected with at least my previous belief in the inheritance. Moreover, in speaking retrospectively of the

[8] I am indebted to a number of people, either for their views on the problems I have discussed here, or for their comments on earlier drafts of this paper. In particular I wish to thank Professors Mary Mothersill, Sue Larson, Terence Penelhum, Roderick M. Chisholm, and an anonymous referee for the *American Philosophical Quarterly*.

Reprinted from *Proceedings of the Aristotelian Society, Supplementary Volume* (Vol. XXXIII, 1959) by permission of the editor and B. A. O. Williams.

pleasure, I shall say that I was pleased because I believed that I had inherited a fortune; or something of this kind.

Hence, the only resort of a causal account of pleasure and its objects will be to say that the cause of my pleasure was my belief in the inheritance. Yet this account in its turn raises difficulties. First, if my belief in the inheritance was the cause of my pleasure, it must have been so in virtue of some law connecting such beliefs with pleasure. But what law? Evidently the belief in an inheritance is not the cause of *any* pleasure, but, at best, of *pleasure at an inheritance;* yet it is this last notion that the causal account was supposed to explain. However, it may be replied to this that there is no need to introduce this notion into the causal law: it will be enough to say that belief in an inheritance is among the possible causes of pleasure, pleasure itself being a state of feeling (for instance), which is much the same whatever its cause. So that when we say of someone "he is pleased because he believes he has inherited a fortune," what we mean is "he is experiencing pleasure, and the cause of this is his belief that he has inherited a fortune."

It would follow from this view that it was *always* the belief that caused the pleasure, even in those cases in which the thing I said I was pleased at really existed. For if not, the statement "I am pleased because I have inherited a fortune" would express a causal hypothesis different from, and incompatible with, the hypothesis expressed by the statement "I am pleased because I believe that I have inherited a fortune." But it is evident that at the time of believing in the inheritance, I could have no grounds whatever for preferring the second of these hypotheses to the first, since it is logically impossible for me to distinguish between what (as I believe) is the case, and what I believe to be the case. Hence there will be two incompatible hypotheses about my pleasure which in principle I shall not be able to distinguish. But it is clear that my retrospective description of the situation as my "being pleased because I believed . . . ," and anyone else's description of it in these terms, are just based on my sincerely thinking or saying at the time "I am pleased because I have . . . "; thus it appears that a necessary condition of the assertion of the true hypothesis would be my previous belief in or assertion of a false one, and this is absurd.

Hence the causal account must hold that it is *always* my belief that is the cause, or at least the proximate cause, of my pleasure; and that the statement "I am pleased because I have inherited a fortune" must be taken to mean "I am pleased because I believe I have inherited a fortune." This is equally implausible, however. For first, it still looks, from the previous argument, extremely doubtful whether I am in a position to arrive at the correct hypothesis, and distinguish it from rivals—at the very least, it seems that it would be a necessary condition of so doing that I had engaged in philosophical reflection; second, it is impossible to see what evidence I could have for the hypothesis, or how I would set about collecting evidence; third, since the statement in question expresses, on this view, a causal hypothesis, it would be corrigible, and it would make sense to say that I had just been mistaken in thinking that it was a certain belief that caused my pleasure; but in general no sense can be attached to this. In fact, something like this incorrigibility extends even to the formulation which does not include an explicit reference to my beliefs. There are, indeed, ways in which I may be mistaken about, or ignorant of, the objects of my pleasure, and it will be one aim of this paper to investigate them; but I cannot be mistaken in saying "I am pleased because I have inherited a fortune" in the same way as I can in saying, for instance, "I have a stomach-ache because I ate some bad fruit."

Thus the object of my pleasure—what I am pleased at, by, or (in this sense) because of—is not to be taken as a cause; nor can my belief in so-and-so be made to function as the cause of my pleasure at so-and-so.

In fact, the whole idea of a man's beliefs being a cause in such cases is a fiction, aided, though not inspired, by a misunderstanding of the form of words "he was pleased because he believed. . . ." Now this form of words, and perhaps a similar misunderstanding, occurs also in another connexion—that of a man's having mistaken grounds for an action. There are other obvious similarities between the two cases. Statements of the form "he did it because he believed that p" are, like the comparable statements about pleasure, ultimately based on the man's own statement, taken to be sincere, of the form "I did it because p"; and statements of the latter form are, again, not open to the charge of being straightforwardly mistaken. It is perhaps worth noticing that there are languages which, in both connexions, do not employ anything like the misleading formula "because he believed" at all, but perform the same function merely by the mood of a verb.

Thus in these respects, at least, there is some analogy between pleasure and its objects on the one hand, and actions and their grounds, on the other. But this analogy will not take us very far. For pleasure, like many other states with which similar difficulties arise, such as fear, is not an action, but more like, at least, a "passion" or something that happens to us. But even if this is denied, the analogy will not work out. Even if we agreed with Aristotle[1] and possibly Prof. Ryle[2] that pleasure in the standard case consists in or accompanies zestful activity, it would have to be the activity, if anything, that constituted the object of the pleasure, for it is this that I take pleasure *in;* but if it is the activity that constitutes the object of the pleasure, this will not be constituted by the grounds of the activity, if any; so that even in this case, the relation of pleasure to its object will not have been explained as the relation of actions to their grounds.

In fact, in many cases it is impossible to discover any activity, the zestful engagement in which constitutes the pleasure. The man who is pleased because he believes he has inherited a fortune may indeed enjoy such "activities" as imagining his improved style of life, planning expensive holidays, envisaging

---

[1] *Eth. Nic.* 1174a 13 seq.

[2] "Pleasure" *P.A.S. Supp. Vol.* XXVIII (1954), pp. 135. *seq.* I am unclear whether Ryle does subscribe to this view; some remarks in this article suggest that he does not, but concentration on the case of activity plays a large part in his arguments against the view that pleasure can be a feeling.

the gratitude of persons to whom he will be generous, etc. But even if we supposed, what seems to be false, that such "activities" were the logically necessary concomitant of being pleased at a supposed inheritance, their zestful performance cannot in fact constitute the pleasure in question. For a man can enjoy such activities (as day-dreaming) without believing that these things will come about. He will enjoy the activities quite differently, and much more, and will give a quite different answer to the question "why are you pleased?" if he really believes that these things will come about, and just *because* he so believes. Hence enjoying such activities is not a sufficient condition of being pleased because I believe I have inherited a fortune, and it does nothing to explain the peculiarities of the latter. So the only "activity" we are left with as the object of this sort of pleasure is the "activity" of believing in these future events, itself; and this will not do, for we give sense to "he takes pleasure in believing it" only where the man does not (really) believe it, or at least has made himself do so, or has refused to be unpersuaded, and these are quite different matters. An activity in which I can take pleasure is surely something in which I can engage or indulge, which I can take up or abandon, and none of these things can in general be done with belief.[3]

In such cases, pleasure certainly cannot consist in any zestful activity. Thus, for more than one reason, the slight epistemological analogy between the grounds of action and the objects of pleasure cannot be directly pursued. How then is the connexion between pleasure and its objects to be characterized?

Let us consider the notion of "pointing to." This will lead is, I am afraid, a long way round, but eventually back to pleasure. It is a familiar point that the mere fact that my finger may be pointing to something, in the sense that a line drawn

---

[3] Though we should not underestimate our capacities in this direction; *cf*. Price "Belief and Will," *P.A.S. Supp. Vol.* XXVIII (1954), Inaugural Address, reprinted in this volume.

from it meets that thing, does not mean that I am pointing to that thing.[4]

It is a characteristic of the sense of "pointing to," in which I point to things, that if asked what I am pointing to, I should be able to give an answer.

Further, that subject to certain qualifications I cannot be mistaken or ignorant, *i.e.*, it makes no sense to say that I am mistaken or ignorant, about what I am pointing to.

Further, that I can point to things of various categories. Consider what can come after "look at . . ."—that thing, the size of it, the shape of it, the number of ants down there, what he is doing, the colour of the sky, the speed he is going, etc.

Last, that by pointing, I can draw someone's attention to these various things; and that the purpose of pointing is usually, if not always, to do just this.

Now it is not true to say without qualification that I cannot be mistaken or ignorant about what I am pointing to. For I can be mistaken, or at least something goes wrong with my account of what I am pointing to, in at least the following cases:—

*a* About the past, I may remember that I pointed, but misremember (or, less usually, completely forget) what it was that I pointed to. This is obvious and uninteresting.

*b* I may point to x, but mistakenly say that I am pointing to y, because I mistakenly believe that x is y. The first case of this is that in which the mistake does not matter, because it was not *as y* that I was pointing to x. The commonest case of this is where I want to point to the attitude, qualities, etc., of x, and identify x as y. ("Look at the wonderful colour of those hibiscus flowers." —"What? There are no hibiscus flowers."—"Oh, I

---

[4] The point is made several times by Wittgenstein in the *Philosophical Investigations*.

meant the colour of that bush over there, whatever it is.")

c This case is like case *b*, except that here the mistake matters, because it is *as y* that I am pointing to x. ("Look! The Queen!"—"It is not the Queen."— "Oh. . . .") Here it is true that I pointed to something, and something of which I could have given another description (*e.g.*, "that lady who just walked in,") but here the pointing is, as it were, withdrawn; and attention drawn to the thing *pro tanto* lapses.

d I may point to x which does not exist at all, as Macbeth might have pointed to the dagger. Here the description given ("a dagger") has to be withdrawn, but in its place a different kind of description can be given ("I was pointing to the dagger I thought was there"). It is noteworthy that "the dagger which I thought was there" is not a description referring to an image, or any similar private thing. It is a description whose place of application is in the external world—for the dagger I thought was there is (if I may be allowed the expression) just the one that is not really there.

So much for mistakes that may arise with my descriptions of what I am pointing to, or drawing someone's attention to. If we consider now the correlative situation, of my having my attention drawn to something by somebody, we see that matters are different since of course I may be just mistaken about what he is trying to draw my attention to. Or the boot may be on the other foot, and I may know better than he about the application of the descriptions he gives, *i.e.*, may be able to correct his descriptions already. But now consider the situation of my having my attention drawn to something, not by a person pointing, but by the thing itself; I may have my attention drawn by and to any of the sorts of things to which I or someone else might point. Now here I cannot make the sort of mistake that arises when someone else does the pointing and I misunderstand him, for that is related to the description he would give, and that does not arise in the present case. Nor can I correct myself, as I can correct him, on the spot; though I may go on to correct myself, or if I share the object of attention with others by pointing, the situation is as described above. The situation is *rather* as with my own pointing; and here it is important that having my attention drawn to something is often a preliminary to my pointing to it, and that the description I would give in pointing to it is often the description under which, as it were, the thing draws my attention to itself. Having my attention drawn to something of course differs from pointing to it inasmuch as the latter is an action and the former is more like something that happens to me. This difference is important; but it is more important that the difference does not affect the status of the descriptions that occur in the two cases. The descriptions or identifications, misdescriptions or misidentifications, I could give of what drew my attention are just those that I might give if I were to draw your attention to whatever the thing is; and just as with pointing the description I give may in one of these ways go wrong, and yet it makes no sense to say that I was mistaken in supposing myself to be pointing to this rather than that, so when I characterise what drew my attention, I may misdescribe it, and yet it makes no sense to say that I was mistaken in thinking that it was this that drew my attention rather than that.

There is one peculiar sort of case that arises in connexion with "having my attention drawn" and cannot arise with "pointing," which may be added to the present list of examples, although it is not strictly speaking a case of mistake or ignorance at all:

> e My attention may be drawn to some feature which I already know to be illusory, but which is striking and worth attention nevertheless. Thus, after I have taken mescalin, my attention may be drawn by the unusual appearance of my carpet. Here I know that I am under an illusion, so of course will not try to point to this extraordinary appearance.

One further case concerns ignorance:

*f* It may be that x has drawn my attention, but that I do not know exactly what it is about x that has drawn my attention.

There is no analogy for this last case, either, in pointing. There must, of course, be some determinacy about what draws my attention, if only because to have my attention drawn is to have it drawn to one thing rather than another; and under the description so proffered I shall be able to point (unless of course the case is otherwise peculiar, by being *e.g.*, of type *e*). It makes no sense to say that I do not know what about it I am pointing to, but it does make sense to say that I do not know what about it drew my attention. There is nothing surprising about this difference: since my purpose in pointing is to draw someone's attention to x, the description I furnish of x will be one which I suppose will effect this purpose, and one that is indeterminate through ignorance would be unsuitable. It is of course true that I can point to, and draw someone's attention to, x (under some description) just because I do not know what (under some other, usually more specific, description) it is: "look at that bird—what is it?" or "that shape in the corner!" This is a partial analogue to having my attention drawn to something and not knowing precisely to what feature of it— but only a partial analogue. For in the pointing case, if I point to x, and ask what it is, any further description I go on to give of it in an attempt to answer the question is in no logically different position from anyone else's suggestion. But the situation is different with the thing that drew my attention. If I go on to try to decide what it was about the thing that drew my attention, it seems that, although others may make suggestions and have theories on the subject, it is for me to decide whether their suggestions are correct. If I do sincerely and wholeheartedly decide that it was a particular feature of this thing that drew my attention to it—*e.g.*, a certain resemblance, even if only a fancied resemblance, of this lady's hat to a familiar landmark—it is doubtful what sense it makes to say that I was mistaken in this diagnosis. The fancied resemblance may turn out to be only fanciful; but I cannot be mistaken in saying that it was this fancied resemblance that drew my attention to the shape of her hat; or that it was the shape that drew my attention to the hat; or that it was the hat that drew my attention to her. At most, I might, in certain very complicated contexts, be said to be deceiving myself; for instance, an inhibited person *might* succeed in deceiving himself into thinking that what drew his attention to a certain girl was the unusual material of her dress rather than its provocative cut. But such cases are perhaps rare.

How it is that one can come to know on reflection that it was *this* feature that drew one's attention to something, I find an obscure question. That such conclusions are not reached by empirical inference, and that one is not establishing an ordinary type of causal proposition, is evident.[5]

Before we return to the direct discussion of pleasure, one further point must be made about "having my attention drawn to." Two importantly different sorts of case have not been distinguished. The first is that in which my attention is drawn to something because I am expecting or looking for something, and the thing which draws my attention does so as a supposed candidate for being the object of my expectation or search. In such cases, obviously, my attention to the object will lapse if it turns out not to be the object in question, and if it is the object in question it will become the object of attention of a different kind, *viz.*, of whatever sort of interest motivated the expectation or search. Second, something can attract my attention as being surprising or (rather differently) intriguing. In this case, attention will lapse if the object turns out not to be a surprising thing at all; or if it is, but surprise is dissipated by explanation; or if, without explaining it, I just get bored

---

[5] This *may* be related to a point made by Miss G. E. M. Anscombe about certain bodily movements: *cf. Intention* (Blackwell, 1957) para. 8. Her phrase "cause known without observation" does not fit the present case; but then I am not sure that it is a very happy description of the case she is discussing, either.

with it or distracted by something else. The most important difference between these two sorts of case is that in the first the object draws my attention as supposedly matching a description (in the broadest sense) with which I am already prepared—a description which would figure in an account of what I was already searching for, expecting, etc. In the second case, the description is not already prepared; the object merely introduces itself, arriving without invitation. It follows from this difference that the situations *a—f* described above do not all arise equally with both types of case; for instance, *f* does not arise with the first sort of case at all.

To return, now, to the case of pleasure. It is obvious that there is a close analogy between the cases *a—f* in connexion with attention, and similar cases in connexion with pleasure. There is in fact a parallel for each case, on the following lines:

*a* First, and again uninterestingly, I may remember some occasion in the past on which I was pleased, but misremember or completely forget what I was pleased at. This is perhaps rare; but less so with the converse case of misery; I may remember the miseries of childhood or adolescence, but forget, because I would now regard as trivial, their objects. This case is not to be taken to include the situation in which present pleasure is based on misremembering—this will be considered later.

*b* I may be pleased at x, but say that I am pleased at y because I falsely believe that x is y; but this does not matter, because x's being y is no element in my pleasure. Thus, I may be pleased by this picture, as a picture, and say that I am pleased by this Giorgione, when the picture is not a Giorgione.

*c* More drastically, I may take pleasure in, or be pleased by, x which I mistakenly think is y, where x's supposedly being y is the basis of my pleasure. Thus, I may be pleased by this supposed Giorgione as being a Giorgione.

*d* I may be pleased at something that does not exist at all, for instance my supposed inheritance of a fortune.

Common to cases *c* and *d* is the feature that the discovery of the truth means the end of pleasure—at least, of *that* pleasure. The distinction between case *c* and case *d* is often merely a matter of expression, and with many cases is would be ludicrously scholastic to try to force them into one class or the other. For instance, I might be very pleased by the arrival at my party of a gentleman whom I took to be a certain distinguished author. This could naturally take its place in class *c*; but someone might argue, very strictly, that what I was pleased at was the (supposed) occurrence of a certain event, *viz.*, the arrival of this author, and that this event has not happened, *i.e.*, does not exist, so that the case belongs to class *d*. It would surely be frivolous to insist on a decision between these two accounts of the situation.

However, a rather more serious point does perhaps emerge here; for it may be objected that the frivolity of an argument on this last question shows a weakness or unclarity in speaking in this way of the *objects* of pleasure at all. Often the most natural formulation will be to say that I am pleased because . . . : *e.g.*, that I am pleased because (as I suppose) this author has arrived, rather than that I am pleased at the (supposed) arrival of this author. Alternatively, the language of activity may be appropriate: I might be taking pleasure in looking at the supposed Giorgione rather than in the supposed Giorgione. Some genuine differences are marked by these different formulations, and the sort of distinction I have been drawing needs refinement to deal with them. But the language of objects of pleasure which I am discussing here is sometimes not reducible to the language of "because," and is rarely not a possible alternative to it; and, as I tried to argue at the beginning of this paper, the language of "because" is a cause of philosophical puzzlement—which the other formulation, properly understood, may help to solve. The language of activity, again, seems more independent, and in some cases not to be reducible to the language of objects; unless it is that in those cases the activity is itself the object of pleasure in the same sense. But, as was argued in the previous discussion of the case of the inheritance, it is also true that the language of objects or of "because" cannot be reduced in every case to the language of activity. I shall not further discuss here the language of activity, which I suspect to be more closely related to the concept of enjoyment than to that of pleasure; in any case, our present concern is with the problems of belief and knowledge in relation to pleasure, and these less notably arise with activities. In so far as they do, it may be that some of the present account can be adapted to deal with them. Thus it seems true to say that if I am engaged in an activity or performing an action, there is one sense in which I must know what I am doing; but this only means that there is some description of what I am doing under which I know that I am doing it, and there may be many others which I might offer of what I am doing which do not in fact apply. It might be under one of these latter descriptions that I was enjoying doing what I was doing (case *c*), or alternatively the misdescription might not matter because it was not *as this* that the action or activity was being enjoyed (case *b*); and so in.

The analogy between the cases discussed in connexion with pointing and attention, and similar cases with pleasure, does not stop here. Similar analogies can be found for the cases *e* and *f:*

*e* I may be pleased by some feature which I know to be illusory, but which pleases me nevertheless. Thus, owing to my myopia, I may find a strident picture agreeably muted; having a high fever, I may find the sour drink pleasantly sweet; after mescalin, I may find my old curtains an exciting riot of colour.

*f* As x may draw my attention, and yet I may not know what it was about x that drew my attention, so I may be pleased by x, and yet not know what it is about x that I find pleasing. Again, with pleasure, as with attention, one finds in such cases the puzzling phenomenon of my apparently being able to discover by reflection what it was.

Thus there does seem to be an analogy between the cases of mistake, ignorance, and illusion that can arise with objects that draw my attention, and such cases that arise with the objects of pleasure. Before leaving the detailed consideration of the analogy however, there is one feature of it that needs further investigation. One notable way in which mistakes can affect pleasure is that my pleasure may be founded on false beliefs about the past or the future. Thus I may be pleased because I suppose the remark I recently overheard to have been a compliment about me, though it was not; or I may be pleased because I think that I am going to see a certain person to-morrow, and, as it turns out, I do not. The case of the supposed inheritance, previously mentioned, is a kind of amalgam of the two, since it involves both the belief that somebody has made a Will in my favour, and the belief that money will be arriving; though it is presumably the latter belief that is the more closely connected with the pleasure. Now, with the inheritance as we have seen, the language of objects can indeed be used; and this case was assigned to a certain class in the analogy, class *d*, of objects which I think exist but do not.

But the situation is more complicated than this suggests. First, there is a certain asymmetry between the past and the future in this respect. In the matter of the future, we must distinguish between the pleasures of anticipation and the pleasures of the event. I can of course have the former without the latter happening at all: either because the event does not happen, or because the event, though happening, turns out not to be pleasurable. These last two possibilities come to much the same thing, so far as the "baselessness" of the pleasures of anticipation is concerned; for the pleasures of anticipation consist in the anticipation of pleasure.[6]

In the matter of the past, it is in general true, correspondingly, that the pleasure of memory consists in the memory of pleasure. The "pleasure of memory" here is not to be confused, of course, with the pleasure of reminiscence, or even of recall;

[6] *Cf.* Plato, Philebus 39d *seq.*

with these, the pleasure is taken in a present "activity", *viz.*, recalling or reminiscing about some past events in themselves need not have been particularly pleasant. We are interested in the "pleasure of memory" in a different sense, of the continuation or revival of the pleasure associated with some past event. But even in this connexion, we must distinguish two quite different ways in which mistakes may arise. The first is the case in which the pleasure is continued or revived by the correct memory of a pleasure originally based on a mistake—as in the case of the supposed compliment. This presents no special difficulty: it is merely, as it were, the inheritance of a mistake. But there is another case, in which, through mistake of memory, I either "remember" a pleasant event which did not happen and which I did not at the supposed time of happening believe to be happening, or misremember as pleasant an event which did happen but was found by me at the time unpleasant; in either case, I may feel present pleasure at the supposed past event. This is not the inheritance of a mistake, but a mistake of inheritance. Of these, the latter is more like the case of a mistake about the future.

Now it is not entirely clear how the language of objects is to be taken in such cases, nor what the analogy with attention will be. The cases can, as was suggested, be crammed into class *d*, thus corresponding to those in which my attention is drawn to the actually non-existent. But this is not very illuminating. However, by extending the notion of attention a little, some better analogies can be found. Where I merely continue or revive a past pleasure originally based on a mistake, this is like having my attention drawn to something and continuing to concentrate on it when the object itself, or rather what I took to be this object, has been removed. More difficult is the case of present pleasure based on mere misremembering; yet here there is the analogy of someone's directing his attention to some event he supposes to have happened, or this event, or perhaps its memory, forcing itself on his attention. With the future, I can indeed have my attention directed to a supposed future event, as I do in expectation or waiting, which (as we noticed above) may be the preliminary to my having my attention drawn to the thing's actual appearance. This, though the analogy is not perfect, is something like the pleasure of anticipation followed by the pleasure of the event. The point needs further investigation, but I should like to suggest that the distinction between the "invited" and the "uninvited" objects of attention has other applications in connexion with the concept of pleasure. For instance, it is connected with the distinction, first drawn by Plato,[7] between those pleasures that consist in the satisfaction of a desire, and those that do not.

In the course of this discussion we have traced some analogies between, on the one hand, the relation of pleasure to its objects, and, on the other hand, the relation of attention to its objects. It can now be suggested that these analogies are not merely analogies: they exist because attention is involved in pleasure, and because the relation of pleasure to its objects *is* the relation of attention to its objects. If I am pleased by something, my attention is, to that extent, drawn to it; and the more I am pleased by it, the more my attention is absorbed in it. It may be remarked here that there are perhaps cases of pleasure that have no object; where one merely feels full of well-being. In fact, the word "pleasure" seems very rarely to be used in such cases, but rather "cheerfulness", "contentment", etc.; or, if it is, the "pleasure" is given a pseudo-object ("pleased with life"). But if they are cases of pleasure, it is noteworthy that they are also cases in which characteristically my attention is not directed to anything in particular.

This is not to say, of course, that being pleased by something just is attending to it, that finding something pleasant just is having my attention drawn to it and held by it, that the pleasures of anticipation just are anticipation; attention can just as well be directed to or held by the unpleasant. It is rather that pleasure is one mode or species of attention.

This connexion between pleasure and attention has been

---

[7] *Philebus* 50b *seq.*

noticed before, *e.g.*, by Prof. Ryle.[8] But Ryle does not discuss what the relation is of attention to its objects, in particular to objects which are mistakenly believed to exist. I have tried to show that the concept of attention is itself sufficiently complex in these respects to illuminate the corresponding complexities of the concept of pleasure. Now it may fairly be asked how much this explains; for, it may be said, since not all attention is attention to the pleasant, the actual relation of pleasure to attention remains still to be explained. This is true—it does. But at least the relation of pleasure to its objects may be somewhat clearer if it is shown that this relation is that of attention to its objects, and if this relation is given some explanation. The last I have tried, very sketchily, to do, in suggesting that the idea of attending to a thing can be based on, though not straightforwardly derived from, the simpler notion of pointing to a thing. In particular, I hope that the introduction of the notion of something's drawing my attention to itself may help to explain how it is that, although pleasure is something that happens to me rather than something I do, nevertheless the characterization of its objects shares epistemological features with the characterization of the objects of pointing, which is something I do rather than something that happens to me. These categories of "something I do" and "something that happens to me" are, of course, much too crude; but it is significant that they are much too crude for the concepts both of pleasure and of attention, and in very much the same ways. For instance, it sometimes happens that my attention is unexpectedly drawn to something because in fact I have been subconsciously looking for it, and very much the same thing can occur with pleasure.

The type of relation to an object that I have been trying to investigate in the cases of pleasure and attention is one of those that some philosophers have investigated under the title of "intentionality"; and though I have deliberately avoided the

---

[8] *Op. cit.*, pp. 139 *seq.*; for pleasure as one mode of attention, see p. 142.

word, I hope the present remarks may suggest a line for clarifying this obscure notion. Some of these philosophers (perhaps Husserl) seem to have held that each type of "state of consciousness" was in the end unanalysable. If not only the relation of attention to its objects, but that of pleasure to attention, could be clarified, it might be found that this view was too pessimistic.

## PLEASURE AND FALSITY

### TERENCE PENELHUM

This paper[1] will consider some possible relationships between pleasure and falsity. Such a consideration is at least relevant to some traditional anti-hedonist arguments. Plato, in Book IX of the *Republic,* and in the *Philebus,* argues that some pleasures are inherently false or deceptive, so that hedonism fails because its objective is incoherent. There is also a tradition in Christian theology, deriving from Augustine, which seeks to represent the sin of sensuality as derivative from that of pride, so that at least some of the pleasures which characterize the life of the sensual man necessarily involve a degree of wilful error, or self-deception, either about the pleasurableness of certain experiences or about their real objects. Typical of anti-hedonist sentiment is the following:

> Look upon pleasures, not upon that side that is next the sun, or where they look beauteously; that is, as they come towards you to be enjoyed, for then they paint, and smile, and dress themselves up in tinsel and glass, gems and counterfeit

Reprinted from *American Philosophical Quarterly* (Vol. I, No. 2, April 1964) by permission of the editor and Terence Penelhum.

[1] This paper was originally presented to the Oberlin Philosophy Colloquium on April 21, 1963. I wish to thank the Oberlin philosophy department for their kind invitation, and to acknowledge a great debt to discussions of the paper's topic with my former colleague Peter Radcliff.

imagery: but when thou hast rifled and discomposed them with enjoying their false beauties, and that they begin to go off, then behold them in their nakedness and weariness. See what a sigh and sorrow, what naked unhandsome proportions, and a filthy carcase, they discover; and the next time they counterfeit, remember what you have already discovered, and be no more abused.[2]

Thus Jeremy Taylor. Such sentiment has many sources, and I make no claim to examine all of them. My purpose is only to explore some of the ways in which, when pleasure is ascribed to someone, it can be said to involve either error or self-deception. I shall proceed as follows. In Section I I shall try to make some working distinctions among pleasure-expressions. In Section II I shall examine ways in which the notion of error can find a place in their uses. In Section III I shall do the same thing for the notion of self-deception. I shall conclude, in Section IV, with a few brief indications of how the results of the earlier sections can be used to help evaluate some anti-hedonist arguments. This last is intended to set the investigation in the context of a traditional problem, but it is not intended to be more than a fragmentary treatment of it.

I shall not at any point be directly concerned with the issue of whether all or any pleasure-idioms should be construed as episodic, or as dispositional, or in some other way; though what I say may commit me incidentally.

## I. Preliminary Distinctions

There are a large variety of pleasure-idioms, and any one of them may be used in more than one way. There is one distinction among them which I wish to make, and which I shall use throughout this discussion to avoid difficulties which might arise if it were neglected. This is the distinction I shall

---

[2] Jeremy Taylor, *The Rules and Exercises of Holy Living*, ch. II, section I. Quoted here from *The Whole Works of the Right Rev. Jeremy Taylor, D.D.*, edited by Reginald Heber and Charles Page Eden (London, Longmans, 1862), vol. 3, pp. 46–47.

refer to, clumsily, as that between *being pleased* on the one hand, and *enjoyment* on the other. In making this distinction in this way, I take the most common use of the expression "being pleased" as typical of one sort of use of pleasure-idioms, and the most common use of the expression "enjoyment" as typical of another sort of use of pleasure-idioms, which I think is significantly different. I do not suppose it is impossible to discover occasions on which we might use the one expression in a way which is typical of the use of the other. And I wish to emphasize, not hide, the fact that there are some pleasure-idioms, including most obviously the word "pleasure" itself, which are used in one way on some occasions and the other on others. It is the two different uses that concern me.

We would expect, and do indeed find these notions to have much in common. (a) Both have *objects,* i.e., there must be something (in some sense of "be") which one is pleased by or at, or is that which one enjoys. (b) Both, further, entail that the subject is *aware* of the object: I cannot be pleased by something of which I am unaware, or enjoy something of which I am unaware. (c) And both are, in some important sense, *passive:* The state of being pleased is something that comes over me, and it is tempting, though wrong, to think of the object of pleasure in this sense as its cause; similarly, I cannot enjoy something at will, but only set about doing it or watching it in the hope that I shall come to enjoy it as it continues.

Yet with these fundamental similarities there go fundamental differences. (a) Although both have objects, the typical objects differ. Being pleased typically has *facts* for its objects; enjoyment typically has actions or events. This must not be forced; certainly I can not only be pleased that the President made such a good speech, I can be pleased at or by the speech he made. But although these are for most purposes interchangeable, the latter pair could, for this reason, be replaced by the "pleased that . . ." construction. Enjoyment-idioms, though, cannot be followed by that-clauses: I can enjoy the President's speech, or listening to his speech, and he can enjoy making the speech, but neither he nor I enjoy the fact that he made the speech. This is partly because I can be pleased by or about his speech without having heard it but only about it; but I cannot enjoy it without hearing it, or reading it—I cannot enjoy it by merely hearing or reading about it, unless of course the account contains extensive quotations. So (b) although both entail awareness of their objects, in the sense that one can neither be pleased at, nor enjoy, something of which one is unaware, one has to specify different forms of awareness for each. All that is necessary for me to be pleased by something is that I should have some actual or supposed cognizance of it, that I should know (or think I know) *about* it; to enjoy it, however, I have to be actively engaged in it (if it is an action) or be paying fairly close attention to it, or rather have my attention drawn by it or be absorbed in it, if it is some event or the action of someone other than myself. There has been some recent argument[3] about the classification of pleasure as a form of attention; this seems to me to fit the concept of enjoyment, but not that of being pleased. I can be pleased by something to which I never gave attention, but about which I have been informed; but I cannot enjoy such a thing. (c) Although in each case the person is passive with respect to the object of his pleasure, this takes different forms. In both cases the object may be something which he has *done,* as well as something which he has seen or which has done something to him. But in making someone pleased, the object has put him into a state of mind which may explain his actions over a considerable period after the occurrence of that which pleases him. These actions may be actions in a full-blooded sense, as when I am pleased by my salary rise and resolve to be more polite to my employer, or actions in a less complete sense, as when my pleasure so overcomes me that I spend the whole of my first higher check on luxuries. Being pleased is a (mild) *emotion.* When I enjoy something, on the other hand, it affects me by

[3] B. A. O. Williams and Errol Bedford, "Pleasure and Belief," *Proceedings of the Aristotelian Society, Supplementary Volume* 33, (London, 1959), pp. 57–92, reprinted in this volume.

holding my attention and distracting me from other things; and this it cannot do after I am aware that it has ceased, even though it may then continue to please me. I can be pleased that it has happened, but not enjoy its having happened.

Akin to being pleased are such states as being delighted (at, that, by), being thrilled (at, that, by), being happy, charmed, amused, excited, uplifted, transported, etc. Enjoyment is akin to being occupied or absorbed in. Some idioms are ambiguous between the two uses, particularly "taking pleasure in," and even "being pleased *with*," particularly when applied to things rather than facts or events. There seem to be clear cases when one type of idiom fits but not the other—I can enjoy some things about which I am not pleased, e.g., a house fire, or a good speech by my opponent; I can be pleased by something which it is logically impossible for me to enjoy, such as my child's examination results, or the upsurge in the economy, and I can be pleased about something which I do not in fact enjoy, such as managing to run five miles or refraining from eating dessert. The very unpleasantness of these activities is a reason for my being pleased at managing them. But in spite of such clear cases, the generic notion of pleasure is no linguistic accident. I would be a strange, inconsistent sort of person if a great many things which I was pleased by I did not in fact enjoy, or if a great many things which displeased me I did in fact enjoy. It is easier to enjoy someone else's fire than it is to enjoy one's own, and it is unseemly to tell him one enjoys it, for this suggests that one is pleased by it.

## II. Error

There are, *prima facie*, two spheres where error would seem to be possible with regard to pleasure. We might make mistakes of some sort about the object; and we might make mistakes about the pleasure that we take in it. I shall explore these possibilities, first using being pleased as the typical idiom, and then using enjoyment.

In recent discussion of the concept of emotion the question has been raised of how far emotions involve an element of rationality or judgment. I agree with Peters[4] that calling something an emotion is classifying it as a *passive* state that comes over us or happens to us, frequently to the detriment of our rational capacities. He goes on, however, to insist that in spite of this emotions have a "cognitive core," consisting in some "appraisal" of their object. That emotions require some (fairly intense) degree of awareness of their objects is no doubt so; but to insist that the concept of an appraisal fits here requires us to admit that it is often not articulate but what he calls "intuitive," and often does not rate the object as, say, beneficial or harmful, but merely as "agreeable" or "disagreeable"— notions which collapse into "generative of favorable or hostile reactions." It is not necessary to slide into verbal legislation here to recognize those essential aspects of emotions that bear upon our present concerns.

An emotion that has an object necessarily involves awareness of that object; and therefore it involves certain beliefs about it. "Involves" is vague, but I would suggest that the emotion presupposes the beliefs in something like the Strawsonian sense. Someone who feels anger at someone else's action, for example, must believe that the other did in fact perform that action. Beyond this point, however, the element of judgment in emotion can vary very widely. At the lower end, it seems possible to have an emotion which is a mere pro or con *reaction* to its object, and does not involve any assessment of it as being beneficial or harmful or as having certain consequences. At the upper end, there may be elaborate and explicit judgments of this sort. I shall use Peters' terms in my own way and speak of that element of judgment which must be present for the emotion to have an object as the *cognitive core* of the emotion, and speak of that element of further judgment or assessment involved in the emotional response to the object as the *appraisal* of the object. Roughly, the cognitive core has to be known to know what the person is (say) angry at; and

[4] R. S. Peters and C. A. Mace, "Emotions and the Category of Passivity," *Proceedings of the Aristotelian Society*, vol. 62, 1961–2 (London, 1962), pp. 111–142.

the appraisal, if present, will enable us, if we know it, to understand why he is angry at it. It would clearly be pedantic to insist that where both are present, a given judgment must belong unambiguously to one rather than the other.

Both in cases where there is an explicit appraisal and cases where there is none, one can ask whether the emotion is *justified*.[5] One can judge an emotion as appropriate or inappropriate to its object, as understandable, as disproportionate, and so on. To decide whether someone's emotion is justified or not in these ways, one must examine the cognitive core of it, and the appraisals it contains. An emotion may be unjustifiable because its cognitive core is false, i.e., if the facts are not as the person having the emotion assumes them to be. It may, further, be unjustified because it is inappropriate to the facts as the subject has understood them. This is very complex. If, for example, there is a clear appraisal of the object, the emotion may be warranted if the appraisal is sound, but yet a critic judge it not to be sound. If, for instance, I were to be outraged at the general's plan of attack because I judged that it showed callousness and would lead to great loss of life, a critic might hold that if these things were true they would justify my outrage but that in fact they are not true. On the other hand, the emotion may be inappropriate even though the appraisal is a sound one. It might be that I am right in judging that my neighbor's unwillingness to prevent his dog from running on my lawn is due to his irresponsibility, but that my anger is disproportionately great. If there is no appraisal in the emotion, criticism cannot take quite this form; instead one has to ask what appraisal of the object *would* justify the reaction in question and then decide whether such an appraisal is correct.

That we judge certain emotions to be fitting, and certain others not, suggests that we have a rough scale with emotions, as it were, paired off against certain sorts of situations. The details of such a scale are inevitably highly controversial and subject to change. Some have even held that *no* emotion is ever

[5] Compare here Mary Warnock and A. C. Ewing, "The Justification of Emotions," *Proceedings of the Aristotelian Society, Supplementary Volume* 31 (London, 1957), pp. 43–74.

justified, but to render this persuasive it has usually been necessary to produce some theory, such as cosmic determinism, to show that the appraisals involved in emotions are always false.

Sometimes, if the emotion is blatantly unjustifiable, or the appraisal wildly unsound, it is suggested that the subject must be wrong as to what the object of his emotion really is. What I wish to say at this point about this move is merely that whatever criteria one may use for determining what the real object of the emotion is, there is no guarantee that it will be found to be more appropriate than the apparent one. The very reverse may be true in some cases.

One standard of a man's rationality is the degree to which his emotions pass these tests of appropriateness. Another standard is the degree to which those that fail the test are reduced or removed by the recognition that they fail it. People do not merely have unjustified emotions; they also have emotions that *they know* are unjustified. I can know that I am unreasonably annoyed with my colleague yet continue to be just as annoyed.

I have indulged in this lengthy preamble about emotions because it seems to me that being pleased can be classified among them. If this is sound, it would follow that to be pleased, one must have an object about, by, or at which one is pleased; that one must therefore have certain true or false beliefs about this object; that one may, though one does not need to, make certain favorable appraisals of it; and that the content of these appraisals would be relevant to the justification of one's being pleased if this were challenged as out of place. All of these consequences seem to me to be correct.

I now wish to turn to the question of the possible scope for error in this sort of pleasure-situation. As I suggested earlier, this would seem to be divisible into error about the object, and error about the pleasure felt toward it.

### (1) Error about the Object
There would seem to be three possibilities here. One might, it appears (a) be in error about the object in the belief which comprises the cognitive core of the pleasure; or (b) be in

error in the appraisal of the object; or (c) be in error as
to what object the pleasure actually has. Noting again that
it is overly-schematic to separate (a) from (b), I shall take
these in order.

(1) (a) *Error in the cognitive core of the pleasure.* We
are often pleased by a supposed fact which is not a fact at all.
Here it is not unheard-of to say that we are erroneously or
mistakenly pleased. Our pleasure is based on, or presupposes, a
false judgment. Pleasure at any agreeable piece of misinforma-
tion will fit into this category, as when I am pleased to hear
the false report that the horse I bet on has won the race. It
is possible to express this sort of situation, if one is careful,
by saying that the object of the pleasure turns out not to
exist. It is not accepted usage to say that one is falsely, rather
than mistakenly, pleased, since this suggests what is *ex hypothesi*
untrue, that one is not really pleased after all.

This account requires further elaboration. Whether or not
the pleasure is mistaken would be decided by seeing whether
or not it ceases when the subject realizes his mistake. If it
does, then it really did depend on the false judgment. But if
it continues, this shows that although the false judgment was
made, the object of the pleasure was not after all the supposed
fact expressed in the judgment, but some other, which has not,
or not yet, been shown to be erroneously believed in. For
example, suppose that I am pleased to see, as I think, that
Miss Smith is coming toward me across the street, and it turns
out that it is Miss Jones. If the pleasure ceases (if only Miss
Smith will do), then it has depended on the false judgment that
Miss Smith is coming. If it does not (if Miss Jones will do as
well) we would tend to say that what I have been pleased
about has not been the advent of Miss Smith *per se*, but the
advent of someone possessing certain personal properties—a
pleasure-object which Fate has now supplied in a manner only
contingently different.

At this point complications arise. It could be said that
when the pleasure continues in such a case it is necessarily a

different pleasure, viz., pleasure-at-the-advent-of-Miss-Jones rather than pleasure-at-the-advent-of-Miss-Smith; in which case I necessarily began with an erroneous pleasure and continued with another, non-erroneous one. It is always partly a matter of verbal choice when we have one pleasure and when another. But there is clearly *a* use in which we would say that we had the same non-erroneous pleasure continuing, so that the judgment it originally presupposed, though largely false, was not false in the sense definitive of the pleasure. I shall stay with this sense for convenience. Even in this sense, there are occasions when we would want to say that even though I continue to be pleased, the pleasure with which I continue is different from the one with which I began, which *was* erroneous. If the person coming toward me turns out not to be Miss Smith but a forbidding official who happens in spite of everything to be bringing me good news, then it would be clear that my continuing to be pleased would have to consist in my first having one (erroneous) pleasure and then having another (non-erroneous) pleasure.

One place for error in pleasure, then, is in the judgment forming its cognitive core. The pleasure can appropriately be called mistaken if the revelation of the falsity of this judgment concludes it, leaving the subject either not pleased at all, or pleased at something else.

(1) (b) *Error in the appraisal of the object.* I might be pleased by something that is indeed so, but which I erroneously appraise. I might be pleased by my appointment to a new position because I mistakenly judge that my personal circumstances will be bettered by it. Here again this could be called a mistaken pleasure if there is reason to think it would cease if the error were revealed.

It might be that a critic would rule that the pleasure was disproportionate to its object, because although the appraisal the subject makes is correct, it is not such as to justify the degree of pleasure which he feels. If I am overwhelmed with delight that my article is accepted by a small-circulation magazine, on the grounds that I shall be slightly more famous than before, the critic might judge the degree of pleasure to be excessive. A critic might hold that a correct appraisal did not justify any degree of pleasure, even when I felt some. An example of this would be my being pleased to hear that someone I disliked had made a decision which I correctly surmised would ruin him, and the critic's objecting to this on moral grounds. In neither such case, however, can we say that the pleasure is mistaken, since no error is involved *ex hypothesi*. The pleasure is wrong or inappropriate or excessive, but this is not the same.

There is another, important, form of this sort of case. I might have a pleasure which I come to see, or see from the start, is inappropriate, yet continue to have it. The cognitive core of the pleasure may be correct, and there be no appraisal, or there be an unsound one, and the subject come to see the pleasure is inappropriate, yet go on cheerfully feeling it. When the Russians sent up a manned satellite before the United States there were some people in countries allied to the United States who were pleased by this. Many realized that their pleasure was inappropriate in the light of their own political interests; yet they continued, irrationally, to feel it. In such a case the pleasure could not be said to depend on a mistaken appraisal, because there was no mistaken appraisal. There are, therefore, non-erroneous irrational pleasures.

(1) (c) *Error about what object the pleasure has.* It looks as though one can easily be mistaken about what it is that one finds pleasing. I can think I am pleased by the triumph of justice when it is really the downfall of someone I dislike, that I am pleased at uncovering truth for its own sake when it is really the chance for scandal. It might be said that if there is any error here it cannot be error about what the object is, since we do not have two objects in these examples, but only one under different descriptions. It is boring to counter this by saying that one is in error about what *aspect* of the object is pleasing. A better, and I think correct, answer is to say that since the characteristic object of being pleased is a fact rather

than a thing, there are two objects being confused here, because there are two facts. It is not so hard to find cases where the duality of objects is clearer. I might, for example, think I am pleased that my students are having a holiday when I am really pleased that I am. Certainly even here there is a close connection between the two objects; but this is easy to explain. One cannot think one is pleased by object $O_1$ when one is really pleased by object $O_2$ unless one is aware of both. And the limits of error here—if error is what it is—are the limits of parallel awareness.

I say if error is what it is. But I do not think it is error in any straightforward sense. The difficulty is that the criteria for the truth of what I say when I say it is $O_1$ rather than $O_2$ that pleases me are the same as the criteria for my sincerity in saying this. If I think $O_1$ pleases me, it does; but if I show by my behavior that it is really $O_2$ that pleases me, this does not merely show I am wrong to say it is $O_1$, but that I am insincere in saying it. Yet we would be unwilling to construe all cases where someone says it is $O_1$ and his behavior indicates it is $O_2$ as cases of simple hypocrisy. Of course there are such cases, when I say it is $O_1$ knowing full well it is $O_2$, to deceive you; and here there is no error on my side at all. But suppose there were a case when I said it was $O_1$ which pleased me, and it was really $O_2$, and I was not simply lying? In such a case I would to some degree mean what I said. Yet my behavior must in such cases indicate, since my words do not, that it is really $O_2$ that pleases me. Yet again, there must be some behavior, in addition to my words, to indicate that it is $O_1$, for if there were only my words, we would be back with straight simulation.

Hence a case where someone says that the object of his pleasure is one fact when it is really another—and we do have occasion to use this sort of description—is a case of conflicting behavior, where the criteria for its being the declared object and the criteria for its being another are both partially satisfied, but the preponderating behavior is against rather than for, the declared object. Since the criteria for the correctness of what he says are also criteria for his sincerity in saying it, simple error is out of place. Since there is a conflict of criteria, simple hypocrisy is also out of place. What we seem to have is a case neither of error nor of lying, but of self-deception.

### (2) *Error about the Pleasure Itself*

Can I think I am pleased when I am not pleased? Can I think I am not pleased when I am? Can I be wrong about *how* pleased something makes me? Can I confuse pleasure with some other mental state?

I can certainly be doubtful whether I am pleased or not. But then it *is* doubtful whether I am pleased or not. The criteria for each are the same, viz., ambiguous behavior vis-a-vis the criteria for really being pleased. I can discover with chagrin or surprise that I am pleased—the hard-boiled father finding himself delighted at his baby's tooth; though it does not seem to follow that the pleasure antedates its discovery.

If I am in no doubt that I am pleased, I am. Only what would put my sincerity in doubt would put my being pleased in doubt. If I say I am pleased when I am not, or say I am not when I am, and I am not just lying, we must, once more, have a case where criteria for both are partially satisfied, those for my not being as I say being dominant, but not altogether so. Error seems to collapse again into self-deception.

The same seems to hold for degree of pleasure: The criteria for the degree of my pleasure being what I say are the same as for my believing it to be what I say. If it is correct to claim that I believe the degree to be other than it is, then my behavior must be ambiguous between the two and my belief neither whole-hearted nor wholly simulated.

A case where is would be correct to say someone thought he was pleased when it was some other state he was in, or vice versa, would seem to be one in which it would be equally correct to say he felt both. An opponent of capital punishment might want to say both that he was offended and that he was pleased by the Eichmann execution. On the other hand, he might *say* merely that he was offended by it, even though we could tell from his eager scanning of the reports that it pleased him. The only difference between the two cases might lie in what was said. It might seem that this is not even *prima facie* a case of mistaking pleasure *for* disgust, but just a case of having both and only admitting to one. But I am inclined to deny the two descriptions differ, since under both there must be some degree of each emotion. For as soon as one reached the point where someone had pleasure and did not have disgust and yet said only that he was disgusted, we would have not the mistaking of one for the other, but straight pretence. So thinking one has one when one has the other is being in conflict between both and saying with some degree of sincerity that one has only the one. Error again collapses into self-deception. Of course I can have both and admit it, but then there is no error whatsoever.

### (3) *Error and Enjoyment*

The differences between being pleased and enjoyment make it necessary to amend many details in the preceding when we apply it to enjoyment. The fundamental patterns, however, are the same, and I can therefore be briefer.

The awareness entailed by enjoyment is the awareness involved in watching or doing and the like, viz., attention. It will, nevertheless, imply beliefs about its object. One may appraise what one enjoys, but often does not; for it is much more a matter of psychological fact that one enjoys certain things than a matter for challenge and justification. It is not a sign of irrationality to enjoy something one judges harmful, e.g., eating proscribed food—though it is irrational to eat it, perhaps. The connection between enjoyment and favorable appraisal is much less close than in the case of being pleased. There is nevertheless *some* connection: It is irrational and frivolous to enjoy too many things one judges unfavorably. And one might enjoy something because one makes certain favorable judgments about it, and it is not damaging to admit that in such cases there would be less clear distinction between enjoying the object and being pleased by it: for the border-line between the two notions would naturally come where I enjoy something because of the favorable judgments I have made about it. Let us turn now to error.

(1) (a) I am obviously not immune even to radical error

about the object just because I am attending to it; and it might be that I enjoy it in part because of my error. I might see something as $O_1$ when it is really $O_2$; so that although it is $O_2$ I enjoy it as $O_1$, and therefore, presumably, mistakenly. Sometimes the revelation that it is really $O_2$ will kill the enjoyment and sometimes not; and the choice whether to say the original enjoyment depended on the mistake may depend on whether there is now something else about $O_2$ on which my continued enjoyment hinges. If in my foreign travels I were to come across two men exchanging swordthrusts and enjoyed watching them under the impression that they were fencing in sport, and then found that they were dueling to the death, this might quench my enjoyment. If it continued, the natural tendency would be to say that the object of enjoyment throughout had been elegant sword-play *qua* elegant swordplay, and that my misinterpretation of its point had no bearing on my enjoyment. This would be the correct move unless something showed that my continued enjoyment had another object. This could happen. If the swordplay degenerated into sordid jabbing and I still enjoyed it, this would suggest that I had come to enjoy the contest as a piece of public bloodletting, and in turn that my original enjoyment of it did depend on my error and ceased when this was exposed. Roughly, when I enjoy something I enjoy it as an object of a certain sort; but it may not actually be of that sort, but only be mistakenly thought to be; when this occurs the enjoyment depends on the error.

(1) (b) I may enjoy something when I am misappraising it. I may enjoy washing my hostess's dishes because I think she is feeling grateful to me; when I find this is not so, I may finish the task in a different frame of mind. The discovery of the false appraisal may not spoil my enjoyment. I may continue to enjoy my dinner even when I realize that it is not after all free from the harmful ingredients the doctor warned me against. Whether the enjoyment has depended on the error would have to be settled as in the dueling example just used. But certainly if I continue to enjoy the dinner I now know is bad for me, *this* does not depend on any error, for there is now no error. In

the case of enjoyment, it is not even irrational to enjoy it, though it would be irrational to ask for more.

(1) (c) With regard to error about what is the object of enjoyment, it is clear that we do sometimes say of people that they think they are enjoying one thing when they are really enjoying another. He thinks, we say, that he is enjoying the arias when it is the prima donna's dress. In such cases, once more, one must be aware of both (that is attend to them together or alternately). There is no reason to say that the real object is more seemly than the apparent one, rather the opposite. Most importantly here, the criteria for its being as the subject says are identical with those for his sincerely saying so; and since the rubric of "He thinks he enjoys $O_1$ but it is really $O_2$" precludes straight lying, it follows that there must be partial satisfaction of the criteria for his enjoying the music and partial satisfaction of those for his enjoying the dress, with the latter preponderating; i.e., self-deception.

(2) The same applies to the question of the possibility of error about the pleasure itself. I can be in doubt whether I am enjoying the concert or not, but then there *is* doubt whether I am. I can discover that I am, though this does not seem to show that I *was*. If I am sure I am (i.e. if I have no doubts, and do not just use the word "sure" about myself), I am. If I say I enjoy it when I do not, or that I do not when I do, then unless we have straight lying we have self-deception. And the man who mistakes enjoyment for disgust would seem to have an unacknowledged conflict between them.

## III. Self-Deception

I have suggested that it is mistaken to construe statements like "He thinks he is pleased at $O_1$ but it is really $O_2$" and the rest as reports of error, and that they are instead reports of self-deception. This is far from being a pellucid concept, and I shall now try to say something in general about it. I hope to show that it is not so odd as it might seem to call these cases examples of self-deception in spite of their not being cases of

error. I shall begin by discussing self-deception about matters
other than the subject's private mental states.[6]

The concept of self-deception has seemed to some to generate paradoxes, to make us claim, for example, that a man
both does and does not believe the same proposition. Such
difficulties come, as has recently been shown, from trying to
understand the idea of deceiving oneself on the model of that
of deceiving others. If we resist this temptation, a non-para-
doxical rendering seems less difficult. Gustavson and Canfield
have argued[7] that self-deception is merely belief in the face of
strong evidence, but I do not think this is enough. Certainly it
is a necessary condition, for if the subject's belief were not
held in the face of *strong* evidence self-deception would be indistinguishable from intellectual indecision. But the self-deceiver
must also *know* the evidence; or else we have not self-deception
but ignorance. Further, if he knows the evidence yet does not
accept what it points to, this might be because he does not *see*
what it points to, and then we have stupidity or naïvete; so the
self-deceiver must not only know the strong evidence, but see
what it points to. But if he has, knows, and sees the import
of, strong evidence, what is left for him to do to believe what
it points to? The notion of acceptance seems to add nothing
in such a context; for the criteria for saying that he really
does see where the evidence points and the criteria for saying
that he accepts the conclusion to which it points are the same.

The only way of avoiding the reinstatement of a paradox
here is to accept the fact which paradoxical renderings feed
upon: that self-deception is a conflict-state. This way we can
settle for consistent description of inconsistent behavior. Someone in this state does partially satisfy the criteria for belief
and also those for disbelief—in particular he will tend to

[6] I am indebted here to the stimulus of the papers by Raphael
Demos, "Lying to Oneself," *Journal of Philosophy*, vol. 57 (1960), pp.
588–595, and F. A. Siegler, "Demos on Lying to Oneself," *Journal of
Philosophy*, vol. 59 (1962), pp. 469–475.

[7] John V. Canfield and Don F. Gustavson, "Self-Deception," *Analysis*,
vol. 23 (1962), pp. 32–36.

declare his disbelief in that to which he sees the evidence points. If he is deceiving himself that something is so when the evidence is against it—a condition we may call self-simulation—he will tend to declare it to be so. If he is deceiving himself that something is not so when the evidence is in favor of it—a condition we may call self-dissimulation—he will tend to declare it not to be so. Now I have already suggested that the criteria for his really seeing where the evidence points and those for his accepting the conclusion to which it points are the same. To this we must add the complementary point that there must be some reason to hold that the self-deceiver does not believe what he asserts (or there would be nothing for him to deceive himself over), and yet there must be some reason to say that he does believe what he asserts (or there would be no deception toward himself, merely lying toward us).

So I would suggest as severally necessary and jointly sufficient criteria for self-deception over matters other than one's own inner states (i) belief in the face of strong evidence, (ii) the subject's knowledge of the evidence, (iii) the subject's recognition of the import of the evidence. These add up to a conflict-state in which there is partial satisfaction of the opposed criteria for belief and for disbelief, with the subject's declarations likely to be against the evidence. It is worth noting that if the subject turns out to have been right after all he is not of course said to have been deceiving himself, but to have had faith.

There is one element which I have not so far mentioned, and that is motive. Usually when we ascribe self-deception to someone we ascribe a motive to him. I do not feel prepared to say that a motive *must* be present, partly because I cannot see any necessary incoherence in the concept of motiveless self-deception in odd cases; partly because insisting there *must* be one, as opposed to saying there almost certainly is, leads into questionable psychological inventions; and partly because the criteria I have listed seem, however oddly, to be enough to establish self-deception without it.

Motives are, however, usual. Normally one would uncover

the motive for someone's deceiving himself by showing that the supposed fact which he denies in the face of evidence is one which he would have reason to wish (or even try to make) otherwise; or that the supposed fact which he asserts in the face of evidence is one which he has reason to wish (or even try to make) to be so; and that he *knows* the supposed fact would be of this sort. One reason for the feeling that there has to be a motive is the fact that we might need to uncover one in order to assure ourselves that the subject really did know the evidence, or really did see where it pointed. For if I am right, we will have ambivalent behavior in all such cases, and this naturally suggests some degree of ignorance or foolishness. If we are unsure, these alternatives can sometimes be ruled out if we discover that the fact he is refusing to admit is one which he has good reason to dislike. On the other hand, this is not the only way of ruling out these alternatives; it may be enough to know that the subject is a generally well-informed and intelligent person. Self-deception is a vice in which only fairly highly rational beings can indulge.

I now turn to the place of self-deception in pleasure. I have previously argued that there are possibilities for straight error over the nature of the object of pleasure, and over the appraisal of it. I have also argued that error is not possible over the being and nature of the pleasure itself, or over which of two or more possible objects it has, and that what we have here instead is self-deception. This gives me two tasks. I shall first look at those places where error is possible and see how self-deception might also occur. I shall then try to justify my contention that those places where error cannot occur are nevertheless places where self-deception can. In both I shall take being pleased and enjoyment together. The first task first.

*(1) Self-deception in Judgments about the Object of Pleasure.* I do not think there is any subject matter about which error is possible but about which self-deception is not, whatever we say about the converse. From this it would follow that if pleas-

ure can presuppose or contain erroneous judgments, it can contain self-deception too. It also seems clear that since pleasure can, in the ways we saw, *depend on* false judgments, this very fact supplies us with an obvious *motive* for self-deception, though not necessarily the only one. The fact that $O_1$ would be more pleasing or enjoyable to me that $O_2$ gives me an obvious motive for judging that it is $O_1$. That it would please me to meet Miss Smith gives me a reason for falsely judging, or telling myself, that it is Miss Smith. (To distinguish self-deception from wishful thinking, one must assume here that the evidence is from the start against its really being Miss Smith.) Further, the fact that a favorable appraisal of the object would render it more pleasing than a less favorable one provides a motive for my making an overly-favorable one. Since I would be more pleased by a new car that was a good buy than one that was overpriced I have a motive for telling myself that it is a bargain.

There are other dimensions to this. The appraisal of the object furnishes justification, if there is any, for being pleased at the object (sometimes even for enjoying it). This generates a higher-level type of self-deception, viz., the invention of reasons which render the pleasures we already take more acceptable to ourselves or to others. A man may tell himself his new car is a bargain in order to justify his pleasure in it, and in order to lend some degree of weight to his arguments with his wife over the expense. In such cases the indulgence in a self-consciously irrational pleasure is a more honest state of mind—the thirst for rationality is a major source of lies.

There is an important asymmetry here between being pleased and enjoyment. (a) When we say that the fact of its being $O_1$ would please me gives me a motive for judging it to be $O_1$, it would of course be very odd to say that I judge it to be $O_1$ *in order* to be pleased that it is. One does not do things in order to be pleased at them. We have to construe such a case by saying that if my being pleased depends on my deceiving myself that this is $O_1$ when it is not, this shows I *want* it to be $O_1$. I do not want it to be in order to be pleased that it is;

I am (mistakenly) pleased that it is because I want it to be. If I am pleased it is $O_1$ without having wanted it to be (an unexpected pleasure), then I am not deceiving myself. (b) The case of enjoyment is more straightforward. For not only can one enjoy things because one wants them, but one can want them because one expects to enjoy them. So enjoyment can provide a motive for self-deception by providing an *objective* for it. But *both* the fact that it has pleased me to believe it is $O_1$ *and* the fact that I have enjoyed it as $O_1$ can give me a motive (an objective) for *continuing* to believe that it is, in the face of new contrary evidence.

*(2) Self-deception about the Pleasure Itself, and about What Object It Has.* I have already dealt with the cases that come under these headings. They are the occasions when it is correct to say that someone thinks one thing with regard to his pleasure but another thing is true, and yet he is not straightforwardly in error. To rehearse briefly: When I think I am pleased by, or enjoy, $O_1$ but really take pleasure in $O_2$, it is necessary that I be aware of both, that I partially satisfy the criteria for taking pleasure in both, that I preponderantly satisfy those for taking pleasure in $O_2$, and it thus follows that I partially impugn my own sincerity in declaring $O_1$ to be the object of my pleasure. If I non-hypocritically say I am pleased when I am not, or that I am not when I am, this entails my partially satisfying competing criteria, and giving ground for partial but not total denial of my sincerity. If pleasure and (say) disgust are confused, then both are present and the denial of one is in part insincere. And so on. If I am sure in such matters, I am right; so, if I am wrong, I am not sure—whatever I *say*. The man who says too loudly in the interval that he is enjoying the Bartok, and who is not being straightforwardly hypocritical, is enjoying it as much as he really thinks he is, though not as much as he says he is. In such situations it is natural enough to speak of the person as deceiving himself that he likes it. Yet some argument might seem to be needed to show we are right

to talk this way when it is wrong to construe these as cases of error, for our language suggests error too.

If such a case is one of self-deception, it differs from the standard cases described earlier in not being belief in the fact of the evidence; since one does not find out from evidence that one is pleased by, or enjoys, something—although others have evidence that may fit or clash with what I say to them. This is the fact that rules out honest error: I do not get the evidence wrong, for I do not use evidence, and yet my sincere statements are criteria for the truth of what I say. So if one can deceive oneself about these pleasure-facts, this is not because one can also get them straightforwardly wrong. Yet we do wish to speak at times of people falsely claiming to have, or not to have, a pleasure, yet not being wholly hypocritical. Calling this self-deception, when the people do exhibit the behavioral ambivalence characteristic of self-deception, does allow this sort of description to have application. And it is necessary that it should, for in such cases we do find what we cannot (logically) find in the cases of simple error, viz., a *motive* for the statements' being false. Perhaps one cannot be mistaken about one's inner states, but one can have reason to wish them otherwise and to dissemble them.

It is easy to see that the pleasure itself could provide the motive for the deception, and that other things also could. I shall content myself with a few random examples. If I really enjoy the prima donna's dress but think it is the arias, the continuance of the enjoyment might be conditional on my not admitting its real object to myself. If I deceive myself in thinking that my enjoyment in something is greater than it is, this could be because I want a greater degree of what I have so far had, which has been less than I had been led to expect. If I deceive myself that I am horrified when I am pleased, it could either be because I realize the pleasure to be morally unjustifiable and can only continue to have it if I disguise it as horror, or because I feel the pleasure to be morally unjustifiable and wish on that ground to be rid of it. The variations are endless; but the last case shows that there are some occasions when we have pleasures that we wish ourselves without. Self-deception does not prove the truth of psychological hedonism.

## IV. Conclusion

I conclude with some applications of the preceding to some anti-hedonist arguments. These are no more than illustrative specimens.

(1) Plato holds that some pleasures are false.[8] I take him to mean that they depend upon error. I have agreed that there are indeed some pleasures which depend upon false judgments, which may be due to error, thus entitling us to speak of the pleasure as erroneous. I would agree further that it would be paradoxical to set out to cultivate pleasures of *this* kind, since it is paradoxical to set out to make mistaken judgments.

We also find in Plato a doctrine that "mixed" pleasures are false. The mixed pleasures are those that attend the relief of discomfort or the satisfaction of physical desires. He seems to hold either that in such cases we think there is a positive object of pleasure when there is not, or that we think we are getting pleasure when we are not. On either reading his argument is confused. On the first reading, Plato seems to suggest that since pleasure must have an object, and would not have one if the only relevant fact were the removal of the discomfort, then if we do have pleasure we must erroneously believe there is some agreeable positive feature, such as a sensation, for which we mistake the negative one. But if I am right that we cannot be simply in error about what the object of pleasure is, it follows that we cannot be wrong in the way he says. And the facts bear this out. When I am pleased by my tooth's no longer aching, I do not thereby think there is some other positive object by which I am pleased. I am pleased by what I say I am pleased by—my tooth's not aching. On the second reading, Plato seems to say that we think we are more pleased

[8] See I. Thalberg, "False Pleasures," *Journal of Philosophy*, vol. 59 (1962), pp. 65–74.

than we really are, even that we think we are when we are not at all, because of the co-presence of discomfort. But whatever complex of experience may produce pleasure, its intensity and reality is the intensity and reality the subject feels it to have. To use his example, if I scratch an itch, even though an unscratched itch is very unpleasant, a scratched itch is as pleasant as can be. Even if the magnitude of the pleasure is due to the magnitude of the distress, the magnitude of the pleasure is as great as the magnitude of the distress makes it seem to be. And it does not seem to be paradoxical, though it may be otherwise unseemly, to adopt a conscious policy of inducing certain distresses to ge the pleasures they generate.

(2) Some anti-hedonists in the Christian tradition have held that certain ways of life, including everyone's at times, involve self-deception because the pleasures in them are not really satisfying. I can only comment insofar as "satisfying" is taken to mean "pleasant." I have allowed self-deception to have wider scope than error, and therefore I think that such arguments have a sounder basis in philosophical psychology than the Platonic ones. It is quite plausible to say, for instance, that the sensualist deceives himself about what he enjoys; or that all of us exaggerate the intensity of some pleasures in order to lose ourselves in them and hide from our mortality and weakness. But caution is necessary. I cannot, for example, deceive myself that my pleasure is in $O_1$ when it is really in $O_2$ unless I am aware of both. Hence anyone who argues that someone who says he is enjoying sensual delights is really enjoying (say) rebellion against God must maintain that the subject is aware of his rebellion against God. This is not shown by showing there is ambivalent behavior on the subject's part, for this would only suggest that there was some other object, not necessarily this one. Similarly, it may be that my exaggeration of my pleasure's intensity is due to my wishing to lose myself in it and not pay attention to my need for God. But that my self-deception has this motive is not shown by the mere proof of some sort of self-deception. It is also necessary to show that I am aware of the religious facts from which it is said I am hiding. There will

always be plausible secular candidates for the title of real object of pleasure, or real motive for pleasure; e.g., rebellion against parents, or simple fear of death. Roughly, one's philosophical psychology will no doubt take its form from one's theology, if one has one; but it cannot lead into it any more than can one's physics.

## THE EMPIRICIST THEORY OF MEMORY

### R. F. HOLLAND

Tho' the mind in its reasonings from causes or effects carries its view beyond those objects, which it sees or remembers, it must never lose sight of them entirely, nor reason entirely upon its own ideas, without some mixture of impressions, or at least of ideas of the memory, which are equivalent to impressions. When we infer effects from causes, we must establish the existence of these causes; which we have only two ways of doing, either by an immediate perception of our memory or senses or by an inference from other causes; . . . 'Tis impossible for us to carry on our inferences *ad infinitum;* and the only thing, that can stop them, is an impression of the memory or senses, beyond which there is no room for doubt or enquiry (*Treatise, I,* Pt. III, Sec. iv).

In speaking of the Empiricist Theory of Memory I mean to refer to a large and variously developed body of thinking, some of whose vertebrae may be observed in the above passage from Hume. It might be protested that this passage is oddly chosen; for what does Hume really have to say here about memory as such? So far from expounding a theory of it, he does hardly more than accord it a passing mention. But the terms in which the reference is made are pregnant with metaphysics: *Ideas of the memory which are equivalent to impressions—an immediate perception of our memory or senses—an*

Reprinted from *Mind* (Vol. LXIII, N.S., No. 252, October 1954) by permission of the editor and R. F. Holland.

*impression of the memory or senses beyond which there is no room for doubt or enquiry.* In particular, there is here the conception of remembering as a subjective experience, together with the suggestion that to this experience belongs a kind of indubitability; and also the analogy between memory and perception, the idea that memory and perception are two more or less co-ordinate forms of awareness or ultimate modes of knowledge. But the Empiricist Theory of Memory is not something which belongs just to the history of philosophy nor is its persistent attractiveness felt only by those who philosophize within the august tradition of Locke, Berkeley and Hume. There is, so far as I know, scarcely any philosophical writing on memory from the time of Hume to the present day in which these conceptions, together with their ramified implications, are not to be found.

## 1. Remembering as a Distinctive Experience

If examples of mental faculties are called for, 'Memory' and 'Imagination' suggest themselves as readily as anything else; and comparison is readily invited between them, so that the question: What is the difference between Memory and Imagination? provides one natural starting point for a philosophical examination of memory. If one asks oneself this question, one is most tempted to begin an answer by saying that when we remember and when we imagine, in both cases alike something comes into our minds: but in the former case whatever comes into our minds represents or refers to an actual past, whilst in the latter case it does not. But if this is said, then straight away something more has to be said. For it seems that the connexion with a past reality which distinguishes memory from imagination does not merely have to exist; it also has to announce its existence to the person who remembers at the time when he remembers. Had it existed clandestinely, as indeed it might have done, then although memory and imagination would have been different, we should never have learned to distinguish them: the difference between them would have been useless, would have meant nothing to us. So it seems necessary to add that, whenever anything comes into our minds, we must have some means of knowing in which cases the connexion with reality exists and in which cases it does not. That is to say, it seems that there must be some mark or sign whereby a remembering state of mind can be distinguished from an imagining state of mind. So that one proceeds to ask: What is this mark or sign? In what manner does the connexion with the past announce itself?

An oddly perplexing question this. But a definite answer to it has been volunteered by more than one philosophical authority. Hume wrote: "A man may indulge his fancy in feigning any past scene of adventure; nor would there be any possibility of distinguishing this from a remembrance of a like kind were not the ideas of the imagination fainter and more obscure" (*Treatise* I, Pt. 3, Sec. v). Bertrand Russell, on the other hand, has said that memory-images, in contrast with images of the imagination, have a characteristic of familiarity, or are accompanied by a feeling of familiarity; and it is because of the presence of this characteristic, or alternatively because of the existence of this feeling, that we are able to know, whenever we remember something, that it is remembering we are engaged in and not imagining. Familiarity is "the characteristic by which we distinguish the images we trust. . . . Some images, like some sensations, feel very familiar, while others feel strange" (*Analysis of Mind*, p. 161).

Faced with these divergent pronouncements one may be inclined at first to try to adjudicate between them. In the case of Hume, an immediate difficulty arises from the fact that each of the contrasts in terms of which he proposes to differentiate between ideas of the memory and ideas of the imagination seems to be utilized already for the purpose of distinguishing some imaginings from others, or for the purpose of distinguishing some rememberings from others, or for both of these purposes. One may have recollections that are clear or unclear, faint or strong, more vivid or less vivid; one's imagination also may be vivid or not vivid, lively or not lively, weak or powerful. The suggestion that the haziest of recollections must be somehow clearer and more vivid than the most powerful products of a lively imagination seems implausible, if not senseless.

In defence of Hume it might be argued that it can still make sense to say that ideas of the imagination are *in general* fainter, etc. than ideas of the memory, just as it makes sense to speak of lead weighing heavier than cork, in spite of the fact that you can have various weights of lead and various weights of cork. A lead roof is heavier than a cork roof, a lead bath-plug heavier than a cork bath-plug; a leaden object always weighs heavier than a cork object *of a like kind*. What Hume said was that an idea of the imagination was fainter, etc. than an idea of the memory *of a like kind*.

But this attempted defence of Hume might be answered as follows. We are able to say that a leaden object is heavier than a cork one of a similar kind because we know that the weight-ranges of these two substances are closely circumscribed and that they do not overlap; and this knowledge rests on the exist-ence of accepted procedures for ascertaining what the weights of different substances are and within what limits they vary. In the case of ideas of the memory and ideas of the imagina-tion there would appear to be no analogous limitation in their respective ranges of clarity etc., since we are accustomed to attribute the extremes of clarity and unclarity to each; and even if there were such a limitation, it is impossible to imagine any criterion whereby their respective clarity-ranges might be shown to stand in an analogous relationship on the scale of clarity in general to the relationship between the weight-ranges of lead and cork on the scale of weight in general. So the qual-ification that the ideas should be of a like kind does not render Hume's story any more plausible.

## 2. Familiarity

Russell spoke of a familiarity which memory images possess and images of the imagination do not; and this might seem at once to be more like the truth. For we know what it is like to come across unexpectedly a scene, face, or picture which strikes us as familiar; the feeling of familiarity which one gets in such situations is often a subject of comment: and if in recalling and visualizing some well-known scene one abstracts oneself from the process and focuses one's attention upon the image as an object something of the same feeling is apt to be produced.

But the artificiality of the situation that is here created should not be disregarded. Was I, before reading Russell and seeking to verify his assertion by making this experiment, ever *struck by* the familiarity of my memory-images? Was their familiarity ever before the subject of comment? No: but neither was the familiarity to me of this room in which I sit. I cannot say that I have ever been struck by its familiarity. Yet it certainly *is* familiar. I was about to say that because the alleged familiarity of my memory-images had never struck me they could not after all have been familiar, since it was the essence of a thing's being familiar that the familiarity should strike one. But this was a mistake. The familiarity of my memory-images could be something like the familiarity of this room.

Only, in the case of this room, the familiarity is something I can explain. The room might easily not have been familiar: it happens as a matter of fact to be so, and the reason for this is that I have spent many hours of my life in it; the furniture has always been arranged in this particular fashion, and so on. Now when I recall a scene by means of an image, my image cannot as a general rule be familiar in this sort of way. For the image is a comparatively fleeting thing: I have never had this particular image before: I may never have had another like it. Of course, the actual scene which I recall may, or may not, be a familiar scene; and if it is familiar its familiarity will be susceptible of an explanation, like the familiarity of my room.

But there are also circumstances in which to say of a thing that it is familiar would be virtually equivalent to saying that one recalls it. Thus I might revisit an art gallery after some of the pictures that were originally on display have been removed and others put in their place. As I walk round I might divide the pictures I see into the familiar and the unfamiliar, those I remember from my previous visit and those that are new. In some such circumstance as this the familiarity of a thing could serve as an indication, perhaps the first intimation, that one remembered it. It may seem that it is in the light of this family of cases that Russell's familiarity must be considered, its function being to indicate remembrance. But one now notices something very curious about the nature of the indication it is supposed to convey, namely that it is not an indication of the remembrance of the self-same object to which the familiarity attaches. The familiarity about which Russell speaks is supposed to belong not to recollected objects, but to our images of recollected objects or to our experiences of recollecting objects. It is these that are supposed to be familiar; yet their familiarity is supposed to point beyond them to something elsewhere. How can this be possible?

There are cases where the explanation of the familiarity of a thing is to be found, not in the fact that one has encountered it before, but in its resemblance to some other object. Thus the Eiffel Tower might appear familiar to the tourist at his first sight of it, if he has previously seen models or pictures of it, or if he knows Blackpool Tower. Its familiarity could here be said, perhaps, to be pointing beyond it to something elsewhere. Here, too, there is no difficulty in understanding how familiarity could function as a kind of sign-post or indicating mark; the first intimation that a resemblance exists, perhaps, or the prelude to a more explicit and self-conscious recognition of the resemblance. Obviously the alleged familiarity of our memory-images invites consideration under this category. When the question is asked: From its resemblance to what does the image acquire its familiarity? an answer is ready at hand: From its resemblance to the remembered object; from its resemblance to whatever it represents.

But is it always necessary for our images to resemble what they represent? Even if it is, will they not do so in imagining no less than in remembering?

The point is that whereas in representing to yourself, for example, an imaginary tower standing in the centre of Magdalen bridge your image is not an image of anything you have ever seen, your representation in a recollection of the actual appearance of Magdalen Tower surrounded by the college buildings is a representation of something you have seen; and it is in this that lies the source of its familiarity.

But the crux of the matter is that familiarity does not by itself indicate its own source: it does not, as it were, bear its own explanation upon its face. Your image of Magdalen Tower may be familiar: suppose that it is familiar just because you have seen Magdalen Tower and are recalling it. However your image of the imaginary tower on Magdalen bridge might also be familiar, possibly because you have amused yourself by creating some such fanciful image as this on many occasions in the past. You may happen to know the explanation of the familiarity in both cases. But if you do not already know it, the mere familiarity by itself will not automatically indicate to you its own appropriate source.

### 3. Remembering and Being Certain About It

It may now seem impossible for a characteristic or feeling of familiarity to do what Russell wished it to do. But that is not to say that some kind of Memory-Indicator cannot exist—only, perhaps, that it tends to elude description. There is still temptation to think that if Hume and Russell failed in their attempts to locate it, their failure was a failure only of a technical kind, and that *something like* what they said must surely be true. One is inclined, for instance, to argue in this way:—

I can remember and know that I am remembering all in the same moment, and even in such a way that it seems impossible for me to be mistaken. Now if I can know in this immediate way that I am remembering when I am, then I must have some means of knowing. Something tells me it is not a wild flight of fancy. But what tells me? This question seems to demand an answer of the pattern: 'I can tell that what I am doing is recollecting by means of *so-and-so*, rather in the way you can tell that a certain motor-car is a Rolls-Royce by the shape of the bonnet.'

We often support a claim to remember by specifying some peculiar or striking feature of whatever is remembered. Thus I might say, with the aim of convincing a sceptic or of settling a doubt which may have arisen in my own mind, "I am quite sure that I remember the Duke of Omnium's motor-car, because it was a Rolls-Royce and had that distinctive bonnet." Only, in this type of case, it is precisely after this move has been gone through that one comes face to face with the question that is one way of launching oneself down the path taken by Hume and Russell; namely, in this instance, the question: But how do you know you remember it was a Rolls-Royce and had that distinctive bonnet? The situation one is in now is no different from the situation in which no doubt has arisen and there has been no call to elaborate upon one's initial recollection or to support it in any way; and yet one is able, without hesitation and with full confidence, to assert that one remembers. How, then, does one know this? Not because of any specific feature belonging to the particular recollection concerned: any such has now been ruled out as irrelevant. Is one not forced to conclude that it is because of some general characteristic belonging to recollections as such? If the attempts of Hume and Russell to describe it seemed to break down when pressed then it was our fault for pressing them too far. We feel that we know well enough the distinction they mean to refer to; and we believe that we are able to locate it in our own experience.

This belief, however, may be caused to appear in a different light by a consideration of some examples. Suppose, in the first place, that you are asked quite simply to imagine a Norman castle with a keep and a moat, and that you find yourself able to comply with this request. You will presumably draw upon your memories of castles you have visited, or heard described, or seen reconstructions of in antiquarian journals. Perhaps you will frame in your mind's eye a composite picture of a castle which will incorporate features drawn from many sources. But perhaps you will simply invoke an image of some actual castle, say Caernarvon Castle, which you are able to picture to yourself by calling it to mind as it is. The request will have been complied with irrespective of whether the castle you have before your mind is one you actually remember or not: whichever is the case you might describe what you are doing as 'imagining a castle.' The concept of imagining thus includes that of remembering. But obviously it was some different application of it from this that Hume and Russell had in mind.

Suppose, then, that the request had been that you should imagine a castle which was not one you actually remembered. What is required here is that your imagined castle should also be an imaginary one—a castle that is imagined in a further, additional sense over and above the one prescribed in the original example. Consider now some of the ways in which you might fail unwittingly to comply with this second request. For a start, you might not know what kind of thing a Norman castle is. Again, although you might know what a Norman castle is, proving this by your ability to recognise one when you see one or by your ability to distinguish between correct and incorrect descriptions of one, you might be unable to picture or draw or describe one to order. These are ways in which you might have failed also to comply with the request in the first example. But in the case of the second request there is a further possibility of failure: you might be picturing to yourself a castle which you believe to be a fictitious one, a product of your inventive genius, while all the time it is some actual castle which you have previously seen and are now, though unbeknown to yourself, recollecting. Maybe you discover the truth later when a friend shows you a picture of Caernarvon Castle and reminds you that you visited it long ago; you realize then with surprise that it was precisely this castle that you had had before your mind. But although our second kind of imagining is something you might think you are doing when in fact you are not, what you cannot do is be exercising your imagination, in this sense of 'imagination,' and at the same time believe that you are remembering. The impossibility here is of a logical kind. For in so far as you believed you were remembering you would *pari passu* be believing yourself to be failing to comply with the request. It is immaterial whether the request is someone else's or your own; and it might, not inappropriately, be said to be your own whenever you spontaneously embark on a flight of fancy. According to Hume, it is precisely to safeguard us from falling perpetually into this impossible confusion that the Memory-Indicator exists: "A man may indulge his fancy in feigning any past scene of adventure; nor would there be any possibility of distinguishing this from a remembrance of a like kind were not the ideas of the imagination fainter and more obscure." To 'feign some past scene of adventure' is undoubtedly to produce an instance of the second of the two kinds of imagining we have distinguished. The idea that one could do this and at the same time think one was remembering were it not for the special character of the ideas involved seems to result, in part at least, from the misconstruction of a logical impossibility as a kind of psychological impossibility. Small wonder that the Memory-Indicator, the allegedly distinctive experience which is supposed to distinguish memory from imagination, should appear to be at once unmistakable and indescribable.

## 4. Sceptical Doubt About Memory

There is, however, another application for the concept of imagination in respect of which it *is* possible for a person to believe he is remembering and yet be imagining. This is the unconscious or involuntary kind of imagining which is spoken of in connexion with mistakes and illusions. In this sense of 'imagine' it could be said of a person that he did not really see a snake in the grass but only imagined he did, or that he did not really remember the church at Hyde Park Corner which he believed he remembered; it was only his imagination. But there can be no scope for a Memory-Indicator to prevent confusion between this kind of imagining and remembering, since it is only where confusion occurs, only where the distinction is not in fact made until after the event, that we can speak at all of something being imagined in this sense. We may on many occasions be quite confident that we are not confused; but it seems that no memory-belief can ever be *proof* against disaster of this kind.

"In the first place, everything constituting a memory-belief is happening *now*, not in that past time to which the belief is said to refer. It is not necessary to the existence of a memory-belief that the event remembered should have occurred, or even that the past should have existed at all. There is no logical impossibility in the hypothesis that the world sprang into being five minutes ago, exactly as it was, with a population that "remembered" a wholly unreal past. There is no logically necessary connexion between events at different times; therefore nothing that is happening now or will happen in the future can disprove the hypothesis that the world began five minutes ago. Hence the occurrences which are *called* knowledge of the past are logically independent of the past; they are wholly analysable into present contents, which might, theoretically, be just what they are even if no past had existed" (Russell, *Analysis of Mind*, p. 159).

The disturbing thought that perhaps we remember, only without there ever having been anything to remember, just as we can be afraid when there is nothing to be afraid of, is a natural corollary of the idea that the essence of remembering is to be found in a private mental transaction. Though it is to be noticed that when he speaks of the logical possibility of a population that remembered an unreal past Russell feels obliged to enclose the word "remembered" in inverted commas, as if from a dim awareness that there is after all some logical impropriety committed by such a statement as "I remember the battle of Matapan though it did not take place". Russell goes on to repudiate the suggestion that the non-existence of the past should be entertained as a serious hypothesis,[1]

---

[1] *Analysis of Mind*, p. 160.

and remarks elsewhere that although "no memory is indubitable . . . our confidence as regards memory in general is such that we cannot entertain the hypothesis of the past being wholly an illusion".[2] Here he leaves the matter, having taken up a position that is curiously reminiscent of Hume's attitude towards the existence of an external world. However, the suggestion that memory, conceived as a source of knowledge or information about the past, cannot be known to be trustworthy has provoked others into attempts to provide special philosophical proofs of its trustworthiness: which reminds one of a famous 'Proof of an External World'.

These philosophical proofs[3] of the trustworthiness of memory constitute an interesting appendage to the main body of the Empiricist Theory of Memory, though the fact that they have invariably been proffered without due regard to the logical peculiarities of the doubt they are intended to allay may foster the illusion that there was here some quite self-contained philosophical problem awaiting solution. But in fact this sceptical doubt about the trustworthiness of memory is a doubt whose settlement is possible only when the motives behind it have been unearthed and when the distorting metaphysical picture of remembering upon which it is nourished has been removed. In this it resembles the Cartesian doubt about the Arch-deceiver, and also the classical doubt about the validity of induction. There are several points at which these doubts run parallel to one another. First, the sense of disconnexion between our experiences of recollecting and the alleged objects of our recollections is like the sense of a hiatus between the 'internal' world of our sensations and the 'external' world of perception. It is indeed, an exacerbated variant of the same complaint; for while the experience of recollecting is a directly accessible part of my or your private mental life, its alleged

---

[2] *Inquiry into Meaning and Truth*, p. 156–157.
[3] See, for example, the articles by R. F. Harrod (*Mind*, 1942) and E. J. Furlong (*Mind*, 1946), and especially the latter's recently published essay, *A Study in Memory*.

object in the public, material universe is not directly accessible; and furthermore, while the experience belongs to the present, the object has been engulfed by the past. A comparable gulf is felt to exist between inductive conclusions and the premises on which they are based, the unfulfilled ideal of direct access having an analogue here in the unfulfilled ideal of deductive certainty; and here, too, the complaint may be aggravated by a temporal disparity, in this case between present and future. Secondly, the lack of any rules to aid us in judging from the quality of our 'memory-experiences' precisely what degree of credence, if any, is to be placed in our various recollections may be compared with our lack of rules for deciding how many peeps, looks or glances shall suffice on any particular occasion for one to be sure that there is *e.g.* a butterfly on the rosebush. Compare too the cases where to our discomfort we are unable to decide or would rather withhold a decision as to the number of instances which shall suffice to render a generalization probable. Thirdly, there is the initially apparent analogy between the sceptic's doubt about memory in general and our ordinary doubts about specific recollections, which makes the question the sceptic asks seem like a *factual* question; and this may be compared with the corresponding effect of the apparent similarity between Descartes' question about the existence of the Arch-deceiver and questions about the existence of ordinary deceivers, or between the question: What is it that justifies any induction whatever? and questions raised in specific contexts about the relative weight of the evidence offered in support of this or that conclusion or the merits of this or that particular method of scientific procedure.

As soon as one considers the kind of steps that might actually be taken, in some situation in everyday life where the truth of the matter is not immediately obvious, to decide, and decide beyond all doubt, about the trustworthiness of a remembrance, part at least of the logical peculiarity of the sceptic's doubt and also of the conception allied to it of what it means to remember should become apparent: for one is in this way forced to recognize what the essential criteria for speaking of a remembrance really are.

Suppose that Smith claims to remember having seen H.M.S. *Nelson* at Dover some time last year, but we are not prepared to take his word for it. Our first step towards establishing the truth or falsity of his claim will be to find out, perhaps by looking up the newspaper reports or other relevant documents, or by asking other people for corroboration, or by inferring from the present state of naval affairs what must have happened previously, whether or not that particular ship was at that particular place at the time mentioned. If it was, this in itself might be enough to enable us to decide to our satisfaction that Smith's recollection was genuine. There is the possibility that it was merely by coincidence that the ship happened to be there; but assuming Smith's recollection to have been reasonably full and precise, the tallying of details would suffice to rule this out. There is the further possibility that when Smith told us his story he may not have been calling the past to mind but, say, reading out notes which he had previously written on his cuff, or passing on to us information he was receiving over a wireless receiver concealed upon his person. We should have to rule out the possibility of trickery of this nature; but we know quite well how to do so. Even then there would remain the possibility that he was employing, not his memory, but some form of clairvoyance. However, I think that all we should need to know, in order to be content to rule out this last possibility, is whether or not Smith had actually been in Dover at the stipulated time and so in a position to have seen the ship he claims to remember seeing. Provided it is established that Smith has had the opportunity of observing, of finding out or learning—the opportunity of doing whatever it may have been necessary for him on some occasion to do in order to be now in a position to remember, then we should not only be satisfied with his claim to remember, but should have no compunction, owing to the extreme rarity of clairvoyance, in correcting him if he should say that he knows what he knows clairvoyantly. In such a case we should insist that he actually remembers, although he may not himself think so. In short, then, the questions which, if satisfactorily answered, enable us to decide with finality whether or not a person remembers are subsumable

under the following two headings:—1. Did what he claims to
remember actually happen? and 2. Is his past history such as
to have put him in the position now to remember it?

Not that an example of this kind, however detailed the
account it might give of the tests whereby the veracity of recollections is established, may be supposed to be efficacious by
itself in allaying the sceptic's doubt. For it is abundantly clear
that his is a doubt that cannot be allayed however much we
multiply our tests and however stringently we apply them; and
an essential part of any answer to him will consist in pointing
this out. His doubt is like that of the man who still professes
that we do not really know there are biscuits in the box, although we have seen them, heard them rattle, smelt them,
touched them, tasted them, and applied to them every conceivable laboratory test, finding our expectations exactly confirmed at every juncture: we have no idea what it would be
like to know in his sense, and can only challenge him to tell us.
However, there seems to be a belief current among those who
have given thought to this matter that the sceptical doubter is
obliged to take over the offensive at this juncture and to provide an *ad hoc* demonstration that our ordinary tests are in any
case inadequate. The argument attributed to him is that all
our proofs that we have on any occasion remembered must at
some point and in some degree involve the use of the memory
on the part of someone or other: hence we cannot ever validate
a claim to remember without falling into a *petitio principii,* and
so we have after all no way of showing conclusively and beyond doubt that our memories give us information about the
past. In Russell's version the argument runs as follows: "Since
memories are not indubitable we seek various ways of reinforc-
ing them. We make contemporary records, or we seek confirmation from other witnesses, or we look for reasons tending to
show that what we recollect was to be expected. In such ways
we can increase the likelihood of any given recollection being
correct, but we cannot free ourselves from dependence on
memory in general. This is obvious as regards the testimony
of other witnesses. As regards contemporary records they are

seldom *strictly* contemporary, and if they are, it cannot subsequently be known except through the memory of the person making the record. Suppose you remember on November 8th that last night you saw a very bright meteor, and you find on your desk a note in your handwriting saying: "at 20 hr. 30 min. G.M.T. on November 7th, I saw a bright meteor in the constellation Hercules. Note made at 20 hr. 33 min. G.M.T." You may remember making the note; if so, the memory of the meteor and of the note confirm each other. But if you are discarding memory as a source of knowledge, you will not know how the note got there. It may have been made by a forger, or by yourself as a practical joke" (*Inquiry into Meaning and Truth,* p. 157).

Now if it be true that in showing any given recollection to be correct we cannot 'free ourselves from dependence on memory in general,' we shall need to inquire what can be the foundation for the distinction which we certainly draw on ordinary life between those recollections which can only be supported by further recollections and those which are supported by something better. To take an example: if I claim to remember putting some money into a box and certain other people saw me do it and later the box is destroyed by fire, then, supposing my recollection to be called in question, there may be no better means open to me of supporting my claim than to bring forward these other people to bear me out by saying that they also remember my putting the money in the box. But suppose that the box is not destroyed. Then I can if necessary fetch it and display its contents. How can it be said in this latter case that my recollection is only supported by other recollections in the way it was in the former case? For the box and the money are there to be seen. Where does the need for further recollecting come in? If it is merely a question of our being on our guard against practical jokes and the like, then have we not other and far superior means of doing this than by the use of our memories—*e.g.* combination locks, electrical fences and burglar alarms?

Broad and Furlong hasten to Russell's rescue at this point:

"When I claim to remember a certain event, I may test my judgment by inferring what events would be likely to follow such an event as I claim to be remembering. If I find that I can remember and perceive these consequences, my memory judgment will be supported by inference. If I can remember and perceive events which are incompatible with these, my memory judgment will be made improbable. But even when I test the memory judgment by present perception and not by memory, I presuppose the general validity of my memory judgments. For I start by inferring that I shall be likely to perceive so-and-so if the event which I claim to remember really happened. And, if the chain of inference be of any length, my guarantee for the conclusion is my memory that the earlier stages of the argument satisfied me" (*Mind and its Place in Nature*, p. 234). According to Furlong, the sceptic can buttress his argument with the claim that "inductive sciences rest on evidence supplied in the long run by memory," and even an anti-sceptic has to admit that "such a simple belief as . . . that the expanse at which I am looking is green . . . presupposes that I know what greenness is; and for such a piece of information I am indebted to memory" (*A Study in Memory*, pp. 11, 16).

Cases are imaginable where it might be asserted, and cases where it might be denied, that a person in drawing an inference has had to rely upon his memory: a man may embark upon a complex chain of inference and, without writing down the initial premises or any of the intermediate steps, successfully reach a conclusion which he might, owing to forgetfulness, have been precluded from drawing; but he could have saved relying upon his memory by setting forth the whole argument in writing. It is from this kind of contrast that the assertion and the denial alike take their sense. To commit oneself to either where no such contrast is in point is to pull the concept of remembering out of shape, so that communication is blocked by its deformity. Broad's contention about the dependence of inference on memory, therefore, if it is not to be dismissed as an obviously false generalization, must be regarded as involving an eccentric use of the word 'memory.' In either case the charge of the *petitio principii* falls to the ground. Furlong's plight is similar. A scientist is imaginable who in propounding some novel theory, not of course before the Royal Society, may have been content to rely for his evidence upon memory: his case would be distinguishable from others where dependence on memory is eliminated. Again, a distinction is to be made between judgments about colour which rest on memory and those which do not. When asked which of two fabrics is Pea Green and which is Apple Green I may succeed in remembering; but if I happen to carry a colour-chart I shall not even try. That both are *green* I can neither remember nor forget. The supposition that all scientific conclusions and all judgments about colour rest on memory, if it is not simply false, involves the use of the word 'memory' in an esoteric and dubious sense.

## 5. Memory as a Mode of Acquaintance With the Past

*a   The 'Transcendental Deduction'.* The absence, in the eyes of the protagonist of the Empiricist Theory of Memory, of any logical connexion between our experiences of recollecting and the past objects or occurrences to which they purport to refer obliges him, after he has either ignored or answered the sceptical doubter, to postulate a connexion of an *ontological* kind. It is, in fact, as a part of the mechanism of this connexion that the Memory-Indicator, be it of whatever sort, has its fundamental *raison d'être*. Its existence was not, as it were, disclosed in the psychological laboratory but rather deduced in Kantian fashion as one of the things which alone make remembering possible.

When a person, to use Hume's example, feigns some past scene of adventure, the scene which passes before his mind's eye conveys to him no knowledge of the past. When by contrast he recalls such a scene it is, one is inclined to say, the actual past which is presented to him and which he is aware of. But how can this be possible? The past has ceased to exist, so apparently he cannot now be aware of it directly, but only through the mediation of the images he now has: they alone can be the contents of the present situation. The problem is to understand how he can get from these present images to past events. In the case of the images in which imaginary adventures are depicted no such step is taken, and one may be inclined to suggest that this is because the images in this case have been more or less deliberately fabricated, built to the owner's specification. It is in the nature of memory-images, on the other hand, to be unalterable replicas of the past, offshoots of past sensations perhaps, which well-up of their own accord and cannot be tampered with. But how do we *know* that our memory-images are representative of the past? We cannot resurrect the past bodily and compare it with our images.[4] The fact that our memory-images are genuine representatives of the past must somehow be conveyed to us, and conveyed by the images themselves: to use a phrase of Bergson's, the representation they provide is one which "bears the marks of its origin". Broad explains the matter as follows:—"the objective constituents of memory situations are not in fact past and . . . they do not even seem to be past. But they do seem to have (and there is no reason to doubt that they actually do have) a certain peculiar characteristic which is not manifested by most images or most sensa. Let us call this "familiarity." Now we are so constituted that, when we are subjects of a cognitive situation whose objective constituent manifests the characteristic of familiarity, we inevitably apply the concept of pastness; and, if we make an explicit judgment, it takes the form: "There *was* an event which *had* such and such empirical characteristics." Familiarity is an empirical characteristic and pastness is a categorial characteristic; but the former "means" the latter to such beings as we are, and this "meaning" is primitive and unacquired. . . ." (*Mind and its Place in Nature,* p. 266).

We need not be deceived by Broad's allusion to Familiarity as an *empirical* characteristic into supposing that his belief in its existence rests upon the result of a psychological investigation.

---

[4] Cf. *Analysis of Mind,* pp. 158–159.

On the Empiricist interpretation of what recollecting involves, its presence, or the presence of something like it, is a sheer metaphysical necessity. It is an indispensable part of the machinery by which is conveyed to us our knowledge of the past. Our images constitute the main part of the mechanism, for they are the primary purveyors of information: but in the absence of Familiarity they would never be taken for such; moreover, their information is useless until it is properly interpreted, and it is the function of Familiarity to do this interpreting. In short, Familiarity is in the first place a signal, and in the second place an adaptor, converting what would otherwise be simply an awareness of something present into an awareness of something past. Without it the two related problems of our knowledge of the past and of the meaning of the past would be insoluble.

One may be inclined at this point to ask how, within the terms of the Empiricist Theory of Memory, an account is to be given of the sort of recollecting in which images are obviously not involved. I might go to a certain drawer and open it in order to retrieve an object I placed there some time ago, and I might while doing this have no image before my mind; or I might be conversing about a disconnected topic and having images related to this disconnected topic.

*b   The Two Kinds of Memory.* The Empiricist remains unimpressed by such feats; for associated with his theory is a segregation from one another of two contrasting kinds of memory, one of which is sometimes designated 'true memory' and monopolizes attention; while the other tends to be dismissed as philosophically uninteresting and umproblematic.

Anyone pausing to scrutinize the various accounts of this dichotomy cannot but be struck by their perfunctoriness. Russell's discussion of it, for instance, is of the flimsiest kind, and he is content to refer his readers to Bergson as an authority.[5] But while Bergson's account (in *Matter and Memory*) is cer-

[5] *Analysis of Mind*, p. 166.

tainly lengthier and more involved than any other, it is so patently full of misconceptions and so ingenuously pressed into the service of a preconceived metaphysical dualism that one stands amazed at Russell's confidence in it. A recent advocate of the dichotomy is A. D. Woozley in his *Theory of Knowledge* —a book which, since it purports to be written for beginners, may fairly be expected to make the ground of the division plain to the uninitiated.

There is on the one hand (Woozley begins, p. 36) such a thing as remembering how to ride a bicycle, to hold a rifle, to swim: this "need not involve any act of thinking". Also there is remembering how to do Pythagoras' Theorem, which does involve an act of thought: similarly, there is remembering the dates of the Kings of England. But there is one "quite different use" of the words 'memory' and 'remember'—"the sense in which I remember meeting Jones at Newhaven last Tuesday . . . or reading *Macbeth* for the first time when I was in bed with mumps at the age of thirteen or fourteen". The contrast is said by Woozley to be that between remembering a soliloquy from *Macbeth* in the sense of being able to recite it, and remembering a particular declamation of this soliloquy. "Remembering in the latter sense is not necessary to remembering in the former sense, although sometimes it may be a help (and sometimes not). . . . The important point, however, is that remembering in the sense in which I can remember a particular recitation of the soliloquy is extraneous to remembering the soliloquy. We are concerned here only with the first, the sense in which remembering is a cognitive act of the mind which occurs *now* and has for its object an event or series of events belonging to the past. . . . We may contrast this sense of 'memory' with others, and we may, as I shall for our purposes, ignore the other senses. . . ."

That is the substance of Woozley's exposition. Notice first how the words 'extraneous to' suggest a fundamental gulf: this iust what Woozley wants. Yet all they mean, as far as the ation Woozley gives us goes, is that the one thing can be ut the other. Thus, to adapt Woozley's example, I might have remembered meeting Jones at Newhaven, but not that it was on Tuesday; or I might have remembered meeting him on Tuesday, though not that the meeting took place at Newhaven: these two recollections would then have qualified for the title 'extraneous to one another.' Notice next how the expression 'cognitive act of the mind' is slipped in, as if it had some explanatory force. The adjective 'cognitive' and the verb 'cognize' may have a vague sort of sense to us by analogy with 'recognize' and from our recollections of a traditional psychological classification. But in what way is the one sort of remembering cognitive while the other is not? What would Woozley give, if we pressed him, as examples of other cognitive acts? One can only conjecture, but the likely things would be seeing, hearing, touching, etc.—any ways of becoming aware of something, of finding out what is there, of getting to know what we did not know before. The suggestion may be, then, that the essential difference between the two kinds of remembering is that in the one case we find out something, whereas in the other case we do not. To which suggestion one might wish to reply that in neither case could it be appropriate to say that we do this. Recalling an event to mind is not a way of discovering, of obtaining new knowledge.[6]

But let us go back to Woozley's contrast between remembering a soliloquy from *Macbeth* and remembering reading the soliloquy for the first time; for we are not yet clear about the criteria by which we may distinguish in practice between the two kinds of memory whose operation is held to be so different in theory. What are the observable differences which, presumably, form the basis of the theory? Obviously the intended contrast cannot be, although some of Woozley's remarks suggest that it is, that between the dispositional and the nondispositional senses of remembering, since this distinction may be applied to each of Woozley's examples equally. We might be tempted to think that the contrast must be that between recollecting one's own private experiences—sensations, emo-

[6] Ryle, *Concept of Mind*, pp. 273–274.

tions, etc.—and recollecting other things. But on applying this to Woozley's example of remembering meeting Jones at New-haven we may wonder whether we have made the 'cognitive' category too narrow. For surely this was not counted as a cognitive act only to the extent that it involved the subject's recollection of his own reactions to the meeting, events quite private to himself? If on the other hand, we try to include in the 'cognitive' category the remembrance of any events whatever, we are likely to find that we are making this category wider than Woozley intended. For instance, although I did not see the last Boat Race I can remember a great deal about it from the reports of other people. But it is not likely that Woozley would allow that in these recollections I am perform-ing 'cognitive acts directed toward' the Boat Race: this sort of remembering, he would presumably say, is not so very different from remembering the dates of the Kings of England. However he would, it seems, allow that I am performing cognitive acts in the case of my recollections of the Rugby match at Twicken-ham, at which I was actually present. Now it looks as if the difference between these two cases lies solely in the manner in which I obtained my information. Why should this difference be thought important?

There is, of course, one way in which I can recall the Rugby match that is not open to me in the case of the Boat Race, and that is by picturing to myself parts of it as I saw them; and it seems likely that it is recollections in which visual imagery occurs that Woozley has mainly in mind when he segregates one sort of remembering from all others as being cognitive. Yet if this is the case, one wonders why he does not say so plainly.

But even now we are only at the beginning of our difficul-ties. For instance, suppose I recall the Rugby match by describ-ing it verbally without the aid of images. Would I still be per-forming a cognitive act? If not, why not? If so, then what about my verbal recollections of the Boat Race? Could we not say that here too there is a cognitive act, only perhaps one which has for its object not the Boat Race itself, but the occasion on which my informant told me about it? This seems queer, for I might easily have forgotten about this occasion while still remembering about the race, or I might have had a whole host of informants on different occasions. Besides, if it be allowed that there is a cognitive act here, it must surely be allowed that there is one in the case of remembering the dates of the Kings of England. But this Woozley denied.

One's suspicion that this distinction between two kinds of memory is to be viewed rather as an effect of the Empiricist Theory of Memory than as a possible cause of it is turned into a certainty by Broad who, in the introductory paragraph to the chapter on Memory in *Mind and its Place in Nature*, writes as follows: "It seems plain that there is one and only one kind of memory which can plausibly be regarded as closely analogous to perception; and this is the memory of particular events, places, persons or things. Let us call this 'Perceptual Memory'. My main object in this chapter is to discuss perceptual memory, to compare it with perception, and to consider some of the epistemological problems to which it gives rise." A group of four other kinds of memory is accorded brief mention later under the heading 'Non-Perceptual Memory', but these are said not really to deserve the name of memory since "in themselves they are modes of behaviour, and not modes of cognition". Broad, then, has offered us two criteria for distinguishing the philosophically interesting kind of memory from other kinds: (*a*) it bears a close analogy to perception, and (*b*) its objects are particular events, places, persons, or things. Why, one wonders, should these two criteria be thought to operate in conjunction with one another?—unless as a result of the crude mistake of supposing that, whereas it is roughly true that the list 'particular event, place, person or thing' exhausts the range of what we can visualize, of what we can have an image of, it is also true that, conversely, the only way we can recall these things is by having images.

c *The Perception Analogy.* Broad's choice of the title 'Perceptual Memory' is significant; for the analogy with per-

ception has dominated the Empiricist Theory of Memory. The
model that is initially adopted is of the mind gazing into the
past and picking out features of the landscape there; looking
back across an expanse of time, analogously with the way we
see across an intervening physical space. The expressions 'cognition' and 'cognitive relation' then suggest themselves as an
appropriate terminology: just as in sense-perception it is said
that we are put into a cognitive relation with the present state
of the physical world, so in memory there is an inclination to
say that we are put into a cognitive relation with the past.
But exactly how does this relationship with the past come to
be established? It is with the raising of this question that the
more sophisticated puzzles and controversies belonging to the
philosophy of perception begin to exert their influence. Discussion may centre on the possibility or impossibility of a
'naive realism' with regard to memory analogous to what has
been called Naive Realism in perception, and to the question:
Are we in some cases *directly* aware of the past? an affirmative
answer is occasionally suggested.[7] But it is more natural for
a kind of representational theory or memory-datum theory of
remembering to be developed, in which images are made to
stand to past events or objects in a relation somewhat analogous
to the relation in which sense-data have been held to stand
towards present material objects. The question which Russell
asks, arising out of the representational theory of memory: How
do we know that our images are representative of the past,
since we cannot resurrect the past bodily and compare it with
our images? has its counterpart within the representational
theory of perception: "How shall the mind, when it perceives
nothing but its own ideas, know that they agree with things
themselves?" (Locke, *Essay*, Bk. IV, Ch. 4, Sec. 3); though
in neither case is the question construed as a *reductio ad absurdum* of the theory. It is, of course, found necessary for

---

[7] *E.g.*, Stout, *Studies in Philosophy and Psychology*, Essay VIII;
Price, *Aristotelian Society Suppl.*, 1936, pp. 24–25; and Woozley, *Theory
of Knowledge*, pp. 52–55.

what are called 'memory experiences' or 'memory situations' to be divided like sense experiences, into those that are veridical and those that are delusive; George IV[8] being made to do for the philosophy of memory what the bent stick in water has been thought to do for the philosophy of perception. But illusions and delusions notwithstanding, our images or memory-data are regarded, like sense-data, as the self-sufficient sources of a primitive kind of information: to be confronted with one is to be confronted with an unmistakable item of fundamental knowledge. This identification of knowledge itself with a kind of quasi-perceptual awareness, called by Russell at one time 'acquaintance',[9] is also an essential part of the theory. It is assumed that to know something is, in all ultimate cases at least, to be actively engaged upon a process of inspection. In one's recollections one is inspecting the past by proxy, and in this way having knowledge of it.

To point out that I cannot, for example, recall a certain visit which I made to London, unless I did in fact make that visit, is to call attention to something that is obvious and seemingly trivial. Putting the point in the terminology of the Empiricist Theory of Memory one might say that memory-knowledge, the knowledge one has in recollecting, is necessarily a knowledge of something one has also known at some time before. With perceptual knowledge this is not necessarily the case. But to a person in whose mind 'perceptual knowledge of the present' and 'memory-knowledge of the past' have been thoroughly assimilated there will seem to be but one important difference between them, namely the one marked by the words 'present' and 'past' respectively—the difference in the temporal status of what is known. It is this that monopolizes his attention and diverts it from the paradox to which his way of thinking

---

[8] Broad, *Mind and its Place in Nature*, p. 231, and Russell, *Human Knowledge, its Scope and Limits*, p. 230.

[9] On page 75 of *The Problems of Philosophy* it is said that "all our knowledge, both knowledge of things and knowledge of truths, rests upon acquaintance as its foundation"; and on page 76 memory is instanced as one kind of knowledge by acquaintance.

about memory gives rise. For if one's attention is firmly focused on the fact that whatever I am supposed to have memory-knowledge of now is necessarily something I have had knowledge of before, a question one is inclined to ask is: Why, if a person once knows something, should he not know it for always? Or suppose one were to ask: Under what conditions, in what kind of circumstances, might a person have to come to know again something he once knew before? An obvious reply would be: When he has forgotten what he originally knew; when he has ceased to remember it. The paradox of the Empiricist Theory of Memory is this: if recollecting is what the theory makes it out to be, then it is a feat the accomplishment of which is neither necessary nor even possible except for someone who has actually forgotten what he is supposed by the theory to be remembering. In the very name Familiarity which they find it natural to use for the distinguishing characteristic of memory-images Russell and Broad give their whole game away. We are dwellers in the present, the present of to-day; but yesterday's present in becoming past is alleged to have turned into a kind of recluse, so that images are henceforth needed to effect an introduction between us and it. The images bring the past before us. But the introduction is attended by an aroma of familiarity. It is as if we knew already what was in store for us: we knew and knew intimately all that the images were to bring, even before they brought it. Their bringing it was, in fact, a work of supererogation, for between old friends introductions are superfluous.

One must evidently relinquish any idea that our images in recollecting can be transmitters of information or independent vehicles of knowledge. If this idea be abandoned then need ceases to be felt for a specific experience which should function as an Indicator, distinguishing those images which do happen to be informers, in recollecting, from those in fancy which happen not to be. For there now appears to be no significant difference between the rôle of images in recollection and their rôle in fancy. In either case, any image that may come before the mind will owe its existence to some knowledge which is possessed by the knower independently of the image; and it will be this knowledge which makes it possible for the image to be created at all, just as it might equally make possible a pictorial representation on paper or a verbal description, each of these being alternative manifestations of the same knowledge. In an earlier example it was supposed that a person be requested simply to imagine or picture to himself a Norman castle, and this situation was compared with another situation in which a person is requested to recall to mind and visualize a specified existent castle. The ability to comply with either request is contingent upon some knowledge which the subject may or may not possess. In the first case he cannot comply with the request unless he has knowledge, and intentionally utilizes his knowledge, of the kind of appearance a Norman castle presents: he must know, and know to this extent, what kind of thing the expression 'Norman castle' refers to. In the second case he cannot comply with the request unless, in addition to this, he has knowledge of whatever castle is specified and unless he intends his image to represent the appearance of this particular castle and no other. This more determinate kind of knowledge is not a prerequisite for compliance with the first request, though if any such should happen to be possessed it would very likely be utilized. It might, if possessed, be utilized again, though in a different way, in the variant case where the request to imagine a castle is supplemented by the injunction that the imagined castle should also be an imaginary one; for here the subject may have to make considerable conscious effort to secure that his visualized castle should represent for him something *other than* the existent castle whose appearance he is familiar with.

If in the three situations outlined in this example we separate what is done from the context in which it is done and proceed to strip the image of the knowledge and the intention that go with it, what are we left with? In the first stage of stripping, the image of the recollected castle is bereft of its specific reference. This castle ceases to be a recollected castle and becomes completely anonymous. The deliberately fabricated castle cannot any longer be regarded as a deliberate fabrication. All distinction between the three performances is lost. In the final stage, the image cannot even be regarded as an image of a castle: it has been reduced to a meaningless concatenation of shapes and colours. One cannot, as Hume thought, contemplate an idea of the memory and an idea of the imagination and, *feigning ignorance of their origins,* begin to distinguish them afresh by means of a difference in their respective qualities.

# PRETENDING

### G. E. M. ANSCOMBE

Offered 'pretending' as a philosophical topic, I should want to distinguish between mock performances and real pretences. The difference, so far as I have noticed, is not pointed to by any of those differences between the grammatical constructions respectively appropriate, sometimes to one nuance of sense and another, sometimes to one word and another closely related one, which are Professor Austin's favourite study. Hence he disregards it,* and lumping dissimilar things together, finds that in "the basic case" the one who is pretending must be giving a "current personal performance" in someone's presence in order to disguise what he is really doing. Mock performances, to specimens of which he devotes a good deal of space, are most naturally exemplified in 'current personal performances' in the presence of others. But it is not at all characteristic of them to serve the purpose of disguising what the performer is really doing. That is a noteworthy characteristic of some real pretences. But for real pretences there is nothing specially basic about a 'current personal performance' in the

Reprinted from *Proceedings of the Aristotelian Society, Supplementary Volume* (Vol. XXXII, 1958) by permission of the editor and G. E. M. Anscombe.
* References to Austin throughout are to his paper on "Pretending" (v. Bibliography). [Ed.]

presence of others. One can pretend to be angry in a letter (this might be mock anger or a real pretence); pretend to marry someone, the 'marriage' being by proxy; pretend to be a meat-eater in a community where vegetarianism is criminally heterodox, by having conspicuous deliveries of butcher's meat made to one's house; pretend through one's emissaries to come to an understanding with a foreign power. Whether the pretending has to be a personal performance sometimes, though not always, depends on whether the doing that is pretended has to be one. It demands a justification, which Professor Austin has not offered, to treat mock performances on the one hand, and cases like these on the other, as deviations from a centre, as fringe cases in which some of the features of 'the basic case' have disappeared. He has perhaps formed this conception out of a prejudice that the identity of a phrase must have something which is 'the basic case' corresponding to it.

I can at present see little intrinsic interest in mock performances. Professor Austin tells us that part of the interest of his considerations is that "philosophers who are fond of invoking pretending have exaggerated its scope and distorted its meaning". In *The Concept of Mind* Professor Ryle discusses pretending, in the sense of giving a mock performance, when he prepares the ground for his attempt to explicate imagination as incipient or inhibited performance. That is a very strange account of imagination. I think it derives from the following suggestion of Wittgenstein's: suppose there were some people apparently playing tennis, but without any ball. Wittgenstein compared the mental image, or the calculation in the head, to this non-existent ball. We should notice that this is not the same thing as comparing *imagining* to the *mock performance* of playing tennis which is here envisaged. It is only the image which is being compared to the ball that there isn't in this game. (What would correspond to the players' strokes to and fro would be *e.g.* the overt setting of a sum and the overt production of the answer.)—I will not pretend to estimate the value of this suggestion, and only mention it to throw light on one of the ways in which 'pretending' has come into current philosophical literature. Obviously pretending is really quite irrelevant here. For though the tennis game without the ball could be called a mock game of tennis, and in that sense the players—in this highly fictitious example—could be said to be pretending to play tennis, the point of the example is not that this is a mock performance or any kind of pretence, but just that it is a tennis-game without a ball. And in Ryle's own attempt to describe imagination, what is of importance is the absence is *first* supposed to throw light on pretending, and this concept in its turn is *then* supposed to throw light on imagination, as if imagination were a species that fell under it.

Leaving mock performances aside, let us consider how 'really pretending' comes into current philosophical discussion. Professor Austin quotes an example, about pretending to be angry.

It is fairly easy to see that the connexion between the meanings of words like "pain" and "anger" and certain types of behaviour cannot be merely contingent. Just what the connexion is, however, is difficult to describe in some cases. *E.g.* it is certainly not that "He is angry" *means* "He behaves thus or thus". And yet acting a piece of typical angry behaviour might serve well as an ostensive definition of "anger". Here the inclination arises to think that if it does so serve, it is working as an indirect indication of something which is simple and yet cannot be indicated directly. This inclination arises because we remember about pretending. Let the following stand for the sort of behaviour that expresses anger:

_____
_____
_____
_____
_____

A man may behave so and not be angry because he is pretending, and the person who understands the ostensive definition ought to understand this. Mr. Bedford, in the passage Professor Austin quotes, *may* be suggesting that the question whether the man who behaves so is pretending or really angry would necessarily be settlable if only there were 'more evidence of the same sort'.* And by "more evidence of the same sort" he *may* mean "more (at least ostensibly) anger-expressing behaviour"—though if he got as far as putting it like that, he would surely *not* think so.

If, then, concentrating on 'behavior that is (perhaps) expressive of real anger' and 'the anger that it is (perhaps) expressive of', we think about pretending, we may feel forced back on a picture like this

where the dot behind the dashes stands for the anger itself. Then the dashes without the dot stand for the behaviour without the anger. This, if there is enough of it, will be pretended anger. We have to say "if there is enough of it" because *e.g.* a scowling face without anger, which looks like an angry face, may be, not a pretence of anger, but just the face someone has when he is thinking hard. But there is behaviour which certainly either is the mark of anger or is simulated anger.—Pursuing our picture, a plain dot without any dashes will be anger which a man does not express at all.

So, it is argued, someone who understands the ostensive definition of anger offered in an imitation of angry behaviour, will take it as an indirect indication of the dot—which cannot be directly indicated by one person to another at all. But with this conception we are forced back to the idea of the private ostensive definition with its absurd consequences—that for all we ever could know the word might stand for a different thing for different people or for the same person at different times; that we can never make more than a probable judgment that someone else is angry; or even that we cannot really make this judgment at all; that our own claim to be angry rests on

* Errol Bedford, "Emotions" (v. Bibliography). [Ed.]

an assumption that we have correctly identified something within ourselves— but without any standard of correctness—and so on.

This, then, is one great locus of the discussion of pretending. Professor Austin proposes to examine pretending just on its own account and out of the context of such discussions. In doing so he has convinced himself that a simple contrast between 'pretence and 'reality' is no good; that pretending has such 'essential features' as that the pretender must be present and active, and there must be something, also 'on the scene', that he is disguising; that there is such a thing as 'the essence of the situation in pretending', namely 'that my public behaviour must be being done in order to disguise some reality'.

Against this I would argue that pretending can no more have that type of 'essential feature' than falsehood or identity or seeming can. Seeming is especially relevant, because the notion of pretending is closely bound up with that of seeming. The best general account of pretending would be something like: *the production of a would-be seeming to be*[1] *what you are not*. That is clumsy, so I will shorten it to 'trying to appear what you are not': cases of this which would not fall under the longer form are excluded. The point of this exclusion is that a man might try to appear what he is not, and not succeed in doing anything—*e.g.*, a very sick man, trying to seem cheerful and too weak even to smile, would have only tried to pretend.

From this general account of pretending we can see why the two more specious implications mentioned by Professor Austin do not hold. As he says, pretending does not imply not being, and really being does not imply not pretending. For *e.g.* a man can pretend to be poisoned when, unknown to him, he is poisoned. In "trying to appear what you are not" the words "what you are not" are governed by the "trying": the whole phrase does not mean: "concerning something which you in fact are not, trying to appear that thing", but: "trying to

---

[1] Like Professor Austin, for brevity's sake I disregard other verbs than 'to be' in formulating this.

bring it about that, without being something, you appear that thing".

This general account of pretending needs an addition to include some cases of trying to make it seem that something is the case which is not. *E.g.*, one might pretend that one's child was under three years old (to avoid paying a fare) by having him dressed in rather babyish clothes and carrying him like a rather younger child, as well as by what one said. All these details would be part of the pretence. In such a case, we have to speak of 'pretending that' rather than 'pretending to' because the subject of what is pretended is not the same as the pretender, and not, I think, for any other reason. Two central features of "pretend" are (1) that the pretender should figure as a principal, in what is pretended *and* in that by which it is pretended; I mean the latter in such a sense that he would *be* a principal if the appearances were not deceptive. This condition may be satisfied even if he is not where the pretence is carried out, if what is done is something that could be done, with him as principal, without his presence, as in the case of the King coming to an agreement with a foreign power. My corollary (that he would be a principal in that *by* which the pretence was made, if the appearances were non-deceptive) can be seen to be necessary from this: if *e.g.*, the King arranged a deceptive appearance that his emissary proposed to murder him, he would not thereby be pretending to be a proposed victim of assassination. (2) Further, there is what might be called a 'rule of sequence of tenses' for "pretending"; if someone has broken some crockery and left it about so that I shall think he *was* angry, he *was* not pretending to be angry; and, unless he does something now to exhibit the smashed crockery as the result of past rage on his part, he *is* not now pretending *to have been* angry.—I suspect that these two facts have misled Professor Austin; he has misconstrued them as a necessity for the pretender to be 'present on the scene' and 'giving a current personal performance'.—Now in the pretence of the fraudulent traveller that the child is under three, the traveller is a principal. I will not consider such cases further; though one has to speak here of 'pretending that' and not 'pretending to', this is only because of the diversity of subjects, and such cases of 'pretending that' should be subsumed under 'pretending to'.

'Pretending' is an intention-dependent concept; one cannot pretend inadvertently. But no special further intentions in whatever constitutes pretending in a given case are specially basic "*as Professor Austin pretends*". Why would that be rude and unfair? Because it implies that he has been trying to make-things-seem-as-they-are-not. There is no hint in that piece of rudeness that the publication of his paper serves to disguise something he is really up to, and it is not the absence of such a hint that turns it into a fringe use of "pretend".

'Seeming' can have no 'basic case'. Let A be the subject of a predicate $x$. Then we can ask "What is it for A to $x$, or to be $x$?" and further "What is it for A (only) to seem to $x$ or to be $x$?" This latter enquiry may well throw light on the first question. And we *could* ask further "Can A be so responsible for phenomena by which he (only) *seems* to $x$, that it accords with the grammar of 'pretending' to say he pretends to $x$?" In cases where that is so, an investigation of 'pretending to $x$' will often help us to understand the concept '$x$' better. But the quite general characteristics of the verb "to pretend" are likely to give singularly little light in an enquiry into 'pretending to $x$'; such an enquiry must be completely dominated by the character of the '$x$' in question.

In the case in hand—that of pretending to be angry— if we consider when and why we may judge that someone was only pretending, we see that it is not only features of his ostensibly angry behaviour that prompt the judgment. If it were, then 'being angry' would be much more like *e.g.*, 'feeling jumpy' than it is. Pure pretences of being angry in person are rarely so successful that a discerning judge will not detect them in the tone and expression of the subject. However, such admirable pretences are possible; so of course the philosopher supposes a case where the performance is perfect. Then perhaps he feels driven either to such a recourse as Mr. Bedford's— "there is a limit that pretence must not overstep"—or to postulating something hidden behind the behaviour. But, as Professor Austin indicates without enlarging on it, there is more to look for besides giveaways in behaviour. Anger has four main features: (1) its object, (2) its expression, (3) feelings, (4) aims. By "angry behaviour" we usually mean things falling under (2), the expression of anger: the angry-looking face and gestures, the stamping or trembling or rigidity, the tone of voice, perhaps the pointless smashing of things. (2) may include elements that bring in (1) and (4). If an angry man expresses his anger in speech, his speech will probably characterise the thing or person or situation or spectacle that he is angry with either as bad in some way, or possibly as something to be overcome or resisted. I suppose that is why Aristotle said that anger was more 'rational' than lust—the expression of anger by an angry man often gives *grounds* of anger. A story of anger —real or pretended—usually includes what the anger was at or supposed to be at, so characterised that the hearer can understand it *as* an occasion of anger. For example, if a man is said to have been angry at the sight of a chair, in a way we do not yet know what he was angry at; we need an explanation which will make it clear whether his purposes or orders have been frustrated, or his vanity insulted, or someone has been proved to have behaved abominably—or what.

There are also characteristic aims of anger—to harm or afflict someone or something, or to overcome obstacles[2] or resist

---

[2] I owe notice of this aspect of anger to Plato, made intelligible by Aquinas who adopted this part of Platonism, getting it apparently from St. Gregory of Nyssa and St. John of Damascus. He does not have a tripartite division of the soul like Plato, but divides the 'sensitive appetite' into two parts, the 'concupiscible' and the 'irascible.' Through the one, he says, the animal is simply inclined to pursue what it needs and to flee what is hurtful, through the other to resist what attacks its needs and offers hurt to it. "These two inclinations do not reduce to a single principle, because the animal sometimes faces hurt against the inclination of desire, so as to oppose what opposes it according to the inclination of anger. Hence the passions of the irascible are even seen to be at war with the passions of the concupiscible. For in general *as desire burns higher anger sinks, and as anger burns higher desire sinks.*" (*Summa Theologica*, Ia, Q.LXXXI, Art II.) To understand the force of this re-

or repel something. A man who was careful to give no sign of anger and did not even have specific angry feelings (sensible commotions) might be implacably angry and arrange some way of harming the man who angered him. Thus, though (2) may pass into (4), as when someone immediately starts strangling the person he is angry with, there *can* be a great difference between the expression of anger and its aims. A man could be said not to have given expression to his anger at all—he merely brought it about that the man who had offended him was ruined or hanged.

What is feeling angry? Let us suppose we find someone who has just been angry and ask him what he felt while he was angry. He may well say *e.g.*, "I felt hot", "I felt cold and trembling", "I felt a rush of blood to the head", "I felt a slight tension in the chest". Yet feeling angry is not any of these things; otherwise we could produce the sensations he characteristically has when angry—*e.g.*, by means of some electrical apparatus—and say: "There, now you feel angry". On the other hand, those sensations were not just concomitants of his anger; he might feel something else, a pain in the stomach, let us say, while he was angry, and not mention it as 'what he felt while he was angry'. The sensations that he mentions are the ones he—intuitively—gives as what he felt *in* being angry. Or again, we may say that he gives his anger as an interpretation of those sensations. But is there nothing else that the *felt* anger is? One kind of reply to this might be: "I felt: 'You filthy swine!' or 'This is too much!' or 'That trick again!' " The words, or the thoughts, are themselves an angry reaction,

---

mark we should imagine someone, about to engage in sensual enjoyment, having to fight to retain what he wanted to enjoy; and then, the battle won, returning to engage in enjoyment.—But, Plato might say, anger is not uniquely concerned with sensitive appetite. That is because of our organisation: "while I was musing, a fire kindled." An abstruse thought can bring my fist crashing down on the table and so also cause all sorts of reverberations in my sensuality. Hobbes' definition of anger as "sudden courage" must be in this tradtion.

and there is no need to postulate, indeed no sense in postulating, another reaction, not the words or the thought, which is the ground of the words or the thought and is the felt anger itself. The fact that the verbal reaction may be a sham does not prove such a need. The mistake is to suppose that since a man can say "I felt angry" we shall find out what anger is by finding out what he felt. In what context does he say "I felt angry"? In the context of some story of events, conversations, thoughts: that is to say, he puts the anger he reports into a context which shews a lot about the anger: and what it shews is not just extraneous. That is why looking for the meaning of "anger" in what a man feels who feels angry yields such dissatisfying results, as if the anger itself had slipped between our fingers and we were left with details, which, while relevant, do not add up to anger.

I am not saying that every case of anger must have all these four features—rather, here we do have a 'full-blown' sort of case with all these features, and other cases lacking some of them. Now imagine an anthropologist saying "The psychology of this tribe is odd: they are angry only, and always, before sitting down to a really good meal." Asked why he says so, he explains "Then, they always shake their fists and assume an expression of hideous rage; after that, they sit down to eat; and they never shake their fists or assume that expression at any other time."—Would it not be absurd for someone so much as to say "They must be only *pretending* to be angry"? Once we have recalled these points about anger, we can see how a diagnosis of pretence could be made in face of angry behaviour which was a quite flawless performance. For example, one might know that the man did not really mind about what he was ostensibly angry at; that it really suited his book extremely well and he knew this. Or that the supposed affliction that he was laying on the victims of his anger was not really an affliction at all but something agreeable and that he knew this.

If someone claims that he was only pretending to be angry

on an intelligible occasion for anger and when his performance had been good if it was only pretence, it is natural to ask why he was pretending that; and an answer telling more about the situation, his attitudes and what he was after will help to convince us that he was pretending.

These facts point to one great difference between anger and pain, and generally between passions and sensations. If a person's performance is good and—as may be the case—there is nothing else to look at, there may be no way at all of telling whether his pain is sham or not, if, say, it is a brief pain or he does not make the mistake of behaving inappropriately when *e.g.*, he does not think he is observed. But it is absurd to say (as Mr. Bedford says in the passage quoted by Professor Austin; which shocks me, though not Professor Austin) that he alone is in a position to give decisive evidence! What he says is no more decisive than his behaviour is. If one thought his groans might be shamming pain, one would hardly accept his word. This however does not mean that there is quite generally a difficulty about knowing whether someone is in pain or not. The difficulty occurs in some cases; and sometimes cannot be resolved. Cases can be constructed for anger too; but there is much more to consider in cases of anger: the whole story of the occasion ('whole story' in the sense of "whole truth" in the law-court oath). Contrast "As I walked along the passage I had a sudden stab of pain in my chest", and "As I walked along the passage I had a sudden stab of anger." Anger what at? "Nothing at all." This man is talking nonsense—unless he means "At X, which I judge to be a nothing." On the other hand consider this case: an actor, who has to act an angry man in a play, says "When I act it, I really am angry." He backs this up by saying that he *feels* angry, and he *means* the angry words in which he recalls and threatens evils. Would not a dispute be stupid about whether he is correct to use the words "I really am angry" or not? 'Say which you like, so long as you are clear about the facts.' *This* situation does not arise for physical pain. For if an actor in *King Lear* said "It's a most extraordinary thing, when they tear out my eyes, I feel an agonizing pain as if it were really so, I almost think I shall have to give up the part," well, we believe him or not, there is not a choice, *after* we believe him, between saying "He really feels pain" and "He doesn't really".

Although I have given reasons for accepting Professor Austin's remark that pretending does not imply not really being and really being does not imply not pretending, I have the impression that his own reasons for saying this lie at least partly in his examples, such as that of the man who was cleaning the windows and at the same time 'pretending to be cleaning them.' Here he relies on a nuance which he explains to us. (It may not exist everywhere where English is native.) But the whole reason why a man can be said to be pretending to be cleaning windows (when he also is cleaning them) is that what he is pretending is not the case. The explanation of the nuance makes this clear. The observer diagnoses the window-cleaner's felonious interest and guesses from this that the window-cleaning is a fake. The diagnosis might be right and the guess wrong—if, say, the man were the regular window-cleaner doing this regular job on his regular day. Professor Austin explains "It is still a pretence [*i.e.*, though the windows *are* being cleaned], because what he is *really* doing is something quite different." But the point of the expression "What he is *really* doing is something different" is that 'what he is *really* doing' falsifies the appearance he presents by cleaning the windows. There are other things he might also be 'really doing' —such as earning his wages or composing verse—which would also be 'different' from window-cleaning but which don't falsify "what he is really at is cleaning the windows" at all. The appearance presented by cleaning the windows is that, in cleaning the windows, he is doing something in some ordinary and proper course of things; and that this is a false appearance is the meaning of the expression "he is pretending *to be cleaning* the windows" in this context.

The two sentences

He is cleaning the windows
He is pretending to be cleaning the windows

may both be true; and as a matter of grammar "is cleaning" is the indicative corresponding to the infinitive "to be cleaning." Does Professor Austin think that *this* is therefore a counter-example to "pretending implies not really being"?* And is it perhaps a fairly important step in his argument, enabling him to reject 'false appearance' as quite central to pretending? If so, this is grammatical superstition.

Why cannot a baby six months old pretend to be in pain? A mother might say "The baby pretends", and we "You mean there's nothing wrong, it only cries to be picked up." Suppose she insists that there is more to it, the baby is a clever one and *really* pretends? Mothers and similar people talk nonsense of this sort. The question is how we know it is nonsense. It is not competence to perform a mental act of pretending that is in question. Wittgenstein would say "Pretending is part of a complicated form of life which the baby is not living yet", but what does that mean? English people are apt to say "The dog is pretending to be lame." Why? He limps, but if he sees a rabbit he rushes after it with no trace of a limp. He was lame and got a lot of special kindness, and is looking for more. We assimilate this behaviour to human pretending. Once these facts have been stated it is not a further hypothesis that he is pretending. The behaviour of the baby is not like enough for the assimilation to be attractive except to mothers, etc. But what is it not like enough to?

The answer to the questions raised here is that you cannot ascribe real pretence to anything unless you can ascribe to it (*a*) a purpose and (*b*) the idea 'can be got by seeming to—'. That is why the baby case is nonsense; the baby's purpose

---

* From the case of the window cleaner, Austin (*Philosophical Papers*, p. 210) concluded: "It looks, then, as though it does not matter if [the pretence-behaviour] does coincide with [the genuine-behaviour-simulated], so long as the contrast between [the pretence-behaviour] and [the real-behaviour-dissembled] is preserved." [Ed.]

may be clear enough, but what reason could there be to ascribe
to it more than the idea 'can be got by roaring'? And even
this means no more than that the baby roars *to be picked up.*
Then why should we say more of the dog than that he limps
to be petted? Why indeed? Only because limping has such a
characteristic appearance, is not just going on three legs but
has an air about it, so that if the limping is voluntary, we may
implicitly think of the presentation of this appearance as
deliberate. We have once more reached a point where we
should say "Say 'he's pretending' if you like, or refuse to if
you like, so long as you are clear about the facts." I emphasize
this; because I am not sure whether Professor Austin would
ever admit that we ought to say "Say such-and-such if you like,
so long as you are clear about the facts"; if he would have
some objection to this, I should like to see it brought out into
the open.

These considerations yield this result: we sometimes ascribe
pretence by way of a comparison, a sympathetic projection on
to a body of facts which we compare with some of the facts of
fairly developed human life. Apart from such sympathetic
projections we must say: we can only ascribe pretence to beings
to which we can also ascribe purposive calculation. That is
not because pretence is generally purposive. It is not; wanting
to seem something that one is not, without any further end in
view, may even form the biggest part of pretending. But it
must be significant that when we ascribe pretending to animals,
it is because we see an advantage gained by seeming. Without
meaning anything absurd (like the mother) we find it possible
to speak of animals', birds' and insects' pretending to be
boughs, leaves, twigs, etc. I think this shews reason to speak
of purposive pretending as 'basic'.

When we consider unpurposive pretending, a new distinction appears between what I will call plain and non-plain
pretending. Unpurposive pretence may be 'just for fun' or 'to
tease' and the like. The description "unpurposive" may be
challenged on the ground that teasing or fun is a purpose, but
I think the challenge would be wrong. It is a specific advantage

served by seeming that is characteristic of the purposive pretending that is 'basic'; fun and teasing are something one
diagnoses as one diagnoses dancing or playing a game, not by
seeing them as results achieved in a certain way.—I will call
pretending "plain" when the pretender unreflectively knows that
he is pretending. A great deal of unpurposive or only very
vaguely and diffusely purposive pretending is non-plain.

What I have in mind is best illustrated by an example.
Here is a dialogue between a schoolmaster and a parent sum-
moned for interview:

> Did James tell you I had to beat him to-day?
> Yes, he said he got beaten.
> Oh, did he tell you what it was for?
> He told me it was for something he had written in his book.
> Hm! I don't suppose he told you what he had written.
> I don't know—what he said was that he wrote "Casson is a
> sod." I gather Mr. Casson is one of the masters.
> Oh! . . . Well, that's not very nice, is it?
> Well, I understand your beating him, but all the same, surely
> this is quite an ordinary thing for a boy to do?
> No, in my experience, not at all normal.
> Let the parent's reply to this be unspoken, since it is: "Stop
> pretending".

In this example, it might be tempting to call the schoolmaster's last remark a plain lie. But we ought to notice that most
likely that is just what it is not. A lie is a plain lie when it
contradicts what the speaker unreflectively thinks. I do not
mean "when it contradicts an explicit thought" since (as is
well known) 'what a man thinks' is not the same thing as 'what
he *is at the moment thinking*'—even if it is only what he thinks
for the time being, in the particular context. But sometimes it
would take some reflection, in the circumstances, for a man to
realise that he knew the contradictory of what he said. Then
what he says is not a perfectly plain lie; he can even be said
to think it.

It is not, however, his saying what he knows to be untrue
that makes our schoolmaster's case one of (non-plain) pretend-

ing. He could pretend in this sense without saying anything
untrue. Further, we often tell untruths that are not lies, in the
sense that they do not contradict what we *unreflectively* know
to be true, without 'pretending' in any sense beyond 'making
out true what (we know) is not'; and, where the content of the
'pretence' is just the content of what is falsely said, there is
no particular aptness about the word "pretending". We say a
thing when we know it is not true, and yet without telling plain
lies, in many ways; one is, by falling into cliché. For example,
a sufficiently learned author speaks in a popular book of
Hobbes' "militant atheism"; we are in a position to know
that he knows that if Hobbes was an atheist he was a crypto-,
not a militant, atheist. But the fact that he wrote that phrase
shews that it would cost him a brief moment's recollection to
realise that he knew this. Here, however, a use of the word
"pretend" really would be a fringe use, as applied to a single
statement; it would come to nothing but: "He says so-and-so,
which he must know not to be true." But there is a sense in
which the schoolmaster is pretending which goes beyond his
telling a (non-plain) lie. What is in question here is *hypocrisy:*
and we are trying to make out what kind of pretending this is.

The following example brings out the contrast between
mock performance, plain pretence, and hypocritical pretence.
A certain nun was the heroine of a devotionally exciting story;
the story was generally known, but not her identity. Once
someone guessed and said "So you are the one!" She, 'with
such simplicity'—so the story runs—'that the other was completely deceived,' laughed and said "So you have found me
out!" Thus she was pretending to be making a mock admission
of something—with a view to concealing that it was the case.
This, then, was a plain pretence. The word "simplicity" bears
dwelling on. It does not merely mean that she laughed and
spoke in a natural way, just like someone who really was
making a mock admission of something that was not the case.
Nor can it mean that she acted without guile, for the contrary is
being recorded. With this word the story-teller is insisting that
the pretence just was a genuine concealment of her identity, and

not *itself* a further pretence of a new sort, as it were saying "See how I am one who wishes to remain obscure." The story-teller probably wishes to suggest that the episode marked a genuine wish to remain obscure; not a pretence of having such a wish. *This* pretence, if the wanting-to-seem was just for its own sake, would be not plain but hypocritical pretence. It is characteristic of this sort of wanting-to-seem that it carries with it an implicit demand for respect for an atmosphere evoked by the pretender, which surrounds not the reality, but the *idea* of such things as being principled, or cultured, or saintly, or rich, or important. There is something of which the schoolmaster is as it were saying 'Respect this'.

This throws light on a further notion, one of the popular senses of *cynicism*. In my sense of "plain", this is a 'plain' pretence of hypocrisy, and is found, *e.g.*, among the clearer-headed politicians.

## ABBREVIATIONS USED IN BIBLIOGRAPHY

*A    Analysis*
*APQ    American Philosophical Quarterly*
*JP    Journal of Philosophy*
*M    Mind*
*MSPS    Minnesota Studies in the Philosophy of Science*
*PAS    Proceedings of the Aristotelian Society*
*PASS    Proceedings of the Aristotelian Society, Supplementary*
    *Volume*
*PQ    Philosophical Quarterly*
*PR    Philosophical Review*
*RIP    Revue International de Philosophie*

# SELECT BIBLIOGRAPHY

ALBRITTON, ROGERS, "On Wittgenstein's Use of the Term 'Criterion,'" *JP*, LVI (1959).

ANSCOMBE, G. E. M., "Two Kinds of Error in Action," *JP*, LX (1963).

AUNE, BRUCE, "The Problem of Other Minds," *PR*, LXX (1961).

AUSTIN, J. L., "Other Minds," *PASS*, XX (1946).

AUSTIN, J. L., "Ifs and Cans," *Proceedings of the British Academy*, XLII (1956).

AUSTIN, J. L., "A Plea for Excuses," *PAS*, LVII (1956–1957).

AUSTIN, J. L., "Pretending," *PASS*, XXXII (1958) reprinted in J. L. Austin, *Philosophical Papers*.

AYER, A. J., "Other Minds," *PASS*, XX (1946).

AYER, A. J., "Can There Be a Private Language?" *PASS*, XXVIII (1954).

BASSON, A. H., "The Immortality of the Soul," *M*, LIX (1950).

BEDFORD, ERROL, "Emotions" PAS, LVII (1956–1957).

BEDFORD, ERROL, "Pleasure and Belief," *PASS*, XXXIII (1959).

BENJAMIN, B. S., "Remembering," *M*, LXV (1956).

BRANDT, RICHARD B. and JAEGWOM KIM, "Wants as Explanations," *JP*, LX (1963).

CAMPBELL, C. A., "Is 'Freewill' a Pseudo-Problem?" *M*, LX (1951).

CHISHOLM, RODERICK M., "Sentences about Believing," *PAS*, LVI (1955–1956).

CHISHOLM, RODERICK M. and WILFRID SELLARS, "Intentionality and the Mental," *MSPS*, II (1958).

DANTO, ARTHUR C., "What We Can Do," *JP*, LX (1963).

DAVENEY, T. F., "Wanting," *PQ*, XI (1961).

DAVIDSON, DONALD, "Actions, Reasons, Causes," *JP*, LX (1963); reprinted in Bernard Berofsky, *Free Will and Determinism*, New York, 1966.

DILMAN, ILHAM, "The Unconscious," *M*, LXVIII (1959).

FEIGL, HERBERT, "The 'Mental' and the 'Physical,'" *MSPS*, II (1958).

FEIGL, HERBERT, "Other Minds and the Egocentric Predicament," *JP*, LV (1958).

FLEMING, BRICE NOEL, "On Avowals," *PR*, LXIV (1955).

FURLONG, E. J., "Memory," *M*, LVII (1948).

GALLIE, W. B., "Pleasure," *PASS*, XXVIII (1954).

GRICE, H. P., "Meaning," *PR*, LXVI (1957).

GRICE, H. P., "The Causal Theory of Perception," *PASS*, XXXV (1961).

GRICE, H. P., "Personal Identity," *M*, L (1941).

GRIFFITHS, A. P., "Belief," *PAS*, LXIII (1962–1963).

GUNDERSON, KEITH, "The Imitation Game," *M*, LXXIII (1964); reprinted in *Minds and Machines*, ed. A. R. Anderson, 1964.

HAMPSHIRE, STUART, "*The Concept of Mind*, by Gilbert Ryle," *M*, LIX (1950).

HAMPSHIRE, STUART, "Freedom of the Will," *PASS*, XXV (1951).

HAMPSHIRE, STUART, "The Analogy of Feeling," *M*, LXI (1952).

HAMPSHIRE, STUART, "Self-Knowledge and the Will," *RIP*, VII (1953).

HAMPSHIRE, STUART and H. L. A. HART, "Decision, Intention and Certainty," *M*, LXVII (1958).

JONES, J. R., "Self-Knowledge," *PASS*, XXX (1956).

JONES, J. R., "The Two Contexts of Mental Concepts," *PAS*, LIX (1958–1959).

JONES, O. R., "Things Known Without Observation," *PAS*, LXI (1960–1961).

KENNICK, W. E., "Pleasure and Falsity," *APQ*, I (1964).

KIM, JAEGWOM and RICHARD B. BRANDT, "Wants as Explanations," *JP*, LX (1963).

MCGUINNESS, B. F., "'I Know What I Want,'" *PAS*, LVII (1956–1957).

MALCOLM, NORMAN, "Knowledge of Other Minds," *JP*, LV (1958); reprinted in *Philosophy of Mind*, ed. V. Chappell, 1962 and in Norman Malcolm, *Knowledge and Certainty*, 1963.

MELDEN, A. I., "Action," *PR*, LXV (1956).

MELDEN, A. I., "Willing," *PR*, LXIX (1960).

MELLOR, W. W., "Three Problems About Other Minds," *M*, LXV (1956).

MORGENBESSER, SIDNEY, "The Justification of Beliefs and Attitudes," *JP*, LI (1954).

O'SHAUGHNESSY, BRIAN, "The Origin of Pain," *A*, XV (1954–1955).

O'SHAUGHNESSY, BRIAN, "The Limits of the Will," *PR*, LXV (1956).

PEARS, D. F., *"Individuals,* by P. F. Strawson," *PQ*, XI (1961).

PEARS, D. F., "Dreaming," *M*, LXX (1961).

PEARS, D. F., "Predicting and Deciding," *Proceedings of the British Academy*, (1964).

PENELHUM, TERENCE, "The Logic of Pleasure," *Philosophy and Phenomenological Research*, XVII (1956–1957).

PLACE, U. T., "Is Consciousness a Brain Process?", *British Journal of Psychology*, XLVII (1956); reprinted in *Philosophy of Mind*, ed. V. Chappell, 1962.

POWELL, BETTY, "Uncharacteristic Actions," *M*, LXVIII (1959).

PRICE, H. H., "Image Thinking," *PAS*, LII (1951–1952).

PUTNAM, HILARY, "Minds and Machines," *Dimensions of Mind*, ed. S. Hook, New York, 1960; and reprinted in *Minds and Machines*, ed. A. R. Anderson, 1964.

PUTNAM, HILARY, "Dreaming and Depth Grammar," *Analytical Philosophy*, ed. R. J. Butler, Oxford, 1962.

RHEES, R., "Can There Be a Private Language?", *PASS*, XXVIII (1954).

RYLE, GILBERT, "Feelings," *PQ*, I (1950–1951).

RYLE, GILBERT, "Pleasure," *PASS*, XXVIII (1954).

RYLE, GILBERT, "Sensation," *Contemporary British Philosophy*, 3rd series, ed. H. D. Lewis, London, 1956.

SCRIVEN, MICHAEL, "The Mechanical Concept of Mind," *M*, LXII (1953).

SELLARS, WILFRID, "Empiricism and the Philosophy of Mind," *MSPS*, I (1956).

SELLARS, WILFRID and RODERICK M. CHISHOLM, "Intentionality and the Mental," *MSPS*, II (1958).

SHAFFER, JEROME, "Could Mental States Be Brain Processes?" *JP*, LVIII (1961).

SHOEMAKER, SYDNEY S., "Personal Identity and Memory," *JP*, LVI (1959).

SHORTER, J. M., "Imagination," *M*, LXI (1952).

SIBLEY, FRANK, "A Theory of the Mind," *Review of Metaphysics*, IV (1950–1951).

SMART, J. J. C., "Sensations and Brain Processes," *PR*, LXVIII (1959); reprinted in *Philosophy of Mind*, ed. V. Chappell, 1962.

STRAWSON, P. F., *"Philosophical Investigations,* by Ludwig Wittgenstein," *M*, LXIII (1954).

SUTHERLAND, N. S., "Motives as Explanations," *M*, LXVIII (1959).

TAYLOR, RICHARD, "Deliberation and Foreknowledge," *APQ*, I (1964).

TEICHMANN, J., "Mental Cause and Effect," *M*, LXX (1961).

THALBERG, IRVING, "False Pleasures," *JP*, LIX (1962).

THALBERG, IRVING, "Freedom of Action and Freedom of Will," *JP*, LXI (1964).

THOMSON, J. F., "The Argument from Analogy and Our Knowledge of Other Minds," *M*, LX (1951).

TURING, A. M., "Computing Machinery and Intelligence," *M*, LIX (1950); reprinted in *Minds and Machines*, ed. A. R. Anderson, 1964.

VENDLER, ZENO, "Verbs and Times," *PR*, LXVI (1957).

WELLMAN, C., "Wittgenstein's Use of the Term 'Criterion,'" *PR*, LXXI (1962).

WHITE, ALAN R., "Different Kinds of Heed Concepts," *A*, XX (1959–1960).

WHITE, ALAN R., "The Concept of Care," *PQ*, X (1960).

WILLIAMS, B. A. O., "Personal Identity and Individuation," *PAS*, LVII (1956–1957).

WILLIAMS, B. A. O., "Mr. Strawson on Individuals," *P*, XXXVI (1961).

WISDOM, JOHN, "Other Minds," *PASS*, XX (1946).

ZIFF, PAUL, "The Feelings of Robots," *A*, XIX (1958–1959), reprinted in *Minds and Machines*, ed. A. R. Anderson, 1964.

# INDEX OF NAMES AND TITLES